T0372796

OPINION POLLS AND VOLATILE ELECTORATES

This book is dedicated to Mel,
and to our children,
Jacob and Oliver.

Opinion Polls and Volatile Electorates

Problems and Issues in Polling European Societies

MATT HENN
Department of Economics and Politics
Nottingham Trent University

 Routledge
Taylor & Francis Group

LONDON AND NEW YORK

First published 1998 by Ashgate Publishing

Reissued 2018 by Routledge
2 Park Square, Milton Park, Abingdon, Oxon OX14 4RN
711 Third Avenue, New York, NY 10017, USA

Routledge is an imprint of the Taylor & Francis Group, an informa business

Publisher's Note
The publisher has gone to great lengths to ensure the quality of this reprint but points out that some imperfections in the original copies may be apparent.

Disclaimer
The publisher has made every effort to trace copyright holders and welcomes correspondence from those they have been unable to contact.

A Library of Congress record exists under LC control number: 98003177

ISBN 13: 978-1-138-32452-7 (hbk)
ISBN 13: 978-0-429-45081-5 (ebk)

Contents

List of Tables

Preface

The research for this book comes from a project which was conceived by the East Midlands Politics Research Group based at the then Trent Polytechnic at the end of the 1980s. Essentially, this sought to examine the extent of polling activities in local and national political affairs, and the contribution that polls make to the democratic process. As a corollary of this, the research focused on the intervention of polling in British politics in terms of its impact on voting intentions, the use of polling data by agencies which commission the research (political parties, pressure groups, and mass media organisations), and the strengths, limitations and weaknesses of established polling techniques and methodologies. However, by the beginning of 1990, the research took a more comparative focus following the dramatic events in Central and Eastern Europe which led to the overthrow of Stalinist bureaucracies there by mass movements of workers and students. The reports of opinion poll results in the European correspondence pages of the British press revealed the truly popular character of the opposition movements, and gave an indication of the role that polls themselves could take in articulating a mass public opinion, generating a sense of statistical community amongst those who opposed the Stalinist regimes, and ultimately in facilitating the democratic process. This sudden profusion of opinion polling contrasted with the virtual invisibility of polling activities in these countries under communist rule, and highlighted the scarcity of research in the field by the American and West European political science communities.

In the knowledge both of this research gap and of the energetic polling activities in the immediate aftermath of the collapse of communism, I decided to investigate the evolution of polling in the unique contexts of countries undergoing processes of political restructuring and revolutionary change. This enabled me to gain some sense of how such events impacted upon the development of polls, and how polls themselves could contribute to the unfolding processes of political democratisation in late-capitalist and post-communist societies. This book is the result of my attempts to analyse these developments.

Matt Henn   Nottingham
                                                                       Winter 1997

Acknowledgements

The responsibility for the work is mine. However, I am greatly indebted to a number of people who have helped in various ways over the long years of this research project. Firstly, to Mike Young and Larry Wilde at The Nottingham Trent University who helped to discipline me in my research. Secondly, to Robert Worcester at MORI who provided introductions to colleagues from other polling agencies in Britain and elsewhere, as well as substantial documentary materials for the research. In addition, I owe much to all my friends and colleagues in Poland, the Czech Republic, Hungary, Romania and Bulgaria, and especially to Cenek Adamec, Piotr Kwiatkowski, Petre Datculescu and Ognian Shentov, each of whom provided immeasurable assistance in organising my fieldwork. I would also like to acknowledge the Faculty of Economics and Social Sciences at The Nottingham Trent University, and the British Councils in Warsaw and Budapest who financed the research. Finally, particular thanks go to my family, and especially to Mel for her tireless support, and for putting up with me generally.

1 Introduction

Opinion polling as an activity is well entrenched in advanced capitalist democracies. Polls are now an integral part of political landscapes, and they are likely to become even more so, particularly in relation to electoral politics in the future. Largely, this is as a result of the functions which they are able to perform in bringing political elites and citizens closer together within political systems. Polls are often characterised as consultative mechanisms through which political leaders can tap into and gauge the needs, interests and demands of the citizenry; for some writers, they ultimately facilitate political linkages and popular input into political decision-making. But polls may also play a significant role in the competition between political elites for power and influence. This is most obvious at the electoral level, where polls are often used as sources of political intelligence by political parties to gain an understanding of the dynamics of public opinion, and to maximise support and votes at elections.

This book aims to examine both the extent to which political opinion polling can contribute to democratic processes in different countries, and the degree to which polling is tied to the developing processes of restructuring and transition which are taking place in contemporary advanced societies. Specifically, the examination will focus on political opinion polling in both late-capitalist and post-communist societies. In doing so, it will consider two key related issues: firstly, how shifting political contexts impact upon the ability of polls to measure public opinion, and in so doing, affect their capacity to contribute to political democratisation in a meaningful and effective way; and secondly, whether polls extend or inhibit democratic processes.

Principally, this analysis is organised around the concept of Complex Politics. This has as its core an analytical framework which focuses upon various aspects of the political systems in both late-capitalist and post-communist societies which impinge directly upon political opinion polling. These are *political culture, party systems, mechanisms for political participation,* and the *policy process.* It is argued that, despite the obvious differences in context and recent history, the complexity of contemporary political environments in which polls operate in both types of political system are such as to display broadly similar issues and problems for opinion pollsters.

In the period between 1945 and 1989, the contexts for polling could not have been more different. In communist societies, there was a marked division between the state and society, with virtually no meaningful public input into the political process. Governments had an avowed mission to transform society according to an overriding commitment to a particular ideology, ostensibly on behalf of the citizenry. In such contexts, there was little scope for opinion polling. Opinion polls were perceived by governing elites as having little or no practical, philosophical or ideological relevance. Essentially, internal public politics did not exist. Politics were generally only public at the international level, with governments either extending friendship to other communist political systems, or engaged in an ideological offensive against global capitalism. Internally, societies were highly politicised in terms of party membership and public propaganda, but there was a notable absence of politics in the sense of publicly competing interests and adversarial opinions. One-party states were the norm, with political priorities limited to one goal (the emancipation of humankind) while class, and hence class struggle, was not officially acknowledged to exist. There was no effective choice between parties; there were no conflicting ideologies concerning how society and the economy should be run; and there were therefore presumed to be no political differences amongst citizens/voters. As Webb (1986, p.11) put it:

> One overriding factor, the predominance of the communist party and its particular philosophy, means that much of the subject matter which was the source of the growth of opinion polling in Western countries . . . reporting divided opinions in the community on political issues, do not happen .

Where polling did take place, it was usually carefully controlled by the political elites, and met with significant scepticism by the public. However, in periods of political reform and liberalisation where there was a modicum of public participation in political affairs, there was heightened polling activity, and the conditions for polling were considerably more favourable than under Stalinist governments.

In capitalist societies during the early decades after the Second World War, political landscapes were more conducive for polling. There was comparatively more public access to, participation within, and attachment to the political process; as a consequence, citizens generally considered the various forms of public politics, including opinion polls, seriously. The competition between rival parties for political office made them more susceptible, accountable, and responsive to public opinion, including the results of opinion polls. And finally, the party systems were usually relatively stable with a limited number of competing parties, and typically they were characterised by strong and enduring alliances between voting groups and these parties. These alliances were based upon relatively homogenous and clearly defined value systems, with stable social and economic contexts. Furthermore, the general economic and social priorities for any government were likely to be agreed across the dominant parties. In this way, the political landscapes were largely stable. As a result, public opinion was relatively fixed and predictable, and therefore relatively straightforward to measure with opinion polls.

However, especially since 1989, political landscapes in both late-capitalist and post-communist societies have become more complex, and in many respects this complexity provides significant challenges for the opinion pollsters as they endeavour to measure public opinion. These circumstances are characterised by the lack of a unified political culture, by heterogeneous value systems, by heightened electoral volatility and the breakdown of traditional voter/party alignments, by the emergence of new parties and shifting party alliances and coalitions, by variegated participation in political affairs, and by greater susceptibility of the parties to public opinion. The post-communist societies represent extreme cases of such situations. There is significant scope for opinion polling activities in such societies, but the political conditions are such that they make it particularly difficult for the pollsters to undertake their work effectively and accurately. One important issue which this analysis raises is the extent to which these processes are taking place in late-capitalist societies like Britain? This book suggests that it is possible to make meaningful comparisons between late-capitalist and post-communist systems as far as political opinion polling is concerned. This is largely because the post-communist systems exhibit certain political features which are apparent in Western societies (such as the emergence of disparate and competing value systems, and the establishment of multi-party systems and so on), while countries like Britain and many of its neighbours in Western Europe are undergoing restructuring processes which are combining to facilitate the development of complex political landscapes more typical in Central and Eastern Europe.

In order to project the course of development of polling, the likely issues that pollsters will need to address in the future, and the shape and nature of the links between polling and the processes of democratisation in late-capitalist societies, it is instructive to refer to the current experiences of pollsters and polling in the transitional states of Central and Eastern Europe. As the processes of political pluralisation and restructuring take place in these former communist societies, this will help to identify the major problems which pollsters are likely to face in countries such as Britain and elsewhere in continental Europe when attempting to gauge political opinions, beliefs, orientations and behaviour as their own societies become more variable and complex.

From such analyses, it is concluded that polls help to extend and strengthen the political linkages between citizens and their political representatives, but that any notion that this facilitates greater 'democracy' is tempered by the control of polls by a small number of elites representing dominant interests. It is found that in both late-capitalist and post-communist systems, polls are often used by politicians and political elites to gauge the mood of the electorate on issues and policies, and monitor voters' reactions to political events. In this way, polls form a useful link between citizens and policy-makers, and provide a vehicle through which the public are able to exert a degree of influence in political affairs. This is particularly the case in post-communist societies, where the new political regimes have limited experience in the art of government. In both types of society however, there is a tendency towards manipulation of the public through opinion polling, in that the data are not so much used for the purpose of incorporating public views into the policy-making process, but rather to set agendas, and as sources of political intelligence through which to develop strategies designed to gain political power and influence. These findings relate to a theoretical understanding of the locus of power in competitive democracies. They suggest that although polls perform a useful channel of popular input into political affairs, ultimately dominant elites continue to wield power in society; by contrast, there is little evidence that polls have shifted political power to the mass of citizens.

Furthermore, the processes of restructuring which are currently taking place in advanced capitalist and post-communist political systems are such that pollsters are confronted with a series of contextual issues which are combining to undermine their ability to accurately measure popular needs and aspirations within contemporary societies. Pollsters will therefore need to re-appraise their methodologies and techniques in the new context of Complex Politics.

Chapter Plan

To address these issues, it is necessary to clarify the scope for, development, status and role of political opinion polling in contemporary societies. In order to do so, an appreciation of the social, economic, political and cultural restructuring which such societies are undergoing is essential. With this in mind, an organising framework is established which focuses on various elements of political systems which are likely to impinge upon the political opinion polling process. Chapters 2, 3 and 4 attempt to do this. Chapter 2 considers the debate concerning the role of opinion polls as agents of democracy. The focus is such that it provides an indication of the extent to which polls have the capacity either to improve or impede democratic processes in contemporary societies. Chapters 3 and 4 then distinguish three polling contexts: capitalist, communist and post-communist. It is possible to identify from these three categories a context for polling which is defined as Complex Politics. This incorporates polling contexts in both late-capitalism and post-communism. It is important to state here that the term

Complex Politics does not refer to some new phase in the evolution of contemporary societies. Instead, it is intended as a means of articulating processes of change and restructuring in late-capitalist and post-communist societies *which relate to political opinion polling*. Consequently, Complex Politics is a *context* for polling, and it is proposed only insofar as it helps us to gain an insight as to the scope for, and ability of political opinion polling in the various shifting political environments of contemporary societies.

Later chapters attempt to provide analyses of the contemporary political landscapes in these Complex Politics societies. Chapters 5 to 7 concentrate on polling in capitalist societies, with an emphasis on Britain. Chapter 5 traces the emergence of opinion polling, focusing on the relationships with the mass media, political parties, and other client agencies. Chapter 6 looks at polling in the context of a transforming British political system. Focusing primarily on electoral politics, it surveys the relative political stability of the 1950s and 1960s and compares this with the re-structuring of later years - the emergence of new political parties and movements, and the alleged break-up of the class-party alliances. In doing so, the discussion explores contemporary theories of voting behaviour and considers the implications they hold for pollsters in terms of the design of political opinion surveys, and in particular of data collection techniques. The implications for these developments are discussed in relation to opinion polling in chapter 7. Here, opinion polling throughout the late-capitalist world is reviewed - Western Europe, the USA, and Australasia - particularly in terms of the performance of polls in some recent elections.

Chapters 8 to 10 examine opinion polling in Central and Eastern Europe. They provide a comparative context by focusing on similar issues to those provided in the previous chapters. This section incorporates material gathered via a postal questionnaire sent out to pollsters in nine countries during 1990-1993, and from qualitative interviews held with pollsters and their clients in Poland, Hungary and Czechoslovakia during 1991, and in Romania and Bulgaria in 1995.[1] The chapter considers the tasks and problems posed for pollsters in post-communist societies. These include issues such as variable and unpredictable public participation in opinion polls, as well as logistical and methodological problems. It also analyses the structural changes which are taking place in these transitional societies, and the impact they are having on political opinion polling. It explores the fragmentation of societies into new socio-economic groups, electoral volatility, and the general polarisation and atomisation of public opinion. Together with the emergence of a complex and undefined party system, it is argued that these factors combine to create a political landscape which is hard to quantify in the opinion polls, particularly in the field of electoral forecasting.

In the conclusion, the key tendencies which relate to polling in both late-capitalist and post-communist societies are reviewed. This serves as a framework for the analysis of the role of opinion polls in contemporary societies, and the degree to which they are both a function of political liberalisation processes as well as facilitators of democratic practice. The conclusion then highlights areas for further research suggested by this book.

Countries Chosen for Analysis

The analyses of the role, status and functions of political opinion polling in this book are confined primarily to capitalist and post-communist contexts, and are based largely upon case studies. To represent post-communist political systems which have developed from their communist roots, there will be a focus on the former Soviet Union, Bulgaria, Romania, Poland, Hungary and the former Czechoslovakia. As an example of a capitalist political system, there will be a focus on Britain, although polling developments elsewhere in Europe, the USA, and Australasia will be referred to. The inference here is that where political landscapes are complex, such as in late-capitalist and post-communist political systems, then pollsters will confront a number of problematic factors which will combine to make their tasks increasingly arduous. At the same time, where political landscapes are less complex, then the problems for opinion pollsters will be less defined. Britain is regarded as a critical methodological case here to test the shift toward Complex Politics in late-capitalist societies. According to Almond and Verba, it came closest to their conception of the ideal 'civic culture' in the 1950s and 1960s. They suggested that there was a high degree of political consensus relating to the post-war British state and its system of government, a strong sense of deference to political authority, and significant trust and confidence in Britain's political institutions and political arrangements (Almond and Verba, 1963, pp.197-198). Furthermore, it can be argued that traditionally Britain has had a comparatively stable, majoritarian system, with a limited number of well-established parties competing for governmental office and forming traditional alliances with blocs of voters. Indeed, Britain possessed, certainly up until the early 1970s, one of the most stable and enduring political systems within the advanced capitalist world (Crewe, 1977). At the heart of this stability, was the largely homogenous nature of society, with cleavages which were based predominantly on social class lines underpinning party-voter alliances. Finally, Britain has always been more tolerant of polls than many of its capitalist counter-parts, such as Spain, Portugal, Italy, Belgium, France, Switzerland, Germany and others where polling is either banned at particular times within the electoral cycle, or else subject to external regulation.

Consequently, if Britain's political landscape begins to display features similar to those found in the post-communist societies, then it can be assumed that those other European capitalist political systems whose political landscapes are more complex historically than Britain's, are likely to undergo such changes more rapidly.   The implications are that, if the developing processes of political complexity serve to undermine the ability of pollsters to effectively carry out their tasks in Britain in ways which reflect the situation in the post-communist political systems, then the situation will be more critical for Britain's more complex late-capitalist neighbours in Western Europe.   Such developments may precipitate the need to reappraise methodological techniques, and develop new styles of measuring public opinion so as to prepare for these shifts toward more complex political landscapes throughout Europe.   The analysis of polling in post-Second World War capitalist and post-communist societies which follows will give an indication of these developments and the likely scenarios for political opinion polling in the future in a variety of European contexts.

Notes

1.   Full details of the methodology used for this study can be found in the appendix.

2 Opinion Polls, Power and Democracy

It [public opinion] believes in the value of every individual's contribution to political life, and in the right of ordinary human beings to have a voice in deciding their fate. Public opinion, in this sense is the pulse of democracy (Gallup and Rae, 1940, p.8).

Introduction

When George Gallup first pioneered the use of opinion polling in the United States of America, he did so with the intention that it would serve to enhance and extend democratic processes and practices by providing a channel through which citizens could participate in political affairs. He advocated a populist notion of government in which voters had significant input into decision-making, and claimed that opinion polls could provide a useful means through which this might be achieved by objectively measuring the views of voters, and communicating these to elected representatives. Ultimately, polls would help to increase the efficiency of representative government, by making these elites more responsive to public opinion, and by facilitating greater popular participation in the political process. This chapter explores these issues, and examines the role of opinion polling in capitalist political systems and the impact they have on the general processes of political democratisation.

Public Opinion, Opinion Polls and Political Democratisation

According to some observers, polls not only provide citizens with knowledge about the political system, and about issues and the performance of political leaders generally, they also enhance the opportunities for citizen influence, and ensure policy-makers are sensitive and responsive to the demands of the populace (Asher, 1988, p.18). Others have argued that "...public opinion polling thrives in a democratic environment . . . that it is the handmaiden of modern democracy" where populations are dependent on governmental provision of public services, and where formalised procedures for monitoring public expression and popular feeling are ordinarily restricted to infrequent elections (Bradburn and Sudman, 1988, p.10).

Underlying this view of the role of opinion polling is an implicit assumption that the nature of political power in advanced capitalist societies is essentially pluralistic, with significant scope for popular intervention in decision-making. It suggests that the political system in these societies is sufficiently flexible to enable the polls to operate as links between the electorate and political representatives, and as mechanisms through which citizens can play a meaningful role in political affairs. In this scenario, polls help to strengthen the general processes of political democratisation. An alternative view maintains that the reality in capitalist societies is that the political systems are largely closed to the mass of the populace, with political power monopolised by small elite groups. From this point of view, the chief concern of those who commission opinion polls is not that they should be used to devolve power to voters, but that they should be used to help gain further political power and influence for themselves. Thus, polls are not conducted to empower wider society, but to sustain the political hegemony of elites.

In order to clarify the relationship between polls and the processes of democratisation in capitalist political systems, it is therefore necessary to gain some sense of where political power is located. A useful point of reference through which to begin such an analysis is Schumpeter's *Capitalism, Socialism and Democracy* (1976), in which he counterpoised two extremes of representative democracy. In the first, a 'classical doctrine of democracy', Schumpeter (1976, p.250) characterised representative democracy as:

> That institutional arrangement for arriving at political decisions which realises the common good by making the people itself decide issues through the election of individuals who are to assemble in order to carry out its will.

The only legitimate source of judgment on major issues was to be found in the will of the people. Government should be by the people and for the people, with politicians articulating and implementing the policy demands of the citizenry. According to this view, public opinion was considered to be the principle dynamic upon which a political system should sustain itself. Thus, the relationship between voters and their elected representatives was one in which the latter should respond directly to the demands of the majority view of the voters on separate policy-issues. Schumpeter located the origins of such a model in the works of 18th century philosophers such as Rousseau, who advocated a participatory model of popular sovereignty based upon a notion of the general will as the only legitimate form of rule (Rousseau, 1968).

In contrast, the theory of 'competitive leadership' defined democracy as:

> An institutional arrangement for arriving at political decisions in which the individuals acquire the power to decide by means of a competitive struggle for the

people's vote (p.269).

Here, Schumpeter claimed that citizens were an ignorant and apathetic mass, which would inevitably be manipulated. The remoteness of the world of international and national affairs from the lives of most people left them in a very weak position to make sound judgments about competing ideologies and policies. Moreover, the general susceptibility of individuals to the pressures of interest groups and the mass media undermined any independent basis for political thought. The increasing use by politicians of advertising techniques to shape voters' ideas further eroded any notion that the 'sovereign people' were or could be either the source of, or indeed a check upon, the powers of the 'sovereign state' (Schumpeter, pp.256-268). Thus, rather than the citizens directing their elected representatives, the reality was that citizens had very little access to real political power, with decisions made on their behalf by elites:

> People can in the short run be 'fooled' step by step into something they do not really want and ...no amount of retrospective common sense will alter the fact that in reality they neither raise nor decide issues but that the issues that shape their fate are normally raised and decided for them (p.264).

Furthermore, Schumpeter claimed that the notion of 'popular sovereignty' was ambiguous. He had a low estimation of the political, intellectual and objective capacities of the average citizen, and argued that the electorate should only have minimal involvement in political affairs sufficient to legitimate the right of competing political elites to rule. There should be a clear division of labour between voters and elected representatives, and voters should avoid trying to instruct or influence politicians. This would enable leaders to define the parameters of public policy efficiently and unimpeded:

> The voters outside of Parliament must respect the division of labour between themselves and the politicians they elect. They must not withdraw confidence too easily between elections and they must understand that, once they have elected an individual, political action is his business and not theirs (p.295).

Schumpeter has been accused of erecting a 'straw man' in his rebuttal of what he terms the 'classical doctrine of democracy', as not even Rousseau suggested that the general will or the common good could be easily established (see Pateman, 1970). However, his value for this analysis is that he sets up two extremes of popular power; through this it is possible to gauge the impact of polls in establishing where power lies on this continuum in contemporary societies, and the role that polls might perform in the democratic process.

George Gallup went some way toward achieving this aim by attempting to explain the possibilities for using opinion polls in political affairs. He acknowledged that in representative democracies it is elites which wield political power, but claimed that polls were a key element of popular input which elected representatives would have to take into account in decision-making; essentially he maintained that polls could help to redress the imbalance of power in society in favour of voters. In this scenario, polls could serve three vital functions: firstly as mechanisms to articulate the general will of the people; secondly to help facilitate the decentralisation of political power from elites to mass popular society; and thirdly to combat the influence of dominant groups in society.

In *The Pulse of Democracy* (Gallup and Rae, 1940), Gallup claimed that in political systems which were governed by elected representatives, there were inevitably procedural mechanisms which served to limit democracy. Essentially, the only meaningful channel available to the citizenry for participating in political life and effecting political change in representative democracies was by voting at elections. Since there were large gaps between these elections, the public (or more precisely the eligible electorate) tended to be effectively disenfranchised during the greater part of the electoral cycle, conferring political power and responsibility on elected elites.

For Gallup, the ideal form of political system would be built upon the principles of direct democracy in which the opinions and priorities of the electorate determined policy agendas, and where elected politicians were responsive and accountable to the citizenry at all times during the electoral cycle, and not just during election campaign periods. In the absence of such political arrangements, he advocated the use of opinion polls in decision-making to help formulate and express the views of the mass electorate, and in so doing, to act as a channel of communication between the governed and the government. Elected representatives would also be insulated from the subjective pressures of the many powerful lobbies which claimed to represent key interests in society. Instead, politicians would be able to by-pass these vested interests, and use opinion polls to consult directly with the voters, and in so doing, to govern more effectively and according to the general will of the people.

Such arguments formed the basis of a populist model of opinion polling and political democratisation. That is, that polls could have the capacity to extend the scope for mass participation in political affairs, while at the same time, decentralising political power away from political and bureaucratic elites. By providing a channel for the articulation by policy-makers of the needs and interests of popular society between elections, polls could also be used to undermine the hegemony of dominant groups which otherwise tended to monopolise the spheres and mechanisms of political influence during these periods (Bruner, 1944 pp.4-5).

In the current context, new forms of communication conferred on entrenched elites even more power in the struggle with unorganised, individualised citizens to influence political affairs; opinion polls could function to redress this imbalance in favour of ordinary citizens. Gallup argued that opinion polls could be the new countervailing form of communication for citizens, serving as a bridge between people and leaders, and circumventing organised elites (Gallup and Rae, 1940, pp.13-14).

However, Gallup stopped short of arguing either that opinion polls should be a proxy for direct democracy, or that elected representatives should be bound to policies which were determined by polling data. In debate with Lindsay Rogers (1949), his chief adversary during the early years of polling in the USA, Gallup maintained that polls could help to facilitate more efficient and responsive government, and yet in doing so he implicitly conceded that ultimately it was political elites which made decisions:

> In my opinion, modern polls are the chief hope of lifting government to a higher level, by showing that the public supports the reforms that will make this possible, by providing a modus operandi for testing new ideas ... Polls can help make government more efficient and responsive ... they can make this a truer democracy (Gallup, 1965, p.549).

This view of opinion polling has recently been articulated by Clemens, who applied Gallup's general populist model of polling to Britain in the 1980s. Like Gallup, Clemens maintained that "...the essence of populism is that public opinion should be constantly made known to the government in power, and that the government should heed it and pay constant attention to it" (Clemens, 1984, p.97). In earlier times, this was not possible. However, with the advent of opinion polling, Clemens claimed that the public was provided with a means through which their views could be heard by politicians above the noise made by organisations whose political power and influence was disproportionately higher than the sum of the individuals which comprised them. In this view, opinion polls provided an instrument through which the public could exercise an ongoing influence over public policy. Governments and political leaders would be held accountable for their actions and policies on a continuous basis, not just at election times. Through the results of opinion polls, voters could be made immediately aware when the actions of political leaders ran counter to public opinion, and consequently they would be able to make informed assessments about the performance of government and of policy outputs when it came to voting at elections. Clemens (1984, p.133) argued that such a situation could lead to a form of continuous populist government, where political leaders were compelled to closely monitor and act upon the views of the public on key domestic issues as these were expressed through the opinion polls:

> In a democratic society, the members of government and politicians generally are
> likely to pay close attention to the public view, and to be influenced by it, because
> they may lose their power and influence overnight.

Roll and Cantril (1972) have expressed concern with this notion that opinion polls should direct public policy in representative democracies. In arguing their case they adopted a position which in part reflected Schumpeter's 'competitive leadership' theory. They maintained that politicians and other political representatives should avoid mistaking the short-range view of the 'mood' of the public for the long-term conception of a 'public interest' because the latter was not readily discernible. The 'public interest' involved taking into consideration the opinions, values and interests of the entire commonwealth, which Lippmann referred to as "...the People, as a community of the entire living population, with their predecessors and successors" (Lippmann, 1955, p.32). The 'mood of the public' however, was comprised of the public as 'voters', whose social and historical base was narrower than the commonwealth, and who could not therefore claim to represent it. What was more, voters' inclinations were towards self-preservation by promoting their own interests, and often they were likely to take hasty and ill-considered positions on issues. If opinion polling data was to inform governmental decision-making, then inevitably this would lead to the adoption of some policies which would be unwise, and occasionally unjust.

Compounding these problems was the lack of competence of public opinion generally in political matters. Roll and Cantril claimed that the public as voters lacked the capacity to direct the actions of political representatives effectively, because they could not realistically possess the technical, scientific or general awareness of all the facts which related to public policy, and nor were they in a position to fully understand the implications of adopting particular policy positions. Therefore, the "...public obviously cannot be expected to be informed and up-to-date in its understanding of complex issues, the implications of alternative courses of action, nor the advantages of specific instrumentalities by which a policy is affected" (Roll and Cantril, 1972, pp. 143-144).

Essentially, this argument held that in most circumstances, public opinion was passive and came into being only as a reaction to problems and policies presented to it by policy-makers and opinion leaders. Consequently, the findings reported in opinion polls did not necessarily reflect the views, aspirations, interests and policy-demands of the electorate; instead, they were more likely to reflect the outcome of the struggle of competing ideologies and of those influential groups, organisations and classes in society who determined which issues should be debated, and the general parameters of discussion. Policy-makers should therefore avoid legislating on the basis of polling data alone.

However, under certain circumstances, opinion polls could assume a limited role as feedback mechanisms between government members and the citizenry. Firstly, opinion polls could give shape to the otherwise largely amorphous views of individual voters, and communicate these to political leaders. Without this formalising process, public opinion would not exist, for an opinion which was not expressed could only be of significance to the individual who held that view (Teer and Spence, 1973, pp.11-12). Secondly, polling data could also be useful in the sense that it is multi-dimensional. At one level, each opinion poll was essentially a snap-shot version of the current state of public opinion. When aggregated however, the results of tracking polls[1] and panel surveys[2] dealing with the same issue or set of issues could measure public opinion over time. This could provide decision-makers with both a coherent representation of citizens' needs and a likely estimation of their future requirements, as well as some assessment of their reactions to policies and events. Furthermore, through the use of carefully constructed supplementary issue questions and attitudinal-scale type questions, the intensity of voters' feelings and reactions to policy could be understood. As a consequence, decision-makers would be in a position to draw informed distinctions between those views which were peripheral to the citizenry, and those which were deeply held. In so doing, they could possess the raw data upon which to make judgments as to whether to follow or lead public opinion.

Ultimately, polling data could also be used to gauge the consistency of public opinion on particular issues over time. Again, the use of tracking polls, attitudinal-type questions, and panel surveys could help in this process. Panel surveys could identify whether a particular response-item supported or contradicted earlier responses, probing why; tracking polls could provide similar data but on a cross-sectional basis, and to different sets of respondents over time. Batteries of attitudinal questions (such as opinion of the Labour Party's position on reforming the House of Lords) dealing with different facets of a multi-dimensional issue (constitutional reform) could help to establish whether a given response was part of a deeply-held value and belief system, or an unformulated response to a question about which the respondent had little knowledge, and which had low priority in the respondent's consciousness.

Therefore, by cumulating and ultimately creating a public opinion around an issue or policy option, polls could provide political decision-makers with the means through which to access the views and reactions of the citizenry between elections. This perspective does not advocate that public opinion should dictate the nature and direction of policy-making, but more that it should inform politicians of the public's mood. In this way, political leaders would be able to govern more effectively.

Furthermore, Roll and Cantril maintained that opinion polls could contribute to the stability of the political process in any given society, by helping to "...alert leaders to stresses in their relationship with the public and uncover the sources of these stresses before it is too late" (1972, p.154). In doing so, opinion polls would firstly ensure that elected representatives would be both highly sensitive and responsive to the electorate's views and needs, and that secondly, they would foster improved linkages between voters and politicians. Such an input-output model of opinion polling and the policy process suggested that ultimately polls could facilitate greater integration of all citizens and social groups in the political system, preventing generalised feelings of alienation from political institutions and processes, and circumventing either the development of political apathy, or the expression of discontent in the form of extra-parliamentary political activity.

It is possible then to summarise the status, role and functions of opinion polls in capitalist societies as defined by those who broadly advocate their use in political affairs. Firstly, they are developed and conducted by independent organisations, using carefully constructed social science tools to monitor and assess public opinion. Secondly, in its natural state, public opinion is atomised, amorphous, and unintelligible. Polls aim to make sense of the plurality of opinions, attitudes and values in society in terms of direction, intensity and consistency, and provide a coherent representation of public opinion for policy-makers. Thirdly, policy-makers can use polling data between elections to gauge the combined views of individual citizens, and distinguish these from the more vocal and expressive views of powerful (but not necessarily representative) organisations, groups and classes in society. Fourthly, polls can provide an effective channel of communication between the governed and governors. That is, they enable politicians to bear in mind the needs and aspirations of citizens in drafting and implementing legislation, and obtain feedback from citizens on the appropriateness, performance and effectiveness of such policy. Finally, polls can function as a link between popular society and the political institutions and structures of government. They provide a mechanism through which popular society can participate in political affairs and as such, they are a tool through which generalised public opinion can be meshed into the political process. Consequently, they serve to bolster political stability in capitalist societies.

Criticisms of Polls

In many respects, this view of opinion polls is considered to be misleading. Some observers have argued that the assumptions that leaders and political elites are responsive to public opinion (as identified by polls), and that public opinion itself is ultimately translated into public policy, are questionable. For instance, Crespi (1989, pp.36-39) compared the results of a series of polls concerning the views of the public on various high-profile issues with the policies of the Reagan administration between 1985 and 1986, and found very little evidence of correspondence between the two. In relation to domestic programmes, indirect military interventions in Nicaragua, and the 'Star Wars' defence initiative, there existed a considerable gap between public opinion and the President's policies. Similarly in Britain, the public concern reported in opinion polls over issues such as the poll tax, health service changes, and privatisation of public utilities such as the water and the electricity industries had no influence upon policy-making under the Conservative administration in the 1987-1992 Parliament.

A further criticism of polls alleges that they give citizens a false sense of being influential when in reality political power is held and exercised by dominant groups, classes and elites within society. Johan Galtung (1967) has suggested that polls do not enable us all to exert our combined will over policy-makers equally. They are not quasi-referendums on issues which politicians respond to, but mechanisms which mask the ability of powerful interests to shape governmental outcomes.

Furthermore, advocates of polling may be criticised for tending to overlook the social pressures which are exerted upon the manufacture of public opinion research. For instance, Lukes (1974) has claimed that through 'non-decision-making', elites are able to exercise power in class societies by controlling the parameters of discussion, and defining which issues are and are not relevant to debate. Marsh cites a number of examples to illustrate how opinion polls which are commissioned by external agencies reflect the biases and ideological assumptions of these agencies by, for instance, the questions asked, and the form that they take (1979, pp.276-82). She claims that:

> The sponsors take all the important decisions. They can choose what to have a poll about, how to word it, when to have it, whom to ask the questions of; and newspaper owners can control how and when and whether it is reported. And . . . each of these decisions can markedly effect the appearance of this public opinion. Something as open to manipulation as this can never be used to further democracy (1979, p.283).

Drawing on this idea, it is possible to challenge Gallup's vision of the role of opinion polls in the democratisation process, as it fails to identify that perhaps polls reflect not the sum of interests within society, but instead the interests of those influential and powerful groups and elites who actually commission and publish polls; they do this in order to influence the political agenda, and ultimately to create issue-priorities for the citizenry and to control opinion formation. Polls should not therefore be seen in terms of any 'populist' notion of political power in capitalist societies, whereby the general will of the public exercises authority over elected representatives. They are not the articulation and aggregation of views from below waiting to be expressed between elections, but rather a social product offered to the public from above by dominant groups and classes.

Another criticism of polls is that, particularly in elections, they can help to determine electoral outcomes by defining what is and what is not appropriate action or behaviour for voters. That is, that polls can be self-fulfilling, by fostering either a bandwagon, or an underdog effect. Essentially:

> A bandwagon effect in an election occurs when the predicted winner in an election poll gains additional votes as a result of the publication of the poll. Conversely, an underdog effect occurs when the predicted loser in an election poll gains additional votes as a result of the publication of the poll (Henshel and Johnston, 1987, p.494).

The possibility of predictions affecting outcomes in electoral politics has been developed in a number of theoretical articles (Simon, 1957; Gartner, 1976; Straffin, 1977; Zech, 1975). Explanations of bandwagon effects from polls have tended to emphasise conformity causes, that is, the information about majority opinion itself causes some people to adopt the majority view. However, there is little empirical evidence to support these findings, although Worcester (1991, p.204) has cited British examples in which a bandwagon, partly generated by the opinion polls, may have helped the Liberal candidates at the 1962 Orpington by-election, and at the Bermondsey by-election just before the 1983 General Election. However, there is a collection of evidence which suggests that polls can affect stated intention to vote in an underdog direction:

> The supporters of the party behind at the polls say they are more likely to turn out to vote, and supporters of all parties say they are less likely to turn out if a clear-cut victory persists (Marsh, 1984, p.52).

Worcester has stated that "...in Britain the effect has always been an underdog effect" (Worcester, 1983, p.30), while Crewe (1986, p.246) has noted that:

> In eight of the twelve post-war elections the final forecast polls have tended ...to over-estimate the actual vote of the out-going government (whether or not it is re-elected) and to under-estimate the actual vote of the outgoing opposition. This has led to suggestions that the polls do have underdog effects, but only on last minute deciders; perhaps they produce a reaction against the prospect of the government obtaining too big a majority or induce complacency amongst the least committed of the government's supporters.

However, while there is little conclusive evidence as well as a lack of agreement concerning the direct effect of bandwagon or underdog roles in polling at elections, many commentators have focused upon the indirect influence of polls (see Henshel and Johnston, 1987, pp.493-511). Here it has been alleged that polls have altered party strategies, affected the morale of activists, and influenced the mass media's expectations of the result. Noelle-Neumann focused upon a broader indirect effect, whereby polls contributed to a "spiral of silence" in which minority views became increasingly unpopular because people were unwilling to express views which they knew were not widely shared (Noelle-Neumann, 1974).

A final criticism of opinion polling rejects the assumption that polls provide an appropriate (and effective) method for representative governments to obtain valid information about public opinion. On the contrary, critics would argue that public opinion is not something that is measurable, let alone agreed across any given society. Crespi (1989, p.6) summarises this position:

> Public opinion is a quality of the political environment, as intangible as the air we breathe, and not susceptible to what are . . . crude 'measurements' of a pseudoscience . . . (Such criticisms) considered nonsensical the claim that tallying the number of people who in a poll say they favour or oppose some proposed legislation tells us anything meaningful about public opinion.

Summary

In spite of these criticisms, political opinion polls continue to play a conspicuous role in capitalist societies. Indeed, as we shall see, the intervention which polls make in late-capitalist societies is becoming increasingly significant over time. Furthermore, they have played an influential role in the general processes of transition which are currently underway in the former communist-led countries of Central and Eastern Europe. However, the question of whether or not polls have on balance had the effect of extending or undermining democratic practices in contemporary societies remains to be seen. The following chapters will explore the extent to which Gallup's vision of opinion polls as facilitators of democratic, populist, and efficient government has been realised.

Notes

1. Tracking polls pose the same questions to different samples of people over a period of time, often years.

2. In panel surveys, a sample of people are selected, and these same people are asked questions repeatedly over time, although the period involved is usually shorter than for tracking polls.

3   The Comparative Context of Opinion Polling

Introduction

This book is chiefly concerned with examining how political opinion polling contributes to the democratisation process in different types of society. To do this requires an assessment of the variety of political procedures and structures which exist in different countries, and the implications they have for the development of opinion polling and vice versa. Polling may be assigned different roles in different societies, and polls may impact upon these political processes in different ways. This chapter sets out the scope for polling in capitalist and post-communist societies, by identifying what are the structures of political power for each type of political system, and what mechanisms exist to link their states and civil societies in the elaboration and implementation of social needs and competing interests in the policy-making process.

The Organisation of Political Power

Classifying phenomena within the social sciences is an inevitably imprecise and somewhat controversial activity. Nonetheless, as Ball (1988, p.38) maintains:

> Classification is essentially an attempt to isolate the most important characteristics of the political system from the less important . . . it is to simplify, to ensure the grouping of like with like, to allow for significant comparison, and thereby extend our understanding.

The discussion which follows compares political systems in capitalist and post-communist societies. However, it seeks neither to over-state the differences between the states and civil societies in capitalist and post-communist contexts, nor to mask any internal differences which exist within any particular type of political system; instead, this approach aims to provide clarity and understanding of the differing historical and contextual landscapes in which polls operate. The categories for this comparative analysis are therefore:

- *capitalist political systems*. This category covers the liberal capitalist systems of Western Europe and the USA which are characterised by representative governments, and regular competitive elections based upon universal franchise. It does not include authoritarian capitalist political systems such as those to be found in Spain, Greece and Portugal before their liberal transitions in the 1970s, Chile under the Pinochet military-dictatorship, or Apartheid South Africa.
- *post-communist political systems*. This category refers to those political systems of Central and Eastern Europe which were formerly classified as communist political systems, but which have undergone a series of structural transformations at a number of levels - economic, political and social - since 1989.[1]

For capitalist political systems, the analysis contrasts early post-Second World War contexts with late-capitalist situations since the end of the 1960s, where it is argued that the processes of change and restructuring impacting upon opinion polls are accelerating and combining to create political environments which are increasingly complex for pollsters to survey. In Central and Eastern Europe, the collapse of earlier communist regimes in 1989 has facilitated the development of forces which have implications for the opinion pollsters in post-communist societies which are similar to those faced by opinion pollsters in late-capitalist societies.

The State and Politics in Capitalist Political Systems

According to Hague and Harrop (1987), majority rule in capitalist political systems is balanced by various constraints upon the exercise of power, so that they have 'limited' governments, and are qualified by a due regard for the acknowledged rights of individuals and minorities. In this way, they are defined as having 'Constitutional' governments. Thus, there is a formal separation of powers between the various structures and agents of the state (the executive and legislature) and political independence of the judiciary, bureaucracy, media, military and police. In addition, basic civil liberties, such as freedom of speech, association, religion, and freedom from arbitrary arrest, are recognised and protected within the political system. Such political systems are also characterised as having 'pluralistic' governments, whereby majoritarian rule tends to operate alongside numerous interest groups which are consulted about, and bargain over government proposals which affect them. More than one political party competes for political power, and the mechanisms available to secure such power are formally open, with established forms of procedure such as periodic elections based on universal franchise.

This conception of the operation of capitalist political systems has been criticised on a number of fronts. Thus Schumpeter has argued that, in such political systems, the direct role of the masses is limited and fairly passive, in that they tend to choose rulers through representative institutions, but do not govern. Democracy is therefore characterised as a 'process', in which elites acquire the power to decide, by means of a competitive struggle for peoples' votes (Schumpeter, 1976, p.269). Lakeman (1974), has condemned the way in which electoral systems operate in some capitalist political systems (especially Britain). The absence of proportionally-based electoral systems distorts the relationship between votes cast for, and degree of political power secured in 'representative' assembles by political parties. She maintains that this tends to result in elective dictatorships. Others have questioned the alleged separation of powers in the United Kingdom (Dearlove and Saunders, 1984) and the openness of the processes of entry and recruitment to positions of political power (Miliband, 1969; Parkin, 1971). A generalised critique of the state and democratic processes in the UK has been articulated by Charter 88, whose programme of political reform suggests that many of the features associated with the term 'capitalist political system' outlined above, are either absent or deficient in the current context. Indeed, Blondel (1969, p.xxxviii) has observed that this is a universal problem:

> Liberal-democracy (capitalist political system) is... difficult to define, as the major components of the combined index (free elections, existence of an opposition, etc) seem to defy rigorous operationalisation.

However, in spite of these problems of operationalisation, Ball maintains that such conceptual categories as 'capitalist political system' and 'liberal democracy' are appropriate; indeed, such categories are "...flexible enough to be able to group together various systems by emphasising certain essential characteristics, and usefully to contrast these systems with other broad categories of political system" (Ball, 1988, p.45). Blondel too, argues for the establishment of broad typologies of political system. Using his notion of the 'distribution of norms', the apparent irregularity of features present in contemporary 'capitalist political systems' can be accommodated. That is, that by asking questions such as "Who allocates values within a society, all members, representatives or elites?" (Democratic-Authoritarian continuum), "How are decisions taken, and are there any restrictions on examination of alternatives?" (Liberal-Authoritarian continuum), and "What is the substantive content of policies?" (Egalitarian-Nonegalitarian continuum), it is possible to locate an identifiable 'cluster' of capitalist political systems which is sufficiently distinct from other types of political systems to enable meaningful comparative analyses (Blondel, 1995, pp.27-47).

Majoritarian Democracy

Within such a framework, two forms of state and society emerge. The first of these is Majoritarian Democracy, characterised by the 'Westminster' model, where a single party forms the government (bolstered by a 'first-past-the-post' or plurality electoral system) without real hindrance from institutions which limit executive power (Lijphart, 1984, pp.1-20). Under such a system, the state is unitary and centralised so that a national parliamentary majority and cabinet can legislate for every geographical area and functional responsibility. This system tended to operate in New Zealand, and also in post-war Britain until 1974. In the latter case, society was relatively homogenous and stable, with one main social cleavage, based on class, which tended to pre-dispose voters toward one or other of the two major (Conservative and Labour) parties. There were, then, strong levels of party identification. Defeat was generally accepted since the election was perceived as fair, and there was a possibility that the losing class and party might secure political power in the next election. Since 1974 however, British majoritarian democracy has been weakened as the traditional class cleavage which underpinned the two-party system declined and new divisions (especially nationalism) emerged. The major parties have also been challenged by nationalist parties in Scotland and Wales, by new political parties such as the SDP and the Green Party, and rejuvenated parties such as the Liberal Democrats, as well as ad hoc single-issue parties targeting vulnerable seats held by the governing party (including recently the Referendum Party, Protect NHS, the Natural Law Party, and the UK Independence Party in the late 1980s and early 1990s). A number of left-wing political parties have emerged ostensibly as a response to New Labour's drift toward the centre of the political spectrum in the mid-1990s; parties such as the trades union-based Socialist Labour Party, and the Socialist Party targeted a number of key seats at the 1997 British General Election, and gained not insubstantial numbers of votes in doing so.

Of course, challenges were made to the major parties during the 1950s and 1960s by smaller (often left-wing) parties (see Butler et al's *British General Election* series). However, such parties never really offered a threat to the Labour/Conservative duopoly of the British party system, because of the strong links between voters and these dominant parties at that time. In this respect, the minor challenging parties attempted to extend the party system *artificially* by presenting themselves as alternatives to the Labour and Conservative parties, when in reality only relatively few voters were prepared to consider breaking ranks with their 'class party'.

What is significant about the emergence of the new parties in the *current* period however is that they are largely a response to changing conditions within the party system, with voters now acting as discerning 'consumers' with few obvious loyalties tying them to the traditional mass-based parties. These contemporary challenger parties then have appeared largely as a reaction to the increasing trend toward what many observers have described as partisan dealignment and/or class dealignment, and the tendency of the electorate to consider voting for non-conventional parties during elections.[2] Furthermore, electoral politics in the current era is characterised by increasing voter volatility and tactical voting, which makes the presence of such parties in marginal seats of particular concern to the established parties.[3]

Consociational Democracy

Lijphart (1984) has argued that in societies in which there are multiple cleavages, a more appropriate form of state organisation is Consociational Democracy, in which the use of power-sharing can be an effective means of securing a stable democracy and of preventing crises. To ensure that minority groups do not opt out of formal politics or withdraw their support from the political system, mechanisms are available to incorporate and integrate all major social groups and interests in decision-making forums, normally on a basis proportional to their numbers. Government is usually by grand coalition, with proportional electoral systems designed to ensure commensurability between the degree of voter support that parties achieve, and the level of political power that they secure in government. A two-chamber legislature normally operates with strong minority representation to veto majority tyranny. There is substantial freedom for each social segment to run their own affairs, and this is encouraged by territorial federalism and by administrative decentralisation.

In Consociational Democracies, the political system, and the relations between its various structures and popular society, are defined within a written constitution which can only be amended under extraordinary conditions rather than by simple majorities. Lijphart maintains that the power-sharing which evolves at elite-level, when combined with the separate, multi-cleavage communities which exist at mass level, guarantees political stability. However, in the current context, developments at a number of levels - economic and social - have combined to undermine the political stability of many Consociational political systems. This is most obvious since 1989. Thus, the emergence of a host of new political parties and movements has weakened the links between established parties and their respective electoral communities in a number of European countries at national and provincial level.

In particular, far-right parties have tended to gain in confidence, prestige and electoral support throughout mainland Europe in the 1990s. In France, the National Front under its charismatic leader, Le Pen, achieved a significant psychological breakthrough at the 1993 General Election, winning 12.2% of the national vote (although, because of the electoral system, failing to take any seats). At the 1994 European Assembly elections, his far-right party consolidated this support with a 10.6% share of the electorate. In the first (multi-candidate) round of the 1995 presidential elections, he secured 15.5% of the vote, only 4.6% behind the eventual second round victor, Chirac. In Germany, the fascist forces have performed particularly well in state elections during the 1990s. The Republican Party for instance gained 10.9% of the vote and 15 seats in Baden Wattenburg in April 1992, with a further 8.3% in Berlin in May of the same year. In March 1993, they secured 8.1% of the electorate at state elections in Hessen, with 9.3% in Germany's second city, Frankfurt. In Belgium the Vlaams Blok won 12.2% of the vote in Flanders at the elections in 1995 for the Chambre de Deputis, and gained the largest share of the vote (26%) in Antwerp. The extreme right Freedom Party (FPO) led by the pro-Hitlerite Haider, won 21% of the vote at the Austrian General Election in January 1996, following the fall of the Socialist SPO and Conservative OVP coalition government. This represented largely a consolidation of their vote from the previous general election, where they secured a 22% share of the electorate, suggesting a 'hard-core' of support of about one fifth of the voting public. The collapse of the traditional Italian parties has led to a complete overhaul of the party system, with the emergence of new and reinvigorated parties dominating the scene, in the form of the nationalist Northern League, the far-right alliance of Berlusconi's Forza Italia with the fascist National Alliance, a left coalition led by the reconstructed Party of the Democratic Left, and a host of radical left and anti-Mafia parties (such as Network, and the Party of Communist Refoundation).

In Canada, the ruling Conservatives were virtually eliminated from national political office by returning only two of their members in the October 1993 national election; meanwhile, the relatively new Reform Party gained 52 seats, and the Bloc Québécois, established as late as 1990 by Bouchard, became the official opposition to the victorious Liberal Party. The relative strength of the Bloc Québécois was again apparent in a provincial referendum in 1995, where it narrowly missed out in its campaign for a separate state by 50,000 votes. In the USA, a new third-force in politics guided by Perot emerged at the 1992 Presidential elections. Its vote of 19% suggested that the traditional two-party system there was beginning to show signs of stress, although, as leader of the Reform Party in 1996, Perot won only 8% of the national vote for the presidency.

The State and Politics in Communist and Post-Communist Political Systems

In order to enable a comparison of contexts for opinion polling, it is necessary to identify a second category - post-communist political systems. Essentially, this label refers to those political systems of Central and Eastern Europe which are currently in a period of restructuring, and a state of flux. These transitional societies have emerged as a response to communist-style organisation of the state and society.

Communist Political Systems

White et al (1990) maintain that four features characterised the former European communist political systems. First of all, there was a generalised commitment to an official ideology of Marxism-Leninism which sought to bring about the establishment of a new type of society based on the economic, social and cultural emancipation of humankind. This transformative ideology required controlled mass participation, under the auspices and guidance of a single (usually communist) party. Thus, the second characteristic feature of communist political systems was that political, and hence state power was highly centralised within one political party, and this party was not open to electoral challenge. Given this effective monopoly over the state and politics, the party was able to pursue its ideological goals by instituting plans to organise the economy along socialist lines; the state had ownership and control over all aspects of economic life, including the means, and processes of production. Thus, thirdly, communist political systems possessed 'command' economies, rather than the 'market' economies typically found in capitalist political systems. Finally, the formal separation of powers which characterised capitalist political systems did not feature in communist political systems. Rather, the party was given a leading role in society and embedded itself in those institutions of the state - bureaucracy, judiciary, mass media, army, and police - which, formally at least, pursued relatively independent roles under capitalism.

However, while these features were by and large present within all of the former communist political systems of Central and Eastern Europe, there were a number of dimensions upon which it was possible to differentiate these societies. Thus Hague and Harrop (1987, p.56) note that, whereas in most communist political systems the means of production had been socialised, in Hungary and East Germany, socialist market economies existed in which industrial enterprises made key strategic decisions on output targets, types of product, prices and wages. Lovenduski and Woodall report that in Poland the principle of collectivisation was rejected in favour of the private ownership of agriculture and land (1987, p.84-85).

The relationship between the party and state also took different forms. Usually the party occupied the leading role within society, whereby all policy-decisions were made according to a 'top-down' formula. However, in the former Yugoslavia, politics functioned within the Titoist doctrine of decentralisation under the 'Basic Law of Workers self-management', with the Yugoslav League of Communists taking a guiding (not leading) role in the economy (Carter, 1982). According to White et al (1990, pp.4-6) it was possible to identify differences between communist political systems along various social and cultural lines. Poland is traditionally Roman Catholic, while many republics of the former Soviet Union were eastern Orthodox or Muslim, and Albania, traditionally Muslim, was officially atheist. Such political systems could also be distinguished by levels of social and economic development.

Despite these inter-national differences, the communist legacy in Central and Eastern Europe is that of an essentially highly centralised political system, with one dominant ideology organised within a ruling communist-style party, which tended to monopolise the state, and through this, the economy, society, and political discourse.

Post-Communist Political Systems

Formerly classified as communist political systems, the post-communist societies can be distinguished from communist and from capitalist types of political system on a number of fronts. Firstly the ruling communist parties have either been replaced, or have re-emerged as re-constructed parties of the left competing for political power in essentially pluralistic party systems. (In reality, many of the old communist forces and personnel have returned to positions of power, albeit with different labels, and usually with a largely 'social-democratic' style programme). Secondly, political pluralisation has encouraged a proliferation of political parties and the establishment usually of complex multi-party systems. The majority of these parties are the product of the political and economic transformations which have taken place since 1989. Often they are populist parties, with no clearly defined political identity, worked out ideology, or consistent political programme. Consequently, they often have no identifiable social base amongst the new electorates, and there are few established party-voter alliances relative to those which can be found in both communist and capitalist political systems.

Thirdly, the economies are in a process of transformation, with changes in the ownership and control of the means of production following the privatisation of industry and agriculture. Such developments have brought about changes in the social relations of production, although typically there are no obvious patterns of social stratification emerging to take the place of the social groups which existed before.   When compared to the relative homogeneity of its communist predecessors, these societies can therefore be characterised as at an advanced stage of social, economic and cultural fragmentation.   There are a number of cross-cutting cleavages apparent, based on class, gender, ethnicity, religion and many other dimensions.   Consequently, the newly emerging electorates are both atomised and volatile in post-communist political systems.

Fourthly, the combination of multi-party systems with heterogeneous and volatile electorates has led to the emergence of government by coalition in most post-communist political systems.   These governments are often temporary and unstable because of a number of associated factors.   These include: a generalised lack of agreement between governing parties on political priorities and issues; an absence of commensurability between government coalitions and the electorate; persistent failures to solve the problems associated with economic restructuring and wrought by the more generalised global economic recession; and finally, the drafting of new political constitutions has led to the establishment of new political structures, structural configurations and relational linkages.   However, these are not stable and are subject to modification.[4]

There are inevitably differences which can be identified between these societies in terms of the areas outlined here.   However, the similarities between these societies are such that it is possible to cluster them together as a single category of political system which can be distinguished from their communist pasts and from capitalist political systems.

Political Polling Complexity

So what are the key features of these political systems which are likely to impinge specifically upon the development of political opinion polling?   The following section addresses this question by examining the *political culture, party systems, mechanisms for political participation* (including elections), and the *policy process* for both capitalist and post-communist political systems in order to analyse how differences and developments at these various levels are likely to impact upon political opinion polling.   It will then be possible to establish the concept of Complex Politics through which to articulate and organise an analysis of the increasingly variable and volatile environment in which opinion polls operate.

Opinion Polling and Political Culture

In this analysis, I assume that the effectiveness of political opinion polling is linked both to the level of political integration within any society, and to the pervasiveness of a mass national political culture, or clearly defined and durable political sub-cultures. This assumption is based on the idea that where there is relative stability in political structures and institutions, there will be (a) a high level of satisfaction with and alignment to political parties, institutions and arrangements, and (b) a clearly focused and defined political consciousness amongst the citizenry, with sets of stable opinions, attitudes and value systems held by different sub-sets of the populace. A combination of these two points provides a context which is conducive for political opinion polling. These are likely to be high rates of accuracy in the data collected, and high levels of performance amongst the polling organisations. Conversely, where a national political culture is deficient or absent, the tasks for opinion pollsters will be more arduous. Such situations include those contexts where there is a newly emerging political system, whose structures, institutions and procedures are relatively unknown quantities amongst the citizenry, or where there is a widespread rejection of the political system, or of generalised perceptions of alienation from political life amongst the citizenry, or of political apathy.

Capitalist societies There are broadly two approaches to the study of political culture in capitalist political systems. The first suggests that in the majority of cases, there is a national political culture, which is the product of that country's historical development, and which is transmitted across generations via socialising institutions like the family. Such behavioural accounts were best expressed in Almond and Verba's *The Civic Culture* (1963). This study of five countries suggested that Britain was closest to an idealised model of a democratic culture, with citizens sufficiently active in politics to express preferences to governments, but not so involved in particular issues as to refuse to accept the decisions made by the elite. Such a civic culture manifests itself in a number of ways, including attachment to established national political parties depending upon one's social, economic or cultural background. Thus, the British party system up until 1974 was characterised by strong alliances between two blocs of voters (the working class, and the middle/upper class) and the Labour and Conservative parties. These alliances were the products of welfare state collectivism which tended to polarise society into two clearly identifiable political camps with distinct political priorities and orientations.

An alternative, marxist approach argues that political culture is the product of an attempt by the dominant class to impose its values on the subordinate class, through formal mechanisms like the media and the education system. The national political culture is therefore the product of an asymmetrical ideological struggle between these classes, and as such is not a stable, enduring feature of capitalist societies. This approach has its origins in Gramsci's concept of 'hegemony', which maintains that a ruling class is only able to enjoy economic and social domination if it is capable of exercising moral and political leadership. However, because this hegemony is imposed, it will always be superficial, and there will always be the possibility of the overthrow of the prevailing political culture (Gramsci, 1971).

Both approaches acknowledge the decay of political culture within capitalist societies since the late 1960s and early 1970s, and a generalised decline in support for political parties, institutions and arrangements. In the current context, the national political culture in the UK has been challenged in a number of ways, and the processes unfolding there are not dissimilar to those emerging elsewhere in Europe and in other late-capitalist countries. These include the decline in support for unitary government, with the strengthening of nationalist tendencies, movements and parties in Scotland and Wales, and the (periodic) intensification of armed struggle over the national question in Northern Ireland; at the same time, there has been a pervasive move toward centralised European integration, at the expense of parliamentary sovereignty. There has also been a decline in the traditional links between class and party, which, when combined with the emergence of new political parties and of electoral volatility, has further weakened the national political culture. This has been reinforced by processes of increasing socio-cultural heterogeneity (with for instance, changes in the nature of the class structure, and the emergence of new cleavages such as those based on regionalism, ethnicity, and life-style). Thirdly, there has been a shift away from traditional forms of political participation toward more non-conventional forms of action. This is largely as a result of dissatisfaction with the political and institutional arrangements of the state, resulting for instance in demands for political reform, and widespread political apathy and feelings of alienation. It will be argued that these features and developments are combining to undermine the notion of a national political culture and of a generalised public opinion. As a consequence, these processes are having the effect of increasingly complicating the political context for opinion polling in capitalist political systems because the values, attitudes and opinions held by voters are neither stable nor therefore easily measurable.

Communist and post-communist societies   The political culture of communist societies was partly shaped through the official ideology which required the party to create communist citizens through an array of educational, and cultural institutions. The political culture therefore was officially 'classless', 'socialist' and 'atheist' - culminating in the development of a completely homogenous society, devoid of the types of cleavages which tend to characterise capitalist societies. In theory then, there should have been little or no scope for opinion polling in communist societies, because there was an absence of divided opinions, the raw material upon which polling thrives. However, in reality there were substantial variations which existed between groups, which combined to undermine the pervasiveness of any mass national political culture in communist societies. White notices a number of cleavages which emerged, particularly in the former Soviet Union, between men and women, the generations, social classes, town and country, different nationalities, and between different ethnic groups in terms of political attitudes and experiences (1990, pp.47-54). These differences were further complicated by White's notion of "two persons in one body" (White, 1979, p.11). Here a 'visible' person repeated the phraseology of the Communist Party officials and authorities, and verbally expressed a commitment to Marxist-Leninist values. Meanwhile, a 'hidden' person retained a set of older, pre-communist values[5]. While the official perception of political opinion polling was that such tools had little or no value in a classless, homogenous society, the reality was that there was considerable diversity within these political cultures, such that there were indeed divided opinions and cleavages which polls could attempt to report. Nonetheless the performance and effectiveness of opinion polling would be undermined according to White's characterisation of communist men and women; that is, that polls could not always predict outcomes or behaviour on the basis of verbal expressions of political attitudes, opinions and values.

Following the transformations which have taken place since 1989 throughout these ex-communist countries of Central and Eastern Europe, there has been an atomisation of public opinion, and a shift in the political cultures. White maintains that the communist value system (that is, the commitment to specifically Marxist-Leninist principles) was never deeply internalised except by relatively small sections of the population. While there was an initial rejection of communism as an ideology and as an approach to political development by peoples of the region, this tended to be coupled with a generalised suspicion of politics in many of these post-communist societies, and an inability or unwillingness to accept the significance of emergent political institutions and democratic mechanisms:

> Overall, the transformations in Central and Eastern Europe brought about an extraordinary fluidity of values, which would take some time to crystallise. The rejection of communism as a set of ideas and as a system of symbols appeared to be complete, but otherwise there was little agreement as to what should replace them (White, 1990, p.69).

Indeed, the re-election of former communist parties to power in many of these post-communist societies undermines even the notion of a unifying set of values built around the rejection of communism. In Romania, the Party of Social Democrats, under the leadership of former communist Central Committee member, Ion Iliescu, and former high-ranking Party officials, has been a dominant force since the revolution which brought down Ceausescu in December 1989. The PSD was the key player in the National Salvation Front which won 263 out of the 387 Assembly seats, and 91 of the 119 Senate seats at the May 1990 General Elections, with 85% for Iliescu himself in the presidential election. At the 1992 elections the NSF split, and Iliescu's left faction - the National Democratic Salvation Front - was returned to office as the single largest party with 28% of the vote (Dellenbrandt, 1994a, p. 213). In November 1992, the Lithuanian communists, under the new label, Lithuanian Democratic Labour Party, were elected to government, gaining a narrow majority of seats in the Seimas - 73 out of 141; their leader, the former anti-Moscow maverick communist Brazauskas, was elected president in 1993 with over 60% of electoral support (Dellenbrandt, 1994b, p. 110).

The landslide victory gained by Solidarity over the communist Polish United Workers Party at the June 1989 election, led to the first post-Second World War non-communist government in Eastern Europe (Grzybowski, 1994, pp. 36-73). However, at the September 1993 elections, the communists' fortunes were reversed: under the name of the Democratic Left Alliance (SLD), the former communists, now transformed into a movement advocating political pluralism and a market economy, secured 171 seats in the 460-member Sejm, and 73 of the 100 Senate seats, and formed a governmental alliance with the Polish Peasant Party who had previously abandoned them in 1989 to join Solidarity (Ka-Lok Chan, 1995; Zubek, 1994). Their power and authority was consolidated with the victory of the SLD candidate Kwasniewski over the former Polish Solidarity Leader, Walesa, at the Presidential elections in November 1995. In the Ukraine, the reconstituted Communist Party secured the largest number of votes (25.4%) at the parliamentary elections in 1994, and returned 86 deputies to the 450 member Supreme Council (Bojcun, 1995).

The performance of the former communists within the re-named Bulgarian Socialist Party (BSP) has been particularly variable. The fall of Zhivkov, First Secretary to the Communist Party and chairman of the State Council, facilitated the movement towards political pluralism, and in June 1990, free elections took place. The BSP won a majority with 211 of the 400 parliamentary seats, compared to the 144 secured by the main opposition group, the Union of Democratic Forces (UDF). However, in October 1991, victory was reversed, with 110 seats for the UDF, and 106 seats for the BSP in the 240 seat reformed parliament. However, the UDF government, faced with a political crisis when its erstwhile coalition partners, the Movement for Rights and Freedom voted against it in a vote of no confidence at the end of October 1992, was replaced by a broad coalition government of technocrats and experts (Bankowicz, 1994). At the General Election in December 1994, the BSP were returned to governmental power winning 44% of the vote, and 124 seats in the 240 seat parliament.

The former communists in Hungary, the Hungarian Socialist Party, won an overall majority at the parliamentary elections in May 1994, under the leadership of Gyula Horn. After being eclipsed by the Hungarian Democratic Forum (HDF), and the Alliance of Free Democrats (AFD) at the first post-communist elections in March and April 1990, the HSP were elected to office on a landslide victory, with 54% of the vote, and 209 mandates in the 386 member parliament, forming a coalition government with the anti-communist, AFD (Racz and Kukorelli, 1995). In Estonia, a mix of former low-level communists and agrarian leaders from the allied Coalition Party and Rural Union won 41 of the 101 legislative seats at the parliamentary elections held in March 1995. The Centre Party, regarded as centre left, won 17 seats. Perhaps the most significant communist resurrection in Central and Eastern Europe has been achieved in Russia. In December 1993, the Russian Communist Party came third in the State Duma elections, behind Russia's Choice, and Zhirinovsky's Liberal Democrats, with 12.4% of the vote, and 48 of the 450 seats (Sakwa, 1995). However, at the Duma elections in December 1995, the communists were elected as the single largest party, winning 22% of vote, and, in alliance with the Agrarians, 189 parliamentary seats.

Thus, there has been a significant decline in the relevance and salience of 'anti-communism' as a factor uniting post-communist citizens. In the absence of this defining variable, the mass publics are typically amorphous, with multiple, yet weak cross-cutting cleavages, and consequently, they are politically and electorally volatile. The implications for opinion pollsters working within such political systems are that it will become increasingly difficult to make sense of public opinion and report meaningful and accurate trends, because of the transitory and often contradictory character of opinions, attitudes and beliefs held and expressed. Coupled with a generalised political apathy which may impact on response rates, the lack of a sustainable and coherent political culture in post-communist political systems is likely to foster a particularly complex context for political opinion polling.

Opinion Polling and Party Systems

The nature of the party system in any society is likely to impact upon the ability and performance of opinion polling in a number of ways: if pollsters are to measure the relationship between the electorate and the political parties, their tasks will be least complicated where the following conditions exist. Firstly, that there are stable and enduring alliances between political parties and groups of voters. Under such circumstances, it should be possible for opinion pollsters to estimate the political behaviour and/or responses of voters to political issues, by reference to certain background characteristics which govern their pre-disposition to a political party and its ideology. Problems will emerge for pollsters however where either (a) they contact 'deviant' voters who express contradictory political orientations, or (b) where the record of one's 'traditional' party has been weak, resulting in either a temporary shift in voting alignments or else in abstention from politics.

Secondly, party competition focuses upon the struggle of a limited number of long-established parties for political power. Here voters are presented with a straightforward choice between their traditional party and other parties whose ideologies are based upon opposing social, economic or cultural interests. Conversely, the greater the level of party choice, the more likely it will be that party commitments will overlap, and ideological distinctions will blur. This will provide a greater scope for voters to switch to alternative 'like' political parties if they are temporarily dissatisfied with the performance of their traditional party. The voter/party relationship will be more variable in the latter situation, providing a more complex context for opinion pollsters than in the former situation. Where there is no party competition there will be no party preferences to compare.

Thirdly, the conditions for polling will be most conducive where political parties have clearly defined political ideologies and programmes. Here voters are able to make a relatively straightforward decision in choosing between parties at an election based on the degree of congruence between party manifesto commitments and their own political orientations, as well as the record of each party's ideology as policy outcomes in government. Under such circumstances, there will be limited electoral volatility, or shifts between voters and their preferred parties.

Fourthly, the outcome of an election should be majority rule by a single party, so that its performance (and the performance of the official opposition party) can be closely monitored by voters. Where governments comprise coalitions of parties, the ability of voters to identify which party is accountable for policy successes or failures will be less effective than in the former situation. This may lead to random voter behaviour at later elections, or indeed to a rejection of all government parties where there are high levels of dissatisfaction with policy outcomes or performance, and a switch instead to other non-governmental parties.

Finally, the tasks for pollsters will be least complicated in those contexts where the political parties are well established, and have a high profile amongst the electorate. Thus, pollsters will be able to monitor the relationship between parties and voters where the nature of the party programme is clearly understood, where the party leadership and its personnel are recognisable, and where voters can critically evaluate the record of a party in government and in opposition. Where party systems are dominated by parties which are relatively new and largely unknown, voters will be unable to make informed decisions at elections. Their voting behaviour therefore is likely to be random and highly unpredictable.

Capitalist societies With these issues in mind, polling is likely to have been most effective in early post-Second World War capitalist political systems, especially in majoritarian democracies like the UK. These had competitive party systems, dominated by two established parties (which were however being increasingly challenged by alternative parties), with relatively differentiated party programmes, and which competed to form single party governments. The dominant political parties had relatively stable social bases of support amongst the electorate, although typically, party loyalties weakened, and electorates became more pragmatic and instrumental. The political context for opinion polling was likely to be less stable and more complicated in Consociational democracies which historically have had multi-party systems, with governments usually based upon a coalition of often disparate parties; inevitably, these coalitions were often temporary and usually unstable. In late-capitalist societies, the party systems in both Majoritarian- and Consociational-style democracies are undergoing processes of restructuring, creating increasingly complex political contexts for opinion polling in which voter-party alliances are fracturing, and established parties are losing their traditional electorates to newer parties.

Communist and post-communist societies Similar developments are taking shape in contemporary Central and Eastern European societies. Prior to the collapse of communism in these countries, the party systems which existed were typically non-competitive and relatively closed single- or dominant-party systems. The ruling communist party in each country was the key political institution. While there was usually some opposition (except in the former Soviet Union), it was neither sufficient nor significant enough to provide any meaningful challenge to communist hegemony (Hague and Harrop, 1987, p.151). Furthermore, while the communist parties were elective in principle, these elections were indirect; each level of the party was elected by the level below, but these were essentially non-competitive contests, with nominations issued from above. The principle of Democratic Centralism ensured that all decisions were binding and once made, no dissent was tolerated. Thus, in a non-competitive party system, the single, dominant party was centralised and hierarchical. In addition, no alternative political priorities or policy choices were made available to the public to consider.

Consequently there was little scope for opinion polls to measure electoral choice, or political preferences. However, there was scope for polls to measure citizen reactions to given policy.

The party systems in post-communist societies which have emerged from these one-party/dominant-party contexts are likely to provide a relative degree of complexity for opinion pollsters. Here, the proliferation of new parties is likely to result in the development of 'party overload' systems, characterised by high levels of party replacement and ongoing processes of party coalition and fragmentation. It is assumed that this complexity in the political landscape will be compounded by the general absence of any coherent programmes or political ideologies put forward by the majority of parties, and that this will result both in a generalised failure to develop political identities, and to appeal to specific groups of the electorate. Consequently, the parties will be unable to form political 'bases' amongst the public, and support will come from shifting, amorphous masses of the electorate, rather than any clearly identifiable groups. Parties are likely to search for the lowest common denominators to attract electoral support, and in so doing, pollsters are likely to confront the problems of 'personality politics' and 'symbolism' where the relationship between the electorates and the parties are likely to be even more tenuous. This is likely to facilitate heightened electoral volatility. These processes are likely to undermine the formation of stable party/voter relationships, and will create problems for pollsters as they attempt to monitor the development of these unfolding party systems, and to estimate likely shares of party support at elections.

Opinion Polling and Mechanisms for Political Participation

Both the quantity and quality of arrangements for the participation of mass publics in political affairs has implications for political opinion polling. In the first instance, it is assumed that the larger the number of channels there are available for effective participation in policy-making and political affairs, the more that citizens are likely to feel attached to the political system, and to make use of these mechanisms either to demonstrate support for regimes, or else to effect change. The citizenry are likely to perceive opinion polling as an additional and useful means through which they can communicate their ideas and interests to political leaders. Response rates in polls will therefore be high. In addition, pollsters can feel confident that most citizens are registered to vote at elections, and that electoral turn-out will be high. Consequently, when asking questions relating to future voting behaviour, pollsters are assured that where voters indicate that they will vote for a particular party or candidate at an election, they will in fact turn out to vote for them; furthermore, pollsters can be confident of high levels of correspondence between what respondents say publicly, and what they think privately. Finally, citizens are likely to be relatively sophisticated observers of political affairs, with high levels of interest in political issues and events. Thus, the findings from opinion polls are likely to represent a fairly close approximation of the views and beliefs of an informed electorate, rather than the product of questions asked in situations where the citizenry have low political cognition, feel alienated from political affairs, or are generally politically apathetic. Where the latter conditions are present, polls are more likely to artificially construct, rather than reflect, public opinion.

Capitalist societies If these assumptions are accurate, the conditions for political opinion polling will have been most favourable in early post-Second World War capitalist political systems. According to pluralist definitions, political power was dispersed amongst various interest groups in society, with open membership the norm. Policy-making apparatuses were sensitive and responsive to the demands of such groups and organisations, and consequently, the latter provided vehicles through which citizens could influence governments. Furthermore, governments were accountable to the voters through the existence of regular competitive elections, based on universal franchise. In addition, because there was open recruitment to political elites, citizens were able to participate within, not just influence, the policy-making processes. However, a very different picture of political participation has been provided by Ginsberg (1982). He focused on elections, and argued that in such societies, elections were a device for expanding the power of elites over the population. They incorporated potential dissenters into the political system, reduced popular participation to a cross on a ballot form, and encouraged people to obey the state. Elections did give a modicum of choice to voters (albeit one restricted to a few broad 'packages' of proposals) and as a result of which, the authority of governments was enormously enhanced. Nonetheless, the channels for popular participation in political affairs were assumed to be more available in capitalist than in communist political systems. As a consequence, conditions were most conducive for opinion polling in capitalist political systems.

However, the citizenry in many late-capitalist societies are becoming increasingly disillusioned with the traditional mechanisms for political participation. They display declining confidence in their political representatives, and will be less likely to take part in the formal arrangements available to influence the political process. For instance, a MORI 'state-of-the-nation' poll commissioned by the Joseph Rowntree Reform Trust in 1995, indicated increasing widespread public disaffection in Britain from politicians and from the political system generally. Such views had shown a sharp acceleration in a 20-year trend, with 75% of the public claiming that "the present system of government could be improved", and 50% believing that Britain's system of government was "out of date", (Rentoul, 1995, p.1; Linton, 1995, p.5). An analysis of the results by Dunleavy and Weir concludes that they reveal a general rejection of established practice across the British constitution, with large majorities in favour of a written constitution, a freedom of information act, a bill of rights, and greater public control over Members of Parliament. Over three-quarters of the electorate believed that voters should have a "great deal" or "fair amount" of power between elections, but fewer than one in ten believed that citizens already possessed this (Dunleavy and Weir, 1995, p.13). The results of a 'Eurobarometer' poll from April 1994 indicate that such disillusion is not confined to Britain. Across Europe, there is a generalised lack of confidence in the existing political set-up, with for instance a net dissatisfaction of 31% amongst EU respondents in terms of their attitude to the way the European Union was being run (MORI, 1994, p.6).

As a result of such widespread scepticism, it is perhaps not surprising that where citizens do engage in political activity, it is often within non-conventional organisations and structures outside of the established political arena. As such, it is likely that opinion polls too will be perceived by the public increasingly as an inappropriate channel for facilitating genuine dialogue with political elites. Polls will be viewed with increasing scepticism and cynicism, with declining and variable response rates typical. As a consequence, the performance, scope, and demand for polls is likely to abate.

Communist and post-communist societies In communist political systems, popular participation tended to have a relatively more 'regimented' character. The traditional Western notion of participation as action resulting in control over political leaders by the rational, informed activities of citizens who have considered the major policy alternatives, was not a feature of communist political systems. In elections, the population tended to be mobilised and controlled from above in pursuit of goals determined by the elite. Hague and Harrop have commented that where 99.9% of voters turn out to cast 99.9% of votes for a single candidate, the object is clearly to mobilise the population, rather than to allow voters a real choice (Hague and Harrop, 1987, p.95). A less sceptical view is provided by Lovenduski and Woodall who suggest that participation was real, and "psychologically satisfying" to citizens, although these citizens usually recognised that such activity did not influence governments (Lovenduski and Woodall, 1987, p.285).

In post-communist political systems, it is expected that the overthrow of one party systems, the introduction of political pluralisation, and the extension of political rights would be greeted with an initial wave of citizen euphoria. This would have the effect of facilitating high levels of political interest and of political participation where previously these were less pronounced or absent. In this context, the circumstances for the development and profile of opinion polling are likely to be favourable. However, if the new political regimes are unable to manage and implement successful programmes for restructuring the social, economic and political systems, the citizenry are likely to lose confidence in the emergent political institutions and processes, and withdraw or feel alienated from political life. Hence the conditions necessary for the growth of opinion polling, as outlined above, will diminish.

Opinion Polling and the Policy Process

The final aspect of the investigation is based upon a series of assumptions regarding the nature of government and the policy process in any political system, and how this relates to the demand for political opinion polling data. Firstly, the conditions for opinion polling will be favourable in political systems which are essentially capitalistic or post-communist. That is, where there is open competition for political power, with more than one political party and with regular elections based on a universal franchise. Here, parties and governments are accountable to electorates. If policy is implemented which does not correspond with the values and interests of the citizenry, or which contradicts their demands, then the policy-makers will be rejected at the next election, and replaced by opposition parties. An opinion poll can provide a tool through which policy-makers can identify voter demands, as well as a feed-back mechanism through which the public's response to policy can be monitored and evaluated. However, post-communist political systems are likely to be variable in respect of this; pluralistic and open regimes may well be replaced by more centralised regimes and vice versa. There are likely to be periods therefore when polls will not be necessary or required by centralised regimes, who will not need (or who will have no desire) to consult the citizenry on policy decisions.

Secondly, polls can be used as a source of political intelligence by political parties and other groups and movements, for developing strategies to secure political power and influence. Where such organisations have core policy positions, polls can identify which issues have a resonance with the electorate and which should therefore be prioritised and publicised, and which policy positions should be hidden from public view. This manipulative function can also extend to the selection of forms of presentation of policy, and of spokespersons and electoral candidates.

Finally, the debates concerning the role of opinion polls in promoting stability by acting as a channel of communication between citizens and political elites, have already been outlined. Without such political linkages, leaders are unable to effectively articulate the demands of citizens in between elections, and therefore risk pursuing policy objectives which run counter to these demands and interests, and which in extreme circumstances may foster the development of extra-parliamentary mass protest.

Notes

1.   See below and chapter 9 for a discussion of these changes.
2.   See Dunleavy (1989) for a review of these processes which are alleged to have taken place.
3.   See chapter 6 for a full discussion of these changes.
4.   For a discussion of these changes in electoral systems across Central and Eastern Europe, see Kuusela (1994).
5.   This is the reverse side of the coin to the British experience at the 1992 General Election, where Conservative voters are alleged to have lied to pollsters about their voting intention in order to disguise their support for a party which had implemented a series of very unpopular economic and social policies (Crewe, 1993b).

4   Opinion Polling and Complex Politics

Introduction

The developments outlined in the last chapter for both late-capitalist and post-communist societies largely parallel each other in terms of their implications for political opinion polling; as far as *political culture, party system, mechanisms for political participation*, and the *policy process* are concerned, many of the features which impact upon polling in post-communist societies are also unfolding in late-capitalist societies like Britain, although the pace and intensity of change in the former is clearly more pronounced and, as discussed below, each type of society has different roots. Thus, we see the advent of a new era for polling which we can call 'Complex Politics'. This refers to political contexts for polling which are variable, unpredictable and undergoing significant processes of restructuring. The culmination of such changes and political complexity are combining to create conditions which make polling a potentially difficult practice. This chapter will explore the concept of Complex Politics and how it relates to opinion polling in contemporary European societies.

Complex Politics

The tendencies towards Complex Politics are emerging in both late-capitalist and post-communist societies, although it is important not to over-state the degree to which they overlap, and to be aware of the obvious differences in context and recent history. Indeed, Crook, Pakulski and Waters have identified three quite distinct models of political change which have shaped the nature of contemporary societies: a West European model, an American Politics model, and Communist etatism (1993, pp.136-138). In the West European model, what has become known as 'new politics' emerged in response to the post-Second World War consensus, which evolved an elitist bureaucratic-corporatist politics. Essentially, this politics was a culmination of the major established interests within societies, which were organised in the large financial and capital associations, the trade unions, various religious institutions, and other such dominant interests. It was a style of politics which articulated and responded to these elite interests, and did so through carefully defined parameters of political activity within formalised institutions and ritualised procedures. The most obvious means through which citizens are able to intervene within the political system under such a model is through elections, but these effectively provide only an indirect route to political power, in that they allow voters to register approval or not of political parties and government, rather than have some direct influence on their programmes and policies. Furthermore, elections (usually) provide only an infrequent input into politics for citizens. Citizens are able to effect change marginally more directly through membership of established and national political parties, but these were usually dominated by those elites who formed part of the bureaucratic-corporatist state. Other than these formalised arrangements and bodies, the only other officially sanctioned mechanisms for political participation open to rank-and-file citizens were less direct, including lobbying parliamentary representatives, petitioning and such like.

As a result of these subtle restrictions, politics was effectively insulated from the pressures of mass action. Miliband provides a useful account of the outcome of such elitist bureaucratic-corporatist arrangements, as 'consensus'-style politics based upon a welfare-state capitalist ideology. Policies were generally geared toward the maintenance of a mixed economy, with the state intervening where necessary to support economic (industrial) activities unprofitable for capital, to introduce welfare policies to socialise labour costs which would otherwise fall on employers, and to act as the key agency of social control to contain pressure and dissent from below (Miliband, 1982, pp.54-93).

In the American Politics model, the political system is comparatively more open to citizens, but access to the centres of power requires financial resources and specialised professional skills, which again reduces the ability of unorganised pressures and weaker interests to influence the political process. In contrast, East European communist political systems were characterised by highly centralised monocentric party-states. Only officially recognised 'legitimate' interests were incorporated into the formal political process, and it was not until the 1970s and 1980s when communist regimes experienced various economic, social and political crises, that 'uncertified' interests asserted themselves as dissident social movements (such as Charter 77 in Czechoslovakia, Solidarity in Poland, Helsinki 86 in Estonia, Eko-Glasnost in Bulgaria, and various other opposition movements advocating human rights issues and political pluralism).

Recent restructuring of these political configurations has precipitated a 'new' form of politics. The movements associated with this 'new politics' display differing orientations to the traditional political set-up. The movements are most accommodating with mainstream politics in America (such as the fundamentalist religious right with the Republicans, and gay activist movements with the Democrat Party). In Western Europe, they tend to distance themselves from, and compete with conventional political organisations and arrangements (the 'ecopax' movements), while they adopted radical anti-establishment positions in communist East Europe (the anti-communist popular front movements of 1989). They are all nonetheless a symptom of restructuring processes which are essentially global in character. This involves chiefly a decline in production-based class cleavages as the defining point of reference for political conflict and activity, and the fusion of politics and culture (that is, with norms, styles, outlooks and values).

Late-Capitalist Complex Politics Contexts for Opinion Polling

The increasing peripheralisation of production-based politics in late-capitalist societies has its origins in the general processes of restructuring of economic, social and cultural life which has been a feature of such societies since the late 1960s and early 1970s. In fact, these processes were first conceptualised as far back as 1959 by Dahrendorf, who noticed a general tendency taking shape in terms of the decomposition and fragmentation of classes, and the emergence of new fault-lines of social stratification. Specifically, he highlighted the differentiation of the dominant group between owners and managers with the emergence of a new 'service class'. Furthermore, he claimed that there was a general atomisation of the working class. This was a result of increasing skill divisions, regional heterogeneity, and ultimately the erosion of its social, economic and cultural specificity through a process of 'embourgeoisement' which contributed to diversity in its lifestyles, values and aspirations (Dahrendorf, 1959, 1969). In part, Dahrendorf's formulations were a precursor to the post-industrial thesis outlined by Bell (1973, 1980). This focused upon the primacy of services, knowledge and information, and the movement away from manufacturing production as the main activity of western economies. In this process, Bell pointed to a general decline in the size and significance of the traditional manual working class, and the growth of new, dominant occupational groupings. These 'post-industrial' classes included those at the leading-edge of the restructuring process: a white-collar service grouping and various professional and technical groups which, he claimed, were the 'custodians' of the scientific and technical knowledge that was shaping the direction of post-industrial change.

While the thesis of post-industrialism has itself been criticised,[1] most commentators recognise that the social structures in Western societies have undergone significant changes over the course of the post-Second World War decades, although the origins, processes, outcomes and extent of the changes are disputed. Thus, Beacham maintains that there has been a general decline in the numbers and conditions of the traditional working class, and a corresponding growth in the numbers and significance of a new 'middle class' - managers, professionals, technicians, administrators, and corporate and state employees[2] (Beacham, 1983; see also Thrift, 1989, and Allen and Massey, 1988). A neo-Marxist account of changes in class formation is given by Rattansi (1985), who observes that the working class in late-capitalist societies is becoming increasingly fragmented by skill, gender, ethnicity, and geography, while neo-Weberians maintain that classes are increasingly differentiated along lines of social status (race, culture and gender), life-chances (occupation and income) and citizenship rights (civil, political and social), rather than relations to production (Parkin, 1979; Barbalet, 1986; Marshall, 1953).

Post-modernists tend to emphasise particular 'historical configurations' within the development of industrial capitalism, each of which generates its own system of social stratification (Waters, 1994, pp. 296-307). In the post-Second World War period, corporate or *Command* societies were the norm, where the development of an expansive and regulatory state generated various political strata, which fused with economic production-based classes into three horizontally-integrated hierarchical blocs: a 'bureaucratic- political- managerial- elite' (which comprised those holding a disproportionate share of power in those organisations that dominate society); an 'incorporated (or middle) mass' of public and private sector white collar workers and primary-labour market manual workers; and a third, exploited and ghettoised 'excluded mass' (or underclass) of state-dependants and marginalised employees (Crook et al, 1992, pp.109-111; Waters, 1994, pp.302-303). However, the generalised withdrawal and marginalisation of the state from economic and social spheres of activity which began at the end of the 1960s/ start of the 1970s throughout the advanced capitalist world, has led to the development of a new historical phase of *Status-Conventional* societies, and a transformation in the nature of these principal blocs. According to Waters (1994, pp.305-306):

> The emerging pattern of stratification will be fluid and shifting as commitments, tastes and fashions change. It will approximate a multiple mosaic of status communities rather than a small number of enclosed social capsules. Membership of any community will depend not on a person's location in a system of production or control, but on status accomplishments, patterns of social worth, established in the spheres of value commitment, the control of symbolic resources, location in circuits of discourse, and sumptuary behaviour.

Pakulski describes these new formations as "imagined communities", in which people (particularly through the mass media) tend to regard themselves as members of solidaristic groupings, with "...shared concerns (for example Greens), habits (for example, non-smokers), tastes (for example, vegetarians), or even some ascriptive characteristics (for example, blacks)" (Pakulski, 1993a, p.285).

Regardless of the differences in which these restructuring processes are conceptualised for late-capitalist societies, the implications for class politics are that there has been a general and incremental 'decoupling' of the links between voters and the traditional mass-based parties. Party trust and class-voting[3] have both declined, particularly in Western Europe. Consequently, there has been a substantial growth in voter volatility and diversity, together with a generalised shift of political action into unconventional forms and new movements and parties. While these new movements are increasingly visible throughout late-capitalist societies, they tend to lack any stable social base. This is partly because, as has been outlined, the social structure is in transition. But it is also because the politics that they orient towards tends to be vague, diverse, and often focusing upon single issues (rather than the ideologically-based programmes which were typical of the traditional class-parties).

Thus, in Britain, the Green Party failed to sustain its electoral momentum after the 1989 European Assembly elections, largely because it failed to communicate to voters that its manifesto extended beyond its environmental agenda. The All Britain Anti-Poll Tax Federation (ABAPTF) co-ordinated a national campaign which represented "...the largest incidence of civil disobedience in post-war Britain" (Tonge, 1994, p.93). The movement was neither coherent nor homogenous, and was conducted through 550 local anti-poll tax unions. At its height 6.1 million summonses for non-payment in England were issued, amounting to almost one quarter of the entire liable population, yet when the government was forced to concede defeat on the issue and abolish the poll tax, the rationale for the continued existence of the ABAPTF was lost. A number of animal rights movements and anti-roads coalitions had significant success in dominating the national news agenda in 1994 and 1995, but the very nature of their campaigns - specific, immediate and short-term - culminated in their having only short, episodic life-spans.

However, to a certain degree, these movements are evolutionary, in that once a campaign has been waged and an outcome established, they tend to transmute into new (usually related) movements. Thus, the Reclaim the Streets "disorganisation" developed out of the London M11 protests and the campaign against the M3 extension at Twyford Down. Furthermore, there is a significant degree of overlap in activities between movements. In 1995, there was a joint action between the Freedom Network (which co-ordinated campaigns against the Criminal Justice Act), the Advance Party Network (of rave party organisers), Reclaim The Streets (anti-car campaign) and the 'coalition' of animal rights groups which had been campaigning against the export of live animals (Sell, 1995, p.16). The Scottish Socialist Alliance was set up in 1996 to articulate and co-ordinate these movements and parties in Scotland. At a founding 'Socialist Forum 96', participants included activists from various trade unions, members of the Labour Party, the SNP, Scottish Militant Labour, various Communist Parties, together with representatives from an array of single-issue campaigns, including peace activists, anti-motorway protesters, animal rights campaigners, gay rights campaigners, and anti-racist groups. As a consequence of these developments, some authors claim that there has been a shift in the values and attitudes of voters towards a concern for 'new politics' issues which underpin such new movements (see for instance, Dunleavy, 1989).

As a consequence of the increasing tendency of citizens to engage in such modes of political action, Veen (1989), and in particular, Inglehart (1981, 1987, 1990) have noticed a changed hierarchy of preferences for citizens which tends to have a significant ethical dimension, and which stresses 'post-materialist' issues such as civil and human rights, peace and quality of life.[4] Because these issues are 'cultural' rather than 'socio-economic', they tend to be universal rather than sectional, implying that there are no specific identifiable groups advocating such priorities to whom the parties could orient. Finally, another difficulty for such movements and parties in establishing a firm social base is because in their rejection of the bureaucratic-corporatist style of organisations, they tend to operate decentralised structures, often with no formal membership criteria, and seek to articulate the interests of a wide variety of diverse protest streams including those perceived as outside the orbit of the traditional mass-based parties.

In short, the processes of restructuring which are increasingly taking place in late-capitalist societies are creating political conditions for polling which are increasingly complex. The traditional style of politics, usually class-based, is on the retreat as a result of changes within the social structure which are eroding the links between the mass-based parties, and their respective electoral 'blocs'. Citizens tend to be concerned with an increasingly diverse set of political priorities, which are often cultural- (value) rather than socio-economic- (class) based. Furthermore, there is an increasing tendency toward support for, and involvement in new politics-style parties and movements, which themselves are often ad hoc coalitions without any formal programme consensus or ideology, and which may orient toward forms of political action which include lobbying, demonstrations, direct action, media events and so on rather than the more traditional channels such as electioneering. As a consequence, the implications for opinion polling in late-capitalist societies are that voters are less predictable and more volatile in their political behaviour and outlook than in previous times, and this is compounded by more diverse party systems which provide greater choice for the electorate.

Furthermore, citizens have a greater repertoire of political activities that they are likely to pursue, although this may not always include voting.

Post-Communist Complex Politics Contexts for Opinion Polling

The post-communist societies which are emerging in Central and Eastern Europe are characterised by their increasingly complex and shifting political environments which, *in terms of the implications for opinion polling*, are not dissimilar from those described above for late-capitalist societies. This is most obvious in terms of the (lack of) relationships between political parties and citizens.

In the first instance, the character of the social structure throughout the region is such that there are few, if any clearly developed referents through which distinctive social groupings or classes can emerge, and which could tie blocs of voters to the nascent political parties. This represents a fundamental break with communist societies, where the pattern of stratification which evolved generated three politically defined strata, and facilitated a distinctive relationship between citizens and the ruling Party. The first, a ruling elite, comprised high Party and government officials, military officers, intellectual leaders, senior professionals, and technical specialists. A middle stratum included professional and white-collar workers, while the third grouping was made up of low-skilled industrial workers, and a partly differentiated peasantry. As Waters states, one's position within this stratification system was largely determined by one's relation to the Party, with membership resulting in preferential access to social, economic and cultural rewards and privileges, and, through the nomenklatura list, eligibility to advancement within the Party and the state itself. Furthermore, the primacy of the Party-State nexus as the key linchpin of the social structure was most evident in that both Party and nomenklatura[5] memberships conferred transgenerational inheritance (Waters, 1994, pp. 301-302). The system which gave rise to this process of social stratification has been termed 'Partocractic', in the sense that the Party-directed state regulates the organisation of economics and culture, emphasising "commitment and political-ideological 'expertise'", rather than administrative or technical expertise (Pakulski, 1986, p. 19).

With the demise of communist regimes and of this highly centralised bureaucratic system of Partocratic Corporatism, the stratification systems throughout Central and Eastern Europe have collapsed, and the development of replacement social cleavages are largely failing to materialise in the void that is left. For political parties, the implications are that there are few readily discernible and stable social constituencies to which they can orient; for the opinion pollsters trying to gauge electoral opinion and the relationships between parties and voters, this situation heralds a period of electoral volatility and complexity, with public opinion an unpredictable intangible, extremely difficult to monitor, assess and forecast. Batt for instance has noted that society "...has disintegrated into a rather homogeneous and amorphous mass (with) social interests in a state of flux and regrouping" (Batt, 1994, pp. 36-37). Bryant has suggested that in post-communist countries like Poland and Hungary, only 'proto-civil societies' exist, in the sense that citizens form largely atomised masses, which have no obvious referents through which they can associate as social groupings or classes (Bryant, 1994, pp. 70-74).

However, one obvious source of social cleavage noted in the literature on post-communist transition which appears to be emerging, is poverty-based. Kolankiewicz claims that the economic reform packages underway in many of these countries have had significant negative social consequences for sections of society within the region in terms of unemployment, low pay, visible homelessness and generalised poverty (Kolankiewicz, 1994, pp. 155-160). Indeed, throughout Central and Eastern Europe, sizeable minorities have perceived their economic situations as in decline. McIntosh and MacIver's analysis of surveys conducted in Hungary, Poland and Czechoslovakia between June 1989 and January 1992 suggested that, after an initial honeymoon period with the early post-communist regimes, public opinion grew increasingly alarmed at the failure of policy-makers to solve economic and social problems. Trends suggested that, over the two-year period, the majority of citizens claimed that both 'life in general' and standards of living had deteriorated since the collapse of communism (McIntosh and MacIver, 1992, pp. 376-378). The persistence of negative economic evaluations by substantial proportions of citizens throughout Central and Eastern Europe has been noted in a number of subsequent studies utilising public opinion data (Duke and Grime, 1994; Mare., Musil, and Rabucic, 1994; Rose and Haerpfer, 1994; White, 1995).

As a consequence of the actual and/or perceived economic hardship faced by these groups, it is possible to identify new cleavages, as the trend toward marketisation of the economies in the region continues. Kolankiewicz dichotomises between the 'winners' and the 'losers' of economic transition (1994, p. 159), while McIntosh and MacIver suggest an ideological cleavage over the role of the state in society, and distinguish between those who prefer a 'state guarantees' society, and those who welcome an 'individual opportunities' society (1992, p. 383). A similar process of cleavage formation is proposed by Cotta, who asserts that the major conflict within these societies has at its source the dismantling of state ownership and centralistic controls, and the development of market economies. This is likely to create divisions between those who either work in, or are dependent on, the public sector ('security-dependent' groups), and those who have a significant stake in the burgeoning private sector ('risk-oriented' groups) (Cotta, 1994, p.120).   Linked to this, Kolankiewicz claims that privatisation has facilitated the emergence of new dichotomous groups, including those who attempt to protect themselves from what they perceive as the uncertainties of economic and social change, and an alternative group who adopt a more entrepreneurial and enthusiastic response to what they regard as opportunities for self-advancement and self-enrichment (Kolankiewicz, 1994, pp.151-153).

However, other cleavage systems have been proposed which suggest that the process and form of social stratification is highly complex, particularly given that many of these cleavages will be cross-cutting. For instance, Schöpflin states that the major segments within post-communist societies can be identified as 'liberal', 'communist', and 'traditional' types. The liberal segment comprises members who advocate free-market economics and individual responsibility. Those within the communist segment demonstrate significant support for continued state intervention within the economy and society, and favour collective action and responsibilities. The final, traditional, segment however is deeply conservative, resentful and dissatisfied; its ideas are "...strongly collectivist, negatively egalitarian or hierarchical, anti-intellectual, and distrustful of politics...(and) it is vulnerable to manipulation by populist demagogues" (Schöpflin, 1994, p.132).

Linked to this third grouping is the phenomenon of ethnic-nationalism, which is particularly salient and enduring in post-communist societies. Smith has argued that there is a lack of 'structure' and a generalised social 'rootlessness' within the electorates of Central and East Europe (Smith, 1994, p.122). As a consequence, he claims that the only real force within society capable of mobilising an identity within the population is ethnic-nationalism. As Batt states: "nationalist politics provides the emotional appeal that can win wide allegiance from a fragmented, atomised society" (Batt, 1991, p.50). This is most inspirational in terms of its focus on community, national self-determination, resistance to external "aggressors" (such as Soviet-imposed political domination during the communist era, and western economic influence in the current context), its reference to historically-celebrated movements and hero-figures, together with symbolism, and language and cultural traditions.   Together, these features distinguish these societies from, and provide perceived status elevation over, 'outsiders'. However, while it is claimed that ethnic-nationalism has the potential to act as a positive catalyst for the establishment of a unifying, consensual, tolerant and democratically-oriented 'civil society', (Batt, 1991, p.50), the reality for post-communist societies is that ethnic-nationalism has largely become a rallying force for reaction and suspicion, and is often associated with extremist, authoritarian and right-wing politics; as a consequence, it has the effect of generating social division and fragmentation (Smith, 1994, p. 122).

This discussion implies that the social structures in Central and Eastern European countries are currently in a state of flux. This is largely a reflection of the generalised shapelessness which is a feature of the transition processes throughout the region. These processes are returned to later in this book, but are encapsulated in the concept of 'liminality' applied by Baumann to post-communist societies. He suggests that in the aftermath of the collapse of communism, these societies, their economies, social structures and politics are entering a phase characterised by their "...unstructured, formless condition, where neither the 'old' nor the 'new' rules apply", and where only uncertainty and unpredictability exists (Baumann, 1994, p. 16). It suggests that, as is the case for contemporary late-capitalist societies, there are few stable social referents through which the public can consolidate into 'blocs'; instead, what is apparent is that, where social cleavages exist, they are generally limited and weak, often cross-cutting, and likely to result in the development of volatile and unpredictable electorates.

It is important not to overstate the parallels here with the processes unfolding in late-capitalist societies, and to be analytically sensitive to the vast differences in context. In late-capitalist societies, these processes are symptomatic of the decay of an established and stable social system which is in the process of *restructuring*, while in post-communist contexts the processes reflect the *unstructured* nature of societies which are emerging from the void left by a virtually complete overthrow of an established social, political and economic order (Smith, 1994, pp. 120-121). The *net effect* in terms of how these changes relate to the relationships between voters and parties however is broadly similar for both late-capitalist and post-communist societies. Essentially, there are few if any developed and durable links between the parties and groups of voters. The electorates are volatile, increasingly sceptical of and disillusioned with political parties and with their performance, apathetic (as recorded particularly in diminishing voter turnout rates, but also in the tendency toward participation in non-parliamentary forms of political action), and likely to reject mainstream democratic-consolidationist style parties, in favour of extremist and/or anti-democratic movements and parties. For Miall, these features are endemic to such societies in transition. He claims that the party systems and civil societies in the region have as yet, failed to consolidate: political parties have yet to develop deep roots within society, and much of the political debate that takes place is restricted to the confines of the nascent, and limited political elites. When combined with the failure of governments to solve the everyday social and economic problems for the masses (which has precipitated a crisis of legitimacy for the new states in many of the countries within the region), it is perhaps not surprising that citizens feel alienated from, and are often opposed to political actors and institutions. As Miall concludes, these societies are therefore often highly charged, and typically volatile (Miall, 1994, p.7).

The governments which emerged following the demise of communist regimes in Central and Eastern Europe were met with an initial wave of optimism and confidence by the public. The prominent forces involved in the overthrow of communist parties largely paralleled the new social movements found in Western Europe. Like their western counterparts, these movements (Solidarity, New Forum, Civic Forum, Public Against Violence, and the Union of Democratic Forces) all developed outside and in opposition to the bureaucratised power structures in communist societies (Lewis et al, 1994, pp.152-153), or what Crook et al term Partocratic Corporatism (Crook, Pakulski, and Waters, 1992, p. 158). These movements were vigorously anti-centralist and anti-totalitarian, and in spite of some differences in orientations, issues and outcomes, they broadly reflected the West European new social movements in terms of their democratic ethos, and anti-corporatist, anti-etatist orientation. Pakulski for instance, claims that Polish Solidarity under communist rule should be viewed "...not only as one of many popular revolts against partocratic elites in Soviet-type societies, but also as a member of a broader family of social movements which also includes the environmental and peace movements in the West ...(which) share concerns about the weakening of democratic participation and the increased bureaucratisation of state machineries" (Pakulski, 1988, p.152). Elsewhere, Pakulski develops the parallels between Western new social movements and Central and East European anti-partocratic movements in his analysis of Solidarity, by identifying the tendency toward 'universal' rather than 'sectional' (class) politics:

> There were few signs of class identity and consciousness among supporters of the movement. If anything, movement participants overwhelmingly adopted a *national* identity and stressed national solidarity (Pakulski, 1993b, p.139).

Furthermore, the anti-partocratic movements focused on the issues of political freedom, national sovereignty, democracy, human dignity, justice, citizenship, human rights, constitutional legalism, as well as the traditional 'class issues' of wages and working conditions. Thus, the anti-partocratic movements provided a generalised focus for the resentments and aspirations of these societies in relation to the agencies of the state, and "...channelled the spirit of 'anti-politics' that encapsulated the revulsion felt against the Soviet-backed dictatorship(s)" into mass opposition movements which ultimately brought about the downfall of the various communist regimes (Lewis, Lomas and Wightman, 1994, p.153).

Waller (1994, pp.45-59) develops the concept of a 'periodisation' of political change, and describes this phase of political transformation as the 'heroic period', where the nation is drawn behind *universal* opposition movements, in a united front dedicated to the overthrow of communist rule. At the following 'transfer of power' phase, government was ceded to the forum movement(s) by the communist leaderships, and laws geared toward the legalisation of free political associations, and the establishment of rules for the holding of competitive elections were implemented. At this stage, the populations within these now 'post-communist' societies demonstrated relatively high levels of enthusiasm for and commitment to the developing political process, and a close affinity with the forum parties. However, Waller claims that this phase of political change was relatively truncated, and he identifies almost immediate signs of decay in the nascent voter/party alliances facilitated by the forum parties' failures firstly to advance beyond the limited ideological position of rejection of communist politics and partocratic organisation, and secondly, to adequately address the question of identifying sectional electoral constituencies. The current phase in the development of post-communist politics can be characterised, according to Waller, in terms of the differentiation of forum parties (Waller, 1994) and what Sartori has described as a situation of 'polarised politics' (Sartori, 1976), and of a tendency toward the transformation of politics from a mass-based, to an elite activity (Baumann, 1994) largely reflecting the model of 'competitive leadership' described by Schumpeter (1976). Indeed the plethora of parties which tend to populate the political scene across post-communist Europe are not a manifestation of stable social and ideological cleavages articulating the interests of various social constituencies, but instead, appear to be reflecting divisions amongst political elites. Furthermore, it is claimed that the current situation is marked by the generalised withdrawal of the public from the political process, and the absence of any voter/party coalitions:

> The situation in Eastern Europe is characterised by the lack of institutionalised relationships between state bureaucracies, elected officials, and socially based interests (Circautas, 1994, p. 36).

This is largely the result of two key factors: firstly, the structural changes which have combined to create socially amorphous electorates as discussed above; secondly, the style of politics adopted by the democratic opposition leaderships who co-ordinated the transfer of power from the former communist regimes. In most cases (Romania excluded) these democratic elites were elected to participate in round-table negotiations with their communist counterparts, rather than to lead an exclusively mass-based revolutionary movement (Friedman, 1993, pp.482-483); the process involved, therefore, 'elite confrontation and negotiation':

> The critical junctures of regime transition and the mechanisms of power transfer remained very much within the domain of elite politics (Lewis, Lomax and Wightman, 1994, p. 155).

Indeed, as Circautas notes, the general orientation of the democratic leaderships at this initial 'transfer of power' stage, and later in the governments established after the first round of elections, was to define politics as an elite activity to be conducted within parliament; as a consequence, there was a general disinclination both to mobilise social constituencies, and to involve popular society in the political process (Circautas, 1994, pp.51-52). As a consequence, the wider citizenry was largely excluded from political activity, except from the routine electoral practice of voting.

Furthermore the democratic elites, in elevating themselves above popular society, effectively insulated themselves from the realities of life experienced by the wider public, and became increasingly de-sensitised to their needs. Baumann (1994, pp.31-33) and Circautas (1994, p.52) suggest that these new political elites made assumptions about the nature of the political process and the political institutions which should replace those from the communist era; they adopted systems based upon western liberal-democracy, and advocated the establishment of laissez-faire free-market economics. However, noting the absence of an appropriate social constituency - a bourgeois-liberal class - the intelligentsia itself had to step into the void left by the collapse of communist society, and substitute itself for this historical capitalist class (Baumann, 1994; Schöpflin, 1994). This had the effect of further alienating popular society from politics, and from both the political groups, movements and parties in power and from those vying for political representation.

In addition, the programmes implemented by the democratic elites tended to have immediate negative consequences for the very people who had brought them to power; for instance, the policies imposed by the Solidarity government geared toward the dismantling of the state and the establishment of free-enterprise had a detrimental effect on the very industrial workers who had played a pivotal role in the downfall of the Jaruzelski government. As a consequence, there appears to have developed across the post-communist societies a "...yawning gap between what the elite can offer and what their genuine or postulated constituencies want and expect", resulting in the paradox that there are "...few if any constituencies in sight for the 'realistic' programmes the elites put together, while potential constituencies still wait for feasible programmes which could forge them into realistic constituencies" (Baumann, 1994, p.31).

The impact of these processes on the relationship between popular society and politics is that the citizenry has tended to withdraw from formal political life creating a void between the public and mainstream politics and political parties. This has had a number of effects. Firstly, throughout the region, voter turnout has fallen over the course of successive post-communist elections. Secondly, despite the fragmentation of the forum parties and the emergence of a party system characterised by intensive party competition and multitudinous parties and political movements, actual membership of such associations is low. Thirdly, elites continue to ignore the mass public in political practice. Furthermore, the notion of democracy itself is understood by popular society "...as seemingly irrelevant bickering, the empty contests for symbols and moral purity that had no bearing on everyday existence, above all with the rapid and continuing economic deterioration" (Schöpflin, 1994, p.136). Ultimately, Baumann concludes that the "'us'n'them' posture" that the public tended to adopt vis-a-vis their former communist leaders, is now a common feature of post-communist societies (Baumann, 1994, p.28).

One final outcome of the inability of mainstream liberal-democratic orientated parties to establish alliances with electoral groupings is the "Brazauskas effect" - the re-vitalisation of former communist parties - and the growth in support for (often extremist) populist nationalist parties and movements (Schöpflin, 1994, p. 137). As mentioned above, there is an emergent constituency for these parties. The consequences of economic reform, and particularly of the programmes of privatisation adopted throughout the region, has displaced large numbers of former state-employed workers and undermined the living standards of state-dependants (particularly the elderly) to create an 'underclass' (Batt, 1994; Duke and Grime, 1994). It has also generated a political back-lash against the advocates of free-market economics and liberal-democracy. Electoral trends throughout the post-communist societies suggest that voters are becoming increasingly sceptical of parties associated with such changes, and are adopting more pragmatic and nostalgic views of the social-economic stability and order characteristic of the communist era. Furthermore, the perceived failure of the early post-communist governments to address the social consequences and economic hardship facilitated by market reform had the effect of generating within the electorates a susceptibility both to charismatic populist leaders, to parties offering "simple and guaranteed solutions" (Baumann, 1994, p.32), and to an ideology - ethnic nationalism - which provides one of the few enduring forces through which to mobilise a collective identity within an otherwise largely unstructured electorate (Smith, 1994, p.122).

Post-communist societies, then, can be characterised by their relative fluidity and lack of structure, both in terms of social organisation and voter-party links. Smith's observations of the immediate prospects for the political systems in these countries largely parallels that discussed earlier in this chapter for late-capitalist contexts. Firstly, he projects continued electoral volatility and public apathy where political processes and party politics are concerned, combined with perceptions of relative political powerlessness and anomie amongst popular society, and a concomitant generalised withdrawal from, and suspicion of 'politics'. Furthermore, he notes a "fragmentation and polarisation of party systems" encouraged by "generous proportional representation systems", which, without the stabilising factors of traditional mass-based parties, is resulting in the development of "centrifugal turbulence" (Smith, 1994, pp.124-125). He cautions that there is a need to be sensitive to differences in context between these developments in post-communist and late-capitalist societies, and indeed, notes some important differences in, for instance the origins and starting points for many of these processes. However, he claims that ultimately "...convergence can nevertheless be discerned" in terms of the end results of these processes (Smith, 1994, p. 120).

For opinion pollsters, the implications of these trends are that public opinion in post-communist contexts - like that for late-capitalist societies - is likely to be persistently volatile: predictable only in its relative unpredictability. The political environment then is likely to remain one characterised chiefly by *political complexity*, with pollsters' given tasks of measuring public opinion a particularly difficult occupation now and in the future.

Summary

The key features of late-capitalist and post-communist societies which characterise 'Complex Politics' contexts for polling are distilled below. I will explore these in detail in the following chapters of this book.

Political Culture: The notion of a national, unified, political culture is difficult to sustain in late-capitalist and post-communist contexts because of intensive restructuring of the economic and social systems. This has facilitated increasing social, economic and cultural diversity and fragmentation and a host of cleavages within the citizenry, together with a generalised absence of any clearly defined value systems. As a consequence, there is a high level of volatility in political values and attitudes, and this is particularly marked at the electoral level. Furthermore there are increasing tendencies towards citizen alienation from political systems, with declining support for traditional political procedures, institutions and organisations.

Party System: The traditional party systems are undergoing a process of restructuring. Competitive party systems are the norm, but in late-capitalist societies the established parties have typically declined in terms of their power, status, and support within the electorate. Both late-capitalist and post-communist contexts are characterised by increased party pluralism, with the emergence of new parties, party replacement, and shifting party coalitions and alliances. Usually party programmes either lack stability, coherence and consistency (and often without any clear ideological basis), or else they are radically transformative. The newness of many of the emerging parties results in their lack of identity within the electorate and consequently impedes the development of any social bases amongst voters. This facilitates a lack of voter-party alliances in electoral politics.

Mechanisms for Political Participation: Political structures and institutions are usually open, and access to political power is available to the citizenry via regular and competitive elections. Mass political participation is limited to electoral turnout which is declining, and there is variegated participation within numerous parties and pressure groups. As we shall see, there is some limited information diffusion, with opportunities for voters to obtain information about the political system via the mass media which is able to exert a degree of autonomy from the state. However, it will become clear in later chapters that the increasing tendency towards de-regulation of the news media has led to declining standards in the quality, professionalism and objectivity of news (and poll) reporting, and is contributing to a general public scepticism of polls.

The Policy Process: There is competition for political office, and the existence of regular elections ensures parties are accountable to the electorate. As a result, parties are increasingly sensitive to public opinion demands when constructing (new parties) or modifying (traditional parties) political programmes and manifestos. However, there is scope for manipulation by the leading political actors, chiefly the political parties: while the public is able to intervene within the political process, it is questionable whether this is real or virtual; consequently, polls do not necessarily provide a mechanism through which the public are able to control political elites. Increasingly, there is a tendency for polls to be used by such elites not to facilitate genuine dialogue with the public, but to manipulate the political process and the political and public agenda to secure power and influence.

Notes

1.   For instance, Allen has flagged-up three major methodological flaws in the post industrial thesis: firstly, the lack of direct evidence offered to substantiate the claim that there has been a shift in demand from manufacturing goods to services; secondly, the type of data employed; and thirdly, the methodological determinism which underpins Bell's thesis of an inevitable historical progression through pre-industrial, industrial, and post-industrial phases of economic and social development (Allen, 1988, pp.112-113). Mandel questions Bell's notion of a post-industrial 'break' from a previous 'industrial era', and argues that the growth of service industries and employment represents a shift in the pattern of capital investment from less to more

profitable activities. Thus, Marxist writers like Mandel emphasise the continuous features of a capitalist system which is reaching its climax under 'late-capitalism', rather than a break with the past (Mandel, 1975.)

2.   However, Goldblatt claims that these observations are partly the product of the methodology employed, in particular, the comparison of occupational categories for the 1971 and 1981 censuses which are not commensurable, and which tend to ignore those not in employment (1983).

3.   Although class dealignment is a controversial concept, and one that is less than universally accepted (see for instance Heath et al, 1985).

4.   These developments will be discussed in Chapter 6.

5.   State positions awarded by the Party patronage system.

5   The Development of Opinion Polling in Capitalist Societies: Britain

Introduction

This chapter is concerned with opinion polling in capitalist political systems. Focusing especially on Britain as a critical case, it considers a number of issues relating to the interplay between politics and opinion polling. It begins by tracing the origins and history of the political opinion polling industry in Britain, identifying the impetus behind its evolution, and the changing patterns of demand for its services. Following this is a consideration of the role and functions of polls in political affairs, with particular reference to the use made of them by mass media organisations and the major political parties. Finally, the chapter concludes with a discussion of the response of political organisations and institutions to periodic calls to ban opinion polls.

The Emergence of Opinion Polling

According to Bradburn and Sudman, opinion polls have been conducted as far back in time as the early 1800s. These straw polls were regularly carried out by newspapers and magazines to report on the political views of the public and to predict election outcomes, with the first such poll commissioned by the *Harrisburg Pennsylvanian* in 1824 during the election contest between Adams and Clay (Bradburn and Sudman, 1988, pp.12-13). However, the methods employed in these straw polls were relatively informal, and were typically based upon either readership ballots, or the convenience selection[1] of respondents (Crespi, 1989, pp.1-2).

Polling as it is now conventionally understood - based upon the systematic selection of representative samples of the public - was not introduced until the 1930s, when Gallup, Roper and Crossley set up agencies in the USA exclusively dedicated to measuring public opinion. These pollsters had all come into opinion polling from a market research background, and considered that the general procedures, methods and techniques used for identifying consumer preferences and for the market-testing of products could also be employed for measuring political opinions, attitudes and values.

The American presidential election of 1936 provided the opinion pollsters with their first opportunity to publicly test the effectiveness and accuracy of their polls. At the election, polls were conducted by all three of these newly established polling agencies, as well as by the Literary Digest journal which carried out what was until then a more typical straw poll. The Literary Digest mailed ballots to over 10 million people drawn from automobile registration lists and telephone directories, and achieved a 25% participation rate. The results of the poll forecast that the Republican candidate Landon would secure a landslide victory over the Democrat Roosevelt by a margin of 57% to 43%. The poll was criticised on methodological grounds. Firstly, it under-sampled the core of Roosevelt's support (lower income voters who had disproportionately low rates of car and telephone ownership). Secondly, it was criticised because of its low response rate.

In contrast, the three opinion polling organisations all used sample survey procedures, and each rightly forecast victory for Roosevelt who eventually defeated Landon by 62.5% of the popular vote to 37.5% (Squire, 1988, pp.126). The relative success of the polls in the election had a profound effect on their status and development, resulting in "...the almost overnight acceptance of public opinion polls by politicians and the general public. From this point, the growth of polls in the United States and Western Europe was rapid, indeed explosive" (Bradburn and Sudman, 1988, p.22).

Polling in Britain

Social Surveys (Gallup Poll) Limited Polls were introduced in Britain in 1937 when Harry Field of the American organisation Gallup approached Dr Henry Durant to set up the British Institute of Public Opinion (BIPO). Durant's first commission for the *News Chronicle* was relatively successful, forecasting the 1937 West Fulham by-election to within 1% of the actual result. BIPO's credibility was further enhanced with its pre-election poll in 1945, which, contrary to general expectations, successfully predicted a victory for the Labour Party, although underestimating the gap by 3.5%. Over time, BIPO (later Gallup) developed a reputation for its quality and accuracy of political polling, which guaranteed a stable relationship with *News Chronicle* until 1960, when the paper ceased to function. Subsequently, Gallup's polls have been regularly published in the *Daily Telegraph*, while it has also conducted work for both the Conservative Party and the Labour Party, as well as various government departments and other academic bodies.

The Daily Express Poll BIPO was joined at the 1950 General Election by the Daily Express Poll. Its final pre-election results in 1950, 1951 and 1955 were fairly respectable, although in 1950 it chose the wrong winner. However, at the 1959 General Election, the newspaper announced that "...The Daily Express has no confidence in its own poll, although it is conducted with complete integrity, and all possible efficiency" (cited in Worcester, 1991, p.10). Following poor results in both 1964 (where once again, it over-estimated the Conservative lead, while Labour slipped into office) and again in 1966, the *Daily Express*' internal poll was closed down (Butler and Pinto-Duschinsky, 1971, p.172).

Research Services Ltd Founded in 1946, Research Services Limited (RSL) is probably one of the biggest market research companies currently in existence in Britain, although its activities in the field of political opinion polling have been relatively ad hoc. RSL's first election polls were conducted during the 1951 General Election campaign for the *Daily Graphic*. However, as with BIPO and the *Daily Express* which also polled the election, RSL over-estimated the Conservative Party share of support, and if not for the peculiarities of the British election system, would have wrongly forecast the electoral outcome. In the event, the return to government of Churchill's party deflected some of the attention away from the error of all three polling agencies. Nonetheless, RSL did not poll during the general elections of 1955 and 1959, although later regular polls for the *Observer* during the period 1964-1970 were more encouraging (estimating the size of Labour's lead to within 1% in the General Elections of both 1964 and 1966). In 1970, Mark Abrams, chairman of RSL since 1951, left the company, and as a consequence RSL moved away from political polling activities. However, in 1979 RSL conducted a series of polls for the *Observer* newspaper. The company's polls forecast unusually high ratings for the Conservative Party, with an estimated lead of 21% in the initial campaign poll. The gulf between RSL's polls and polls from other companies was received with scepticism by readers and commentators alike, and as a result RSL discontinued its political polling activities.

Under the direction of Mark Abrams, RSL also forged a somewhat unstable relationship with the Labour Party. Its progress depended both upon which ideological wing of the party ('Gaitskellite' or 'Bevanite') controlled the National Executive Committee at any one time, and upon the continued presence of RSL's Chairman himself. Thus, when Abrams departed in 1970, the ties between pollster and party were severed.

National Opinion Polls   Labour was not the only political party to employ a company for the purpose of specifically undertaking political research. In 1957, National Opinion Polls (NOP) was established as a subsidiary company of *Associated Newspapers*, and took over from the *Daily Mail's* own internal poll. In 1963 under R.M. Shields, NOP was commissioned by the Conservative Party to conduct a "10,000 case study, the major emphasis of which was to identify Conservative defectors, (and to) measure attitudes towards the two major parties and the leaders" (Worcester, 1991, p.24). This encounter was brief, however, and in December 1965 Humphrey Taylor (himself a former executive of NOP) formed the Opinion Research Centre in conjunction with Conservative Party Central Office. Since 1989, NOP have conducted polls for the Labour Party, and provided the bulk of Labour's quantitative work during the 1992 and 1997 General Election campaigns.

NOP's association with the newspaper industry began with the *Daily Mail* during the General Election of 1959, and continuous polling for the paper lasted until the General Election of 1983. The length of the relationship is neither surprising nor remarkable however, when one considers that Associated Newspapers (later the Daily Mail Group) owned both NOP and the *Daily Mail*. Since the beginning of 1990, NOP has also polled regularly for the *Independent* newspaper, and more recently, for the *Sunday Times*.

In terms of forecasting general election outcomes, NOP's performance is comparable to that of other opinion pollsters, and generally satisfactory. However, like most of the other polling organisations (except ORC), it too did not escape the disaster of the 1970 General Election, choosing the wrong winner, and misjudging the size of the gap between Labour and the Conservatives by a margin of 6.5% (this however, does not compare with the 9.4% error of Gallup, and the 11.1% error of Marplan). Again, in February 1974 NOP picked the wrong winner, although the Conservatives did secure a higher share of the popular vote (by 0.8%) but lost out in seats to Labour. In October of the same year, NOP refused to acknowledge its eve-of-poll result as a prediction (although most commentators perceived it as such). This was fortunate, because it over-estimated the Labour lead by 11%. NOP performed significantly better at later General Elections in 1979, 1983 and 1987, with errors on the lead of -0.2%, +2.0%, - 4.0% respectively. However, as we shall see in Chapter 7, all the major pollsters, including NOP had their credibility severely damaged at the 1992 General Election when, against all polling expectations, the Conservative Party was returned to government with a margin of victory of 7% over Labour.

Opinion Research Centre   The Opinion Research Centre (ORC) was set up in 1965 at the behest of the Conservative Party, although it was not until 1970 that its ability as a political polling agency could be judged at a general election. In terms of crude results, ORC's forecast of a Tory victory over Labour with only a 1.4% under-estimation of the margin of victory, seemed to confirm its status as a leading actor within the industry. The other companies (Harris, NOP, Gallup, and Marplan) all forecast a Labour victory, and erred on average by 7.9% on the party gap. However, ORC's final forecast was based on results from only 257 respondents re-called from an earlier survey and adjusted for turnout. ORC's results in February 1974 were disappointing, underestimating Labour's share of electoral support by 2.2%. The error was exaggerated when Labour in fact won the election by virtue of securing a larger share of Parliamentary seats, but fewer votes than the Conservatives. This error forced ORC's founder member Humphrey Taylor to admit in the *Times* that "...we very much regret that we misled a great many people into believing the Conservatives would win by a comfortable majority" (cited in Worcester, 1991, p.46). In October, ORC over-estimated Labour's margin of victory by 3.9%.

Throughout its brief career however, ORC was successful in securing a series of major clients, including the Conservative Party (1965-1979), the *Sunday Times*, the *Times* and the *Express Group* of newspapers. When Humphrey Taylor departed for the USA in 1977 to join the Louis Harris polling agency however, the fortunes of ORC as a leading, independent political polling company slumped, losing its newspaper sponsors to MORI in 1977. During the 1979 General Election, ORC still polled for the Conservative Party, but failed to produce an election forecast, and in 1983 was taken over by the pollsters, Louis Harris Research Limited.

The Harris Research Centre The history of Louis Harris Research Ltd (now the Harris Research Centre), has been relatively successful. This might appear somewhat surprising, given that its early forays into the field of political opinion polling were notably irregular, infrequent and inaccurate. Thus, its first three pre-election polls (conducted on behalf of the *Daily Express*, for whom it had worked since 1969) were conspicuous by their rather disappointing record: in 1970 and later in February 1974, Harris' predicted winner actually lost; in October 1974, the margin of victory for Labour forecast by Harris was over-estimated by 4.9%; while in the 1979 election, the company did not conduct an eve-of-poll study.

However, its long standing relationship with the *Daily Express* (until 1983) enabled Harris to establish itself as a key player within the industry. Following its take-over of ORC in 1983, it polled regularly for the *Observer* (from the General Election of 1987 until the newspaper was taken over by the *Guardian* in October 1993), and occasionally for both *TV-am* and *Weekend World* (during the 1983 and 1987 General Election campaigns). Meanwhile, it has engaged in exclusive work for the Conservative Party during the 1979, 1983, 1987, and 1992 elections.

Marplan Previously a conventional market research society, Marplan's origins date back to 1959, although its first election-based study was not undertaken until 1962 (for the *Sunday Times*). In the 1966 General Election, it carried out a series of constituency polls for the *Sunday Times* and the *Coventry Evening Telegraph*. In 1968, Marplan was commissioned to produce a regular quarterly political survey for the *Times*. However, this association with *The Times* was short-lived when, following the disastrous eve-of-poll party estimates of 1970, they produced an 11.1% error on the Conservative and Labour gap, which was "...the worst general election forecast ever recorded in Britain" (Worcester, 1980, p.37). Inaccurate forecasts in both February and October 1974 failed to inspire confidence amongst commentators and clients alike, and it was not until 1979 that Marplan's fortunes changed, and its reputation as one of the five leading political polling organisations was confirmed.

Marplan conducted a series of private political surveys for the SDP during the 1987 General Election campaign, focusing upon twelve key marginal seats. However, the extent to which these polls can in any way be regarded as private is questionable, because the results of ten of the surveys, all indicating a strengthening support for the Alliance, were leaked to the *Today* newspaper which was consistently sympathetic to the Owen-Steel team. Meanwhile, the technical details of the surveys were unaccountably omitted. It was difficult therefore for readers to clarify the reliability of the polls, and to establish whether the forecasts were credible or not (Butler and Kavanagh, 1988, p.137).

Following the 1983 General Election, Marplan began long-term monthly polling for the *Guardian* newspaper. However, in January 1989 Marplan was taken over by The Reflexions Group Ltd. This company's ambivalence for opinion polling resulted in Marplan's polling team leaving the company to form International Communications and Marketing Research (ICM) Ltd. ICM continue to poll for the *Guardian*, and also worked for the *Sunday Correspondent* from October 1989 until the paper's demise a year later in October 1990, as well as for the *Sunday Express* during the 1992 General Election campaign. At the 1997 General Election, it conducted private polling research for the Conservative Party.

Market and Opinion Research International In 1969, Market and Opinion Research International (MORI) was set up as a joint venture between NOP and the American Opinion Research Corporation. Within a matter of months (October 1969), its director Robert Worcester had been approached by the Labour Party to help steer their election campaign. MORI conducted two surveys for the Labour Party during the campaign, but as Butler and Pinto-Duschinsky noted, the findings had little relevance for strategy because "...the party in fact seemed to lack the skill to commission polls that would be of much real use to it, still less to digest or give effect to their finding" (Butler and Pinto-Duschinsky, 1971, p.190). In subsequent elections however, this proved to be less of a problem, with the Labour Party becoming more adept and sophisticated in its use of MORI's data. MORI have also polled for the Green Party, and the Rainbow Alliance Party (Dobbs, 1992).

MORI's success in establishing a long-term relationship with a political client has been duplicated in the media world, turning out polls regularly for the *Sunday Times* since 1975, and for the *Evening Standard* from 1976 until 1986. In the 1983 campaign, it provided polls for the *Daily Express, Daily Star, Sunday Times, Evening Standard, BBC* and *Yorkshire TV*, while in 1987, for the *Times*, again the *Sunday Times* (for whom it currently produces regular polls), and continuous (Scottish) regional polls for *The Scotsman* since 1977. Its first media-sponsored general election poll was undertaken in 1979, when MORI was commissioned by the press (*Sunday Times* and the *Express Group*) to conduct an eve-of-poll forecast which managed to estimate the size of the Conservative lead to within 1.6% of the actual result. MORI's subsequent performances at general elections, local elections and by-elections have helped to establish it as one of the five leading organisations involved in the political opinion polling industry.

Audience Selection Ltd As far as political opinion polling is concerned, the 1979 General Election was unique, in that it was the first in which nation-wide polls (Marplan for the *Sun*) were conducted using random telephone interviewing methods (Butler and Kavanagh, 1980, p.269). By 1983, the adoption of this method by Audience Selection Ltd (ASL) looked set to revolutionise the industry, challenging the orthodoxy of face-to-face interviewing using quota samples, and the dominance over the polling industry by the big five companies for whom this technique was perceived as the most reliable, and therefore the most preferred means of gauging public opinion.

ASL was set up by a leading market research company, AGB, in 1980, as the first stand-alone telephone polling agency. Its first test at polling the public's voting intentions was in the campaign period of May to June 1983, when considerable attention was focused upon the results which they provided for their clients, the *Sun* and *TV-AM*. The results, which indicated advances for the Alliance, were received with some scepticism by ASL's pollster rivals, as well as by many academics and Members of Parliament. Critics claimed that the polls were inevitably biased because they under-sampled the Labour vote: with only 75% telephone penetration in Britain in 1983, it was a widely held view that those sections of the electorate without telephones were likely to be disproportionately low income groups, and generally sympathetic towards Labour (Butler and

Kavanagh, 1984, p.127).   Others, including such prominent Members of Parliament as Labour's Dennis Healey, and the Conservative's Cecil Parkinson, suggested that ASL were involved with the SDP (for whom the pollsters also conducted polls) in a concerted campaign to mislead the electorate about the strength of the Alliance and presumably, to try to encourage a bandwagon effect of some kind. Added to this was the criticism by Labour Member of Parliament Tony Benn, who accused the *Sun* and by association its pollster ASL, of publishing a survey in his Bristol East constituency in an attempt to undermine his election chances (Butler and Kavanagh, 1984, p.131).

In the event, ASL's final national election forecast failed to convince commentators and readers of the polls that the 1983 General Election heralded the dawning of a new era in the development of political opinion polling: its results forecast that the three main parties, Conservative, Labour and Alliance, would win 46%, 23% and 29% of the vote respectively, when in reality the final vote was 43%, 28%, and 25%.

ASL's poor performance had a negative impact upon its fortunes. At the 1987 General Election, the SDP chose Marplan as their pollsters, and the *Sun* opted not to publish ASL's eve-of-poll-forecast, whose precision was surpassed only by MORI with an average error on the Labour/Conservative gap of only 2%. From June 1987 until November 1993, ASL continued to produce a regular sample of national voting intentions as part of their omnibus survey, although without a formalised link with either the news-media or the political parties.

Summary The development of the political opinion polling industry in post-war Britain is summarised in Table 5.1 below. The industry has experienced a marked increase in growth over time in terms of the number of actual political opinion polling organisations, the volume of campaign polls conducted, and the demand for polls by the mass media. Earlier, it was noted that the initial impetus for political opinion polling derived from the journalistic requirements of newspapers in the USA. Similarly in Britain, it has been media sponsorship which has provided the publicity bandwagon for polls. Indeed, some polling organisations were actually set up by news media organisations, with the specific intention of providing news stories and unique angles on current affairs stories (The Daily Express Poll and National Opinion Polls).   Today, polls are a common feature of newspaper coverage of political issues (especially during election campaign periods), and increasingly they are commissioned by television programmes for this purpose.

Table 5.1   **National Opinion Polling in British General Election Campaigns 1945-1997**

Election Year	Number of Polling Organisations	Number of National Campaign Polls*	Number of Media Sponsors of National Campaign Polls
1945	1	1	1
1950	3	11	3
1951	3	n.a	3
1955	2	n.a	2
1959	4	20	4
1964	4	23	5
1966	4	26	8
1970	5	25	7
1974(Feb.)	6	25	10
1974(Oct.)	6	27	13
1979	6	26	11
1983	6	47	14
1987	7	54	15
1992	8	50	18
1997	5	47	14

* Only polls asking respondent's voting intention included.

We have also noted the effect that the political parties have had on polling. These parties have recognised at a very early stage the potential advantages in using polls to monitor the public's reactions to issues, events and candidates, as well as employing the data to help guide them in developing strategies to improve their image, and market their policies. Long-term party-pollster relationships have endured as a result, and indeed one organisation (Opinion Research Centre) was established as a collaboration between the Conservative Party and others precisely because of the functions which the Party perceived it could perform in its campaigning work.

It is as a result of these developments that polling has expanded over time, and become such an established feature of the contemporary political landscape in Britain.

Polls and The Political Process in Britain

The following discussion examines why there is such a demand for polls by the mass media and political parties, and in doing so, considers the relationship between polling and the mass media organisations, and the ways in which the major political parties have used and reacted to the opinion polls. In this way, we will be able to see the impact that polls have on the political process in Britain.

Polls and The Mass Media

As we have seen, the development of political opinion polling in Britain is closely tied to the priorities of the mass media. In fact there is a symbiotic relationship here - polls help to increase the readership and viewership of media organisations, which in turn stimulates the demand for polls, increases public awareness of them (especially in the context of elections), and ultimately helps to reinforce their role within political affairs. Before considering the nature and origins of this media-polling relationship, it will be useful to consider the ways in which the mass media operate in countries like Britain, so that we can understand the context and demand for media polls.

According to one view, in capitalist political systems private media proprietorship prevents the state from monopolising the means of communication. A proliferation of media organisations, a plurality of ownership, and the separation of ownership and control ensures professional and objective reporting of political affairs, and a variety of viewpoints available for public consumption. Thus, where partisanship is expressed, there will be countervailing sources of alternative media bias, which results in a balance of overall media reporting.

In this process, the state plays a supervising role by ensuring open competition within the mass media industry, as well as the impartiality and quality of coverage and dissemination of political news and information. The state does not seek to control or censure media coverage of political issues, except where publication would threaten the national interest (Whale, 1977). Even in the public sector, where the *BBC* is bound by government legislation to provide both a high quality public service and balanced and responsible coverage of issues and events, the state is being increasingly superseded by market mechanisms. While television and radio possess a large degree of freedom and independence from government control, it is competition from the commercial sector, and the need to secure a share of the market-audience sufficient to justify continued state-funding and licensing, which regulates the *BBC*.

This pluralist conception of the mass media, its relationship with the state, and the process through which the flow of political information passes to the electorate, have been criticised by elite theorists and neo-marxists alike. For instance, Murdoch and Golding (1977) dispute the notion of a free, competitive media industry, and argue that throughout the post-war period, there has been a persistent trend towards a concentration of media ownership and control, and of multi-media empire building. Furthermore there are significant organisational and cultural linkages between media organisations and the state. Schattschneider (1960) maintains that this direct collusion leads to a 'mobilisation of bias', which serves to suppress certain issues which question the fundamental assumptions upon which society is organised, and ultimately determines the political information available to the electorate.

Thus, broadcast news, like the images and messages conveyed to the public via the press, is ultimately socially produced, and reinforces the dominant culture - the values, biases and prejudices of ruling groups within society (Glasgow University Media Group, 1980). Nonetheless, the press is perceived as relatively more overtly partisan than the television in its coverage of political news, not least because the traditional system of broadcasting as a universal public service is easier to monitor, and there are more formal structures in place to limit the extent of bias. However, the recent trend has been towards the marketisation and deregulation of the broadcasting media, particularly with the Broadcasting Act of 1990[2]. This development represents a further drift towards the fragmentation of the national audience, the relegation of serious political analysis, the general popularisation of the broadcasting media, and its loss of integrity as an objective vehicle for political communication.

However, in spite of the differences between the pluralist and the elite theorist/neo-marxist analyses of the mass media, it is possible to contrast the operation of the mass media industry and the role of the state in regulating its affairs in capitalist political systems, with the situation which previously existed in communist political systems. Victor Afanasev, editor-in-chief of *Pravda* from 1976 until 1989, describes the underlying principles of the mass media in communist societies:

> Our enemies not infrequently criticise the Communist Party for monopolising the guidance of the political information system ... However, the guidance of this important sphere of public life is both the party's right and its obligation ... Our party is the ruling party: and is therefore called upon to carry out the guidance of all spheres of life in a socialist society, including the ideological sphere ... the defense of the party's policy and ideology is at the same time also the defense of the most sacred ideas and interests of the people (cited in White, Pravdo, and Gitelman, 1992, p.176).

In Britain then, there is *relative* media independence from governmental control. This operates within the framework of a limited system of competition, which is generated and sustained by the ability of organisations to accumulate capital in the form of profits from the sale of political information via newspapers and advertising revenue for commercial broadcasting media. In this process, state organisations like the *BBC* are encouraged and ultimately compelled to operate within this media marketplace to justify their status and financing.

Political opinion polls, while an expensive form of journalism (Worcester, 1991, p.181) assist in this process. Media organisations commission polls to gain advantage over their rivals in securing the market audience. The ability to transform the results of voting intention data into front-page headlines and top-line broadcasting news items (not just as feature and background stories, but as major election campaign news) provides an irresistible attraction to all media organisations (press and broadcasting, public and private) of even the simplest of poll stories, "...given the combined circumstances of a short campaign and intense media competition" (Crewe, 1993b, p.474). By the early 1980s, the media's fascination and preoccupation with election polls was described in terms of facilitating the advent of a new stage in the evolution of political opinion polling - 'saturation polling'. Crewe (1986, p.234) defines this as:

> The unremitting attention that was devoted to reporting, analysing, comparing, averaging, explaining, interviewing politicians about, and speculation upon - the polls.

As a consequence, the results of published polls may themselves become newsworthy political issues. Crespi, for instance maintains that "...views of the general public on political issues and events are treated as the primary subject matter, worthy of attention in their own right" (Crespi, 1980, p.464). Thus news editors use polls not merely to illuminate or explain political issues or events, but to report on public opinion for its intrinsic interest as news. This serves to define and limit the topics which are asked, and the data which is ultimately reported to the public.

Boorstin defines polls used in this way as pseudo-events, as artificial items of news that are "planned, planted or incited" specifically in order to be reported (1961, p.40). He criticises polling for offering images of "...public opinion...[that are] synthetic, believable, passive, vivid, concrete, simplified and ambiguous as never before" (1961, p.232). Furthermore, polls used in this way have the capacity to distort people's perceptions of politics and social life:

> Having been polled as a representative of the public, [the citizen] can then read reports and see how he looks. As polls become more scientific and detailed - broken

down into occupations, counties, income groups, religious denominations, etc - the citizen can discover himself [and the opinions which he "ought" to have or is likely to have] ...Public opinion - once the public's expression - becomes more and more an image into which the public fits its expression ...It is the people looking into the mirror (1961, p.238).

As a result of this process, public opinion itself becomes partly the product of a chain-reaction inspired by the mass media and its use of opinion polls.

There is more scope within the press than broadcasting for polls to be used in this way. Unlike the *BBC*, the press is privately-owned and has no tradition in which it is compelled to operate as a public service within the constraints that such a status imposes. Furthermore, unlike both public and commercial broadcasting, the press enjoys relative autonomy from the state. It therefore has the capacity to decide for itself which topics should be polled, and how the results should be disseminated. However, the pressure to attain high audiences is increasingly as much a feature of broadcasting as it is for the newspaper industry. According to Crewe, this almost inevitably leads to a situation where polling data, whether consciously or unconsciously, will be massaged prior to public dissemination both by the press and by the broadcast media. The effect may in extreme circumstances contribute to the production, rather than the communication, of political information, and in the creation of a distorted and artificial political reality for readers and viewers alike. As he notes, this is most evident in the reporting of polls. Crewe (1986, pp.249-252) presents five propositions to support his case:

(i) "However static public opinion actually is, the polls enable the media to maximise the impression of flux and change";
(ii) "However clear the outcome and trend, polls allow the media to hedge their bets";
(iii) "However improbable a poll finding is, the media will always publish (broadcast) it";
(iv) "Whatever the state of public opinion, the media have a strong incentive to commission polls";
(v) "The more polls there are, the more likely they are to become an election issue".

This amplification of the significance of opinion polls in the political process by the mass media (especially during election campaign periods) is likely to prove problematic where the treatment of data by journalists and/or editors is either ill-informed, unsophisticated, or manipulative. Worcester (1991) describes the flaws in the interpretation, analysis and reporting of polls by such inexperienced media personnel. At a general level, journalists may tend to overemphasise the impression of change which marginal shifts in a run of polls may suggest, by failing to take account of sampling fluctuations. This exaggeration of voting volatility is likely to be particularly marked during a close contest between the leading parties, and all the more misleading for being so.[3] Furthermore, while the pollsters may attempt to guard against the use of data in this way and insist on the publication of a poll's technical details, the advice is often ignored, and in the case of secondary reporting of polls, virtually impossible to control. This latter point is particularly serious in the case of television reporting of polls, where limitations in terms of copy deadlines and time combine to ensure that the reporting of such information for verification of a poll's validity and reliability is very often absent.

The pollsters have limited input on the actual text of media reporting and on the final headlines. They may be able to make suggestions on the content of the draft copy, but at the final stages it is the sub-editor who usually decides what gets printed, and in what format. As a consequence, headlines may misrepresent the findings of political opinion polls by "...implying change where no trend has been measured ...emphasising the unimportant ...highlighting the insignificant ...(and by) quoting out of context" (Worcester, 1991, p.185). Furthermore, in the actual text of a newspaper article, or on a radio or television report, journalists are often required to make sense of and simplify complex statistics without prior training in this area. A combination of these two factors may result in a distorted picture of the state of public opinion filtering through to the electorate via the mass media; during the 1992 General Election campaign, voters were presented with a virtually constant stream of media headlines and reports signalling a hung parliament as the most likely electoral scenario, with Labour as the largest party:

> **Figures Would Give Kinnock Commons Majority of 20** (McKie in *The Guardian,* 18th March).
> **History Points To Hung Parliament As Voters Are Unmoved** (McKie in *The Guardian*, 28th March).
> **Hung Parliament Looms** (Helm and Palmer in *The Sunday Telegraph*, 5th April).
> **Major Increases Popularity As Hung Parliament Looms** (Lewington in *The Sunday Express*, 5th April).
> **Polls Put Kinnock In Number 10** (Wapshott in *The Observer*, 5th April).
> **Unchanged Labour Lead Confirms Hung Parliament** (McKie in *The Guardian*, 8th April).

Ultimately voters were misled by this reporting, not least because "...the polls were regarded not as snapshots taken at one point in the campaign, but as predictions of what would happen on polling day" (Butler and Kavanagh, 1992, p.153). Given that the electorate generally paid close attention to the polls (Worcester found that half-way through the campaign, 40% of voters registered an interest in the polls [1992b, p.1]), the way in which the media select and report polling data has important consequences for how voters perceive the course of elections.

In the current era, where electorates are typically becoming increasingly volatile, instrumental, sensitive, and receptive to political news and events, the misuse of data in this way has serious implications for electoral politics. Given the prevalence of tactical voting in countries like Britain and elsewhere in Europe, the increasing voter awareness of and exposure to these poll reports may have an influence on people's voting behaviour.

The often contradictory relationship between the pollsters and the mass media organisations who sponsor them, is summarised by Weiner (1977, p.675):

> The tension between academic survey techniques and the pressures of journalism has remained the prime characteristic of polling organisations. While the pollsters are indeed concerned with the 'scientific measurement' that their promotion suggests, their concepts and operations are constrained by journalistic conventions and resources. Polls must produce *news* - items of immediate interest such as explicit election forecasts - with limited time, staff, and money.

While pollsters may attempt to cajole their clients into a more informed, professional and valid use of polls, the underlying needs of the media to maximise profits and their share of the audience often results in the use of polls as part of a strategy to provide entertainment, rather than to educate the public on political issues. As pollsters Webb and Wybrow (1974, p.265) have observed:

> Our main sponsors, the newspapers and T.V. are continually pressuring us to forecast seats, and are likely to supply their own forecasts in the face of our resistance.

Worcester reports for instance that at the 1992 General Election, the public "...were clearly misled by the seat projections done by the broadcasters and their psephologists, not the exit polls" (1992a, p.3). Thus, the Harris exit poll pointed to a Conservative majority of 12 seats (compared to an actual result of a 21 seat majority); *ITN* massaging of the data actually suggested that the Tories would be 21 seats short of a majority.

To create a space between themselves and their media clients, the pollsters have combined to form various associations. The purpose of these associations is to preserve their integrity as independent research organisations, to maintain high standards in data collection and dissemination, and to set up a mechanism for self-regulation. At an international level, the World Association of Public Opinion Research (WAPOR) exists to "...establish a world-wide meeting ground for those working in the area of survey research" (cited in Worcester, 1991, p.207). Similar associations include ESOMAR (Europe) and in Britain there is APOPO.[4]

These associations have codes of practice concerning how polls should be conducted, rules of practice between the researchers and respondents, as well as guidelines on how best to report the results of opinion poll studies. This latter aspect is designed to "...protect the public from misrepresentation and exploitation in the name of research" by ensuring that the final results are an accurate and valid representation of the data (Worcester, 1991, p.209). The codes aim to prevent the misuse of polls by uniformed or unscrupulous media editors and journalists, and suggest for instance that reports based on political opinion polls should include full technical and methodological details (fieldwork dates, sample sizes, number of sampling points, margins of error and so on). However, these codes are only a guide for the media, and in practice cannot be enforced by the pollsters themselves who ultimately have little control over how their results are communicated to the public. Thus the independence that the polls have from the media, the state, and the dominant values which both tend to reflect, is only relative, and ultimately depends on the extent to which the media is both willing and economically able to accommodate codes of practice set up by the pollsters.

The post-war experience in Britain suggests that the pre-conditions for growth in polling are essentially three-fold. Firstly, it depends upon the extent to which private companies are able to make commercial gain and profit through investment in this form of political research. Even state-owned media enterprises use opinion polls to maintain and increase audience ratings. In the current context, the *BBC* is undergoing a process of restructuring which is resulting in the commercialisation of its services. As a result, it is likely to use polls in a more structured and systematic way in the future to help it compete for viewers and listeners. Opinion polls may themselves become newsworthy items, and help to popularise political events and issues (especially elections) even where these are predictable, and are perceived by voters to lack salience. This situation ultimately depends upon the mass media's relative autonomy from state interference, and the operation of a capitalist market economy.

The second condition is directly related to the first. That is, that the openness of the political system, and the lack of constraints upon, or censure of political information, enables the mass media to poll on virtually any political topic, and publish these as they see fit in order to help maximise audiences. In the absence of any restrictive state regulations, there is greater scope for the mass media to use polling data imaginatively for these purposes. The misuse of polls will only be minimised where the pollsters themselves are able to form associations and/or devise codes of conduct to create a space between themselves and the mass media. However, experience suggests that pollsters are unable to enforce standards within the media unless the latter voluntarily enter into an agreement to work within boundaries of good practice as defined by the pollsters.

Finally, the more volatile the electorate and the consequent unpredictability of electoral outcomes, the more demand there will be for polls by the mass media. Under such circumstances, opinion polls are likely to be perceived by news-editors as effective tools for monitoring changing public opinion and voting behaviour. They will aim to take advantage of the increasing trends toward the development of highly sensitised electorates, as well as large pools of discerning and inquisitive tactical voters who will use newspaper and broadcast polls to satisfy their appetites for political information.

Polls and The Political Parties

To a large extent, the pattern of growth in opinion polling is likely to be shaped by the nature of the party system which operates, as well as the demand for public opinion information by the political parties. The latter will be determined by:

(i)   how pragmatic or ideological the parties are, and therefore how receptive they are to the idea of using polls to develop policy, and make revisions to party programmes;

(ii) how useful the parties consider opinion polls are for helping them to develop strategies to gain electoral advantage over their rivals.

By tracing the relationships which have developed between the political parties and the opinion pollsters in Britain, we will be able to develop an understanding of the role of opinion polling in the political process.

Polls and The Conservative Party Kavanagh has claimed that "...private polling is now inseparable from the marketing orientation of contemporary election campaigns" (Kavanagh, 1993, p.526). The earliest reference to public opinion research in the Conservative Party Archives is given in the suggestion by a research officer to Joseph Ball in 1930 that a questionnaire should be distributed to "...persons competent to answer it, such as social workers, teachers, scout leaders etc. It would not be necessary for all these persons to be Conservative, though it would be necessary for them not to be active members of the Labour Party" (cited in Street, 1992, p.108). After the Second World War, the Conservative Party's interest in using information about the electorate's views, including polling data, led them to establish the Public Opinion Research Department (PORD) in 1948. A significant part of PORD's activities involved collating data from various sources on the general state of public opinion, reporting on voters' reactions to party political broadcasts, and providing election forecasts. In 1949, PORD commissioned a survey on 'The Floating Vote', which focused on the political loyalties and issue positions of 5000 voters. As Street notes, data was reported in a monthly *Public Opinion Summary* and distributed to party officers, Government ministers, Members of Parliament, and election candidates; a 'Confidential Supplement' "...combined more sensitive information and had a restricted circulation to ministers, the Chief Whip, selected officers and department heads, and members of the Liaison Committee" (1992, p.108).

By 1958, the Conservative Party were commissioning their own private opinion polls on a regular basis, and began employing NOP for this purpose in 1962. However, as Worcester notes these early surveys "...confused rather than clarified" (1991, p.24) the party's campaign strategists, and in 1965 Humphrey Taylor of NOP set up a joint polling collaboration with T.F. Thompson from the Conservative Central Office, by establishing the Opinion Research Centre (ORC). Polling data was used at each level of party policy- and decision-making. In the 1970 General Election campaign, findings from a series of continuous panels on the causes of changes in voting behaviour, identified that the C2 group of skilled manual workers was especially volatile, and these results "...affected party policy, election strategy, and advertising" (Worcester, 1991, p.40). In 1979, polling data helped to shape the Conservative's policies on council house sales, which ultimately formed one of the pillars of the Thatcherite ideological commitment to replacing collectivism with individualism, and developing a property-owning democracy.

During the 1983 General Election campaign, the Conservatives made extensive use of polls, retaining Harris (formerly ORC) under John Hanvey, who reported to Chris Lawson and Keith Britto at Central Office. Large scale 'State of the Battle' polls were conducted weekly, and were supplemented by a series of 'quickie' polls, which measured the response of voters to the party's campaigning and marketing strategies (Butler and Kavanagh, 1984). However, by 1987, the impact of the polls on Conservative electioneering had declined in significance: as one senior party worker observed, the influence of the polls was only relatively marginal, in that, "...they told us we were on course and, if things had been going wrong, they could have given us invaluable early guidance on specific weaknesses" (cited in Butler and Kavanagh, 1988, p.136).

Nonetheless the Party expanded its polling research in 1992, and increased its expenditure on polls from £200,000 in 1987, to £250,000. The Conservatives supplemented their polls from Harris with qualitative research conducted by Dick Wirthlin, who had previously worked for Ronald Reagan's Republican campaign team in the US presidential election of 1984. Wirthlin's research sought to probe voters' values, and in so doing, was designed to contribute to "...a general campaign strategy and suggest phrases and themes for party communications" (Kavanagh, 1993, p.521). However, there was some resistance to and scepticism about this work. It was only partially incorporated into the Conservatives' electioneering strategy, before the Party chairman Chris Patten dispensed with the research, and returned instead to the more conventional style opinion polling with Harris. A series of issue-based studies were conducted, not to guide or dictate policy, but to inform the Party of their strengths and weaknesses, and to help in the electoral struggle to dominate and shape the political agenda. As Kavanagh states "...The polls did not decide the contents of policy but they influenced presentation and were a means of monitoring the success of the campaign" (Kavanagh, 1993, p.523).

Polls and The Labour Party Probably the most documented pollster-party relationship grew out of the projects which Mark Abrams and RSL conducted for the Labour Party in the 1950s and the 1960s. In the early years after Gaitskell's election as Party leader in 1955, there was much resistance to polling amongst particular sections of the Party on ideological grounds. Essentially, the organised left-wing under Bevan held a deep distrust of Abrams because of his social democratic credentials; his attempts to use polls to revise and up-date Party policies and commitments were widely perceived as measures designed to undermine and discredit Labour's socialist traditions. Furthermore, as Abrams conceded, much of the scepticism which existed within the party originated in its inability to exploit polling data effectively:

> The party simply had no machinery that could have taken survey findings and used them to help shape effective political propaganda (cited in Worcester, 1991, p.25).

Throughout the 1960s, Labour's polling activities were rejuvenated. Under a new political regime, Abrams was commissioned to undertake a number of studies for planning and propaganda purposes. Polls in marginal constituencies helped to identify key target groups within the electorate, and further polls were conducted to identify which issues were salient amongst voters, and which should be stressed in canvassing and marketing campaigns. A major study in 1962 for instance highlighted the declining influence of class and levels of party identification, and uncovered the emergence of large groups of uncommitted and floating voters. The data was used by the Labour Party to develop strategies designed to win over these voters (Teer and Spence, 1973).

However, the association between Abrams' RSL and the Labour Party was essentially an ad hoc one. In 1969, the party turned to MORI for their polling work, and by 1972, MORI was conducting regular political surveys for its part in a relationship which lasted up until the General Election of 1987, after which it was replaced by NOP. As was the experience for RSL, MORI's contracts with Labour were dependent upon the ideological complexion of and balance of political forces within the party's various levels of decision-making. Kavanagh claims that "...MORI was frequently a casualty of internal party strife" (1993, p.512). While successive Party leaderships were generally enthusiastic about polling, the Party NEC, dominated by the left-wing throughout the 1970s and early 1980s, were generally sceptical and ambivalent. This debate within the Party about the usefulness and desirability of polls virtually mirrored the positions of the 'Gaitskellites' and the 'Bevanites' in the 1950s. Thus, in 1983 MORI's contract with the Party was not renewed until very shortly before the election campaign; as a consequence, the polling information generated by MORI's studies had little impact upon Labour's election strategy. The lesson was not lost on the new Party leader Neil Kinnock who sought to place opinion polling at the heart of the Party's electioneering machinery throughout the period in the run-up to the 1987 General Election. According to Butler and Kavanagh (1988, p.133):

> There is little doubt that the link between pollster and party was the closest and most intelligent that has been achieved in recent British politics.

Prior to the 1987 campaign, Labour set up the Shadow Communications Agency (SCA) to provide the major source of advice and expertise for the Party, especially on matters concerning advertising and media strategies. Shaw (1992, p.2) describes the role of opinion polling in this process:

> The basis of modern electioneering is the regular scrutiny of public opinion: this sets the parameters of policy development, shapes advertising strategy, moulds the choice of campaign themes and messages, and in the formation of overall campaigning and communications strategy, provides the yardstick of flexibility.

In practical terms, polls were used in a variety of ways to assist Labour's post-1987 campaigning and communications strategy. Firstly, polls were used to educate the Party about the reasons why it had lost the election, and to reposition the Party through its Policy Review.[5] Secondly, polling data helped to renovate the Party's image (by demonstrating to the electorate that it had modernised, was trustworthy and had united around a strong, collective and capable leadership). Thirdly, polls were employed to help Labour try to control the political agenda (by gaining maximum media coverage and dominating this). Finally, polls identified the Party's target voters - polls "...were inspected to detect shifts in patterns of partisan preferences, opinions and values in order to locate those segments of the population potentially most receptive to Labour's case" (Shaw, 1992, p.12). In the run-up to the 1992 General Election, an SCA strategy document *SCA Presentation* was prepared using NOP polling data. Essentially, the report asked: Who is the target market? What is the key to their voting behaviour? How do we influence them? The results formed the basis of Labour's 1992 campaigning strategies.

The experience of the SCA, and in particular its use of polls for electioneering purposes, provides a useful case-study in which to identify the extent to which politicians (and political parties) have come to rely on polls for political intelligence. It is this breadth of functions which polls offer which accounts for the continued demand for public opinion polling data by the political parties. As Kavanagh (1993, p.518) explains:

> Polling is used in particular by parties to test and enhance their images, target voters, present policy, track issues and themes, and generally improve their political communications with voters.

Furthermore, for the governing party, polls may provide an important, perhaps crucial source of data as to the most opportune time to call a general election. In Britain, the election date is determined by the Prime Minister, who has the power to dissolve government and call an election at his/her discretion at any stage within a five year parliamentary cycle. However, the practical input that polling information can provide on this matter is not always heeded. For instance, Prime Minister Edward Heath ignored ORC's advice to call an early election for January 1974, even though their polling data highlighted a widespread public dislike of trade union militancy. As Worcester notes "...the effect of a month's delay was to throw away the key advantage of surprise that a British Prime Minister enjoys" (Worcester, 1991, p.44). Nevertheless the polls are acknowledged to have been a major factor in persuading the Conservatives to set early election dates in 1983 and 1987. A set of poll results in marginal constituencies indicating a fall in Conservative support in February 1992, convinced Chris Patten and John Major to announce an April 9th election before a Labour bandwagon could gain any momentum. As one Conservative advisor put it:

> In setting the date, on a scale of one to ten, I'd put polls at eleven (cited in Butler and Kavanagh, 1992, p.135).

The extent of this demand for opinion polling information by the political parties can be illustrated with reference to Table 5.2, which provides a numerical index of the growth of private polling for Labour and the Conservatives between the 1979 and 1992 General Elections. As we can see, the figures suggest that there has been considerable growth in demand for polls by the two major political parties over this period.

Table 5.2   Patterns of Expenditure (£'s) on Opinion Polling by Labour and the Conservatives in British General Election Campaigns 1979-1992

Election Year	Conservative Party Expenditure	Percentage Increase	Labour Party Expenditure	Percentage Increase
1979	60,000		25,000	
1983	96,000	60.0	100,000	300.0
1987	200,000	108.0	120,000	20.0
1992	250,000	25.0	200,000	66.7

The discussion in this section on polls and the political process suggests that there are essentially two issues which account for this development of private political opinion polling. Firstly, the uses and functions of these polls. They provide an input as raw material for the marketing and campaigning strategies of the parties, particularly during very close and competitive electoral contests where the electorate is allegedly becoming increasingly volatile, and receptive to images and the presentation and content of policies. In this context, there is likely to be debate within the parties as to the extent to which such private polling represents an abdication of a party's role in leading and educating the public. To a degree, these controversies reflect the debate discussed in Chapter 2 between advocates of the 'classical doctrine of democracy', and those who adhere to a more 'competitive leadership' model.

Secondly, it has been seen that relatively stable relationships have developed over time between the parties and the pollsters, but there have been cases and moments where these links have remained only very tenuously. Particularly in the case of the Labour Party, it has been seen that polling is linked to the ideological character of a Party and the balance of forces between revisionists and traditionalists.

Regulating The Impact of Political Opinion Polling on The Political Process

The final factor involved in the development of the opinion polling industry in countries like Britain is the degree of tolerance of the political system, and the pressures which exist for regulating polling activities, or for imposing outright bans on the polls.

In many West European countries there are regulations enforced by national legislatures banning the publication (but not the conducting) of polls. In France, legislation introduced in 1977 prohibits the publication or distribution of public opinion polls, as well as public comment on them for one week prior to each stage of an election. Similar bans exist in Spain (5 days), Belgium (30 days), and Portugal (90 days). Voluntary bans are observed by the pollsters in Switzerland, and in Germany on election-day itself (Worcester, 1991; Kellner 1992). In Belgium, the law was introduced in the early 1980s, and challenged by the magazine *Knack* which published a poll four days prior to the 1985 General Election quoting article 18 of the 1831 constitution which states that "...the printed press is free; censorship can never be introduced" (cited in Worcester 1992c, p.9). In Britain, no such regulations exist, although there have been periodic calls to ban polls by politicians from across the political spectrum. Furthermore, in 1985, proposals for the 'harmonisation' of European Law to regulate polls were considered by the Council of the European Parliamentary Assembly committee, but their investigations concluded that such actions were unnecessary (Worcester, 1991, p.201).

The key consideration raised by opponents and sceptics of political opinion polls is the effect that they might have on the political behaviour of the citizenry, particularly in terms of any 'bandwagon' or 'underdog' effects that they may have at elections. It was noted in Chapter 2 that while there is little available empirical evidence to test the credibility of both the bandwagon and underdog propositions, this is a subject of considerable dispute. In an era of alleged *partisan dealignment*, large pools of voters are likely to have weak party attachments, and be prone to voting shifts or tactical voting on the basis of their sensitivity and receptiveness to various sources of political information including opinion polls (Crewe, 1986, pp.245-246).

The issue of whether or not polls should be banned is likely to be even more sensitive in the future, given both the use made of polling data by some journalists and media organisations, and the occasional slump in public confidence of polls when they are perceived to have performed badly in an election contest. Indeed, at both the 1987 and 1992 British General Elections, data from MORI indicated that 25% of British voters supported a ban on opinion polls in the final seven days of an election campaign (Worcester, 1992b, p.l). However, there was a significant fall in the proportions of people who advocated banning the polls in 1997, with only 16% in favour (Worcester, 1997, p.lxxvii). Advocates of opinion polls would argue however, that "...the concept of mature citizenship in a democracy and a ban on the publication of pre-election polls are diametrically opposed" (Koschnick, 1980, p.59). Furthermore Kavanagh (1983, p.212) has argued that there is little scope either for any collusion between the pollsters and the mass media or any direct massaging of the data:

> An obvious check against abuse is competition between independent polling organisations.

Irrespective of the claims and counter-claims of those who support or oppose bans on polls, the technicalities of implementing embargoes and bans on the publication of pre-election polls would prove difficult to enforce. As Worcester (1992c, p.9) notes:

> Polls cannot effectively be banned: if they were, the political parties would do even more polling than they do now - and leak even worse than they do now; secondly, stockbrokers, jobbers and other City financiers would do private polls and leak them (or make them up as they sometimes do now); third, foreign media would commission private polls in Britain and publish them overseas, and of course, the results would be transmitted and reported subsequently in this country.

Summary

This chapter has focused on Britain as a critical case study to demonstrate the development of polling in capitalist political systems. The commodification of political opinion polls, and their perceived and actual usefulness and functions both for competing political parties and for mass media organisations ensures that there is continued demand for polls.

In such countries, the competition for governmental office is relatively open, with periodic elections based upon a universal franchise. Because they are relatively accountable to voters (during election campaigns at least), political parties will be susceptible to public opinion. Parties need to be alert and sensitive to voter demands and grievances in order to fashion and present their policies in electorally appealing ways. Opinion polling performs a significant role in this process, and also helps parties as they attempt to target resources and political capital in the most efficient and effective ways to maximise electoral support. Furthermore such data may be used to frame the political agenda around issues where parties have actual or potential strength, and where their opponents are electorally vulnerable.

As a consequence, there has been a steady expansion of polling, and polls have assumed a significant role in political affairs and set down deep roots into the political landscape. However, given that there is a buoyant demand for polls by the parties and the mass media organisations, there may also be problems in terms of how the data is actually disseminated to the public. The mass media in particular may have an agenda for the use of polls which contradicts and undermines the good practice which pollsters seek to achieve. As a response, pollsters may form associations, and produce professional codes of conduct in an attempt to establish some autonomy between themselves and their clients. Ultimately however, these codes of conduct are dependent upon the integrity and co-operation of the clients.

Notes

1. Convenience sampling is based upon the selection of groups of the population who do not meet any necessarily pre-defined criteria, but are merely immediately (and therefore conveniently) accessible.

2. The Broadcasting Act of 1990 was essentially a package of measures designed to re-define the control and operation of broadcasting media operations, with the objective of creating "...a substantial liberalisation... and greater reliance on the viewer, rather than the regulator to sustain range and quality" (former Home Secretary, Douglas Hurd, cited in McIlroy, 1989, p.127). For commercial television, the IBA was to be replaced by the Independent Television Commission, to enforce lighter programme requirements, and *ITV* franchises were to be put out to tender every ten years, and secured on the basis of highest bids rather than strict content criteria. The Act sought to reduce the reliance of state-run broadcasting on the licence-fee, and influence the concept of 'direct charges'. This shift towards individualism and consumer choice-based regulation within the *BBC* would be shored-up by greater marketisation of the service, with both moves toward privatisation of broadcasting transmissions, and the injection of independent contracting into programme production. The Act was criticised by the Labour Party as "...a giant retreat from the concept of public service broadcasting. Its result will be less diversity and lower standards" (cited in McIlroy, 1989, p.127).

3. As we shall see in Chapter 6, some pollsters have taken steps to 'artificially' reduce reported voter volatility by weighting voting intention data to compensate for large numbers of respondents who 'disguise' their party and issue preferences. However, the media tend to emphasise (often exaggerated) unadjusted poll data, particularly in report headlines; adjusted data is typically given only secondary status in news reports, and 'hidden' in the text.

4. The Association of Professional Opinion Polling Organisations was formed in February 1987, comprised of the major polling companies (MORI, Marplan, Harris, Gallup and NOP) to make polling data available to each other and to bona fide enquirers.

5. The Policy Review was an exercise designed to reappraise Labour's traditional programmatic commitments, and to broaden its appeal to recapture the C2 voters and win over sections of the middle class large enough to win victory at the next general election. For Patricia Hewitt, one of the key architects of the Policy

Review, "...Giving people good reasons to vote for us is vital. Removing (at least some of) the reasons why people vote against us is also essential" (Hewitt, 1988).

6 Complex Politics and Opinion Polling in Late-Capitalist Britain

Introduction

This chapter is concerned with how political restructuring affects opinion polling in capitalist societies. In doing so, the chapter considers in particular two of the four aspects of Complex Politics examined in chapters 3 and 4: these are opinion polling and political culture, and opinion polling and party system. Focusing on Britain as a critical case, the chapter begins by looking at the comparatively stable relationships which evolved between the classes and parties until the end of the 1960s and the performance[1] of the opinion pollsters in this context. Following this, there is a consideration of the restructuring of the British party system at a number of levels, and a discussion of how these might raise problems for the opinion pollsters. There is then an examination of the apparent transformation of the electorate, which considers the variety of models which have focused on changes within the class structure, and the apparent emergence of new cross-cutting cleavages within, and ideological changes amongst, the electorate. These are allegedly undermining the traditional alliances between blocks of voters and the major parties. It is in this context that a discussion of the perspectives which need consideration by opinion pollsters is undertaken, by outlining those aspects of heightened voter volatility which might impinge upon or even impose limitations on, the ability of pollsters to survey the public's political mood effectively. This will help to examine the ways in which developments in techniques and practices might help to compensate for the emergence of a more complex political landscape in the future.

Complex Politics Conditions for Polling: Britain as a Critical Case

It has long been thought that Britain has one of the most stable and enduring political systems among post-war West European capitalist states, especially in relation to electoral politics. Indeed, up until the early 1970s, the British political system was seen as settled, with electoral battles being predominantly (and routinely) two party affairs: As Crewe et al noted, "...since the second world war two parties - Conservative and Labour - have alternated in exclusive incumbency of government office on the basis of an evenly balanced duopoly of electoral support and parliamentary seats" (Crewe, 1977, p.129). Hence their combined share of the poll at general elections for the period 1950 until 1970 was approximately 90%[2] - and in 1955 the Conservatives and Labour secured 96.6% of votes (see Table 6.1).

Table 6.1   Electoral Support in Great Britain for the Conservative and Labour Parties, 1950-70

Year of General Election	Conservatives (%)	Labour (%)	Conservatives & Labour combined (%)
1950	43.0	46.8	89.8
1951	47.8	48.3	96.1
1955	49.3	47.3	96.6
1959	48.8	44.6	93.4
1964	42.9	44.8	87.7
1966	41.4	48.9	90.3
1970	46.2	43.9	90.1

Source: Crewe, Sarlvik and Alt (1977, p.130)

To a large extent, the dominant position of these two parties was reinforced by the nature of the electoral system itself (the 'Plurality' or 'First Past The Post System') which tended to hinder the political aspirations of any emerging challengers. More significant however, were the close relationships which developed between the electorate and the political parties - relationships which were both defined and determined by social class-based cleavages, summed up in Pulzer's maxim that, "Class is the basis of British party politics; all else is embellishment and detail" (1967, p.98).

Since the beginning of the 1970s however, the political complexion of Britain has been undergoing a process of transformation which has been manifested in a series of dramatic changes within the party system. In the 1980s for instance:

The Conservative Party won three successive general elections, with 43% of the vote but steadily increasing Parliamentary majorities. Labour's electoral fortunes reached a low point in 1983, unprecedented since the party first competed nationwide in the

1918 election ...(and) third party voting for the Liberal and Social Democratic parties in Alliance swelled almost to parity with Labour's vote in 1983 before receding (Dunleavy, 1989, p.173).

Such changes have rendered problematic the core assumptions of the mainstream analyses of politics, "...especially those concerning the instrumental nature and the structural-class determination of political processes" (Crook, Pakulski, and Waters, 1992, p.138). Instead many commentators have argued that there have been a number of social and political changes resulting in a restructuring of the relationship between the political parties and various electoral groupings. This has led to an increase in voter volatility, the development of new but more transient patterns of electoral linkages, and the rise of new political forces and alliances. These developments represent a significant contrast with the past as far as the conditions for opinion polling are concerned. The following discussion considers the genesis and evolution of these changes, and the implications which they herald for opinion polling in Britain.

Class and Electoral Politics in The Post-War Period

When analysing post-war politics in Britain, commentators typically emphasise a process of major restructuring at the end of the 1960s in the nature both of the party system and of the electorate. While contemporary electoral politics is generally considered to be far more volatile than it was in the past, the party system which emerged in the immediate post-war period was comparatively stable, and supported by both 'class alignment' and 'partisan alignment'. Class alignment reflected the fact that people tended to vote for a particular party on the basis of their social class. Partisan alignment referred to the psychological loyalties which predisposed voters to particular parties, and which resulted in a situation whereby voters considered themselves to be supporters of that party. Together, these two phenomena comprised a 'party identification' model of voting behaviour.

According to Butler and Stokes (1974) individuals identified with a particular political party as a result of political socialisation. Political loyalties were transmitted from parent to child, and later were sustained and reinforced by friends, neighbours, and work-mates who occupied the same position in the social structure. This tendency toward party identification was particularly useful to voters as it enabled them to rely on others to help them solve the problems of interpreting what were in essence very complex political realities; essentially, because voters had little interest in politics, they tended to adjust their opinions on policies and issues to fit the positions of their 'natural' party. Thus individuals generally tended to absorb and replicate class values, class allegiances and class issues which oriented them toward their class party.

The depth of this party identification is well illustrated by Table 6.2 which shows that the pattern of voting for manual and non-manual workers which developed during the 1950s and 1960s was both stable, and apparently class-based. Throughout this period, approximately two thirds of the electorate voted for their predicted and natural class party.

However, while social class tended to be associated most strongly with party choice, a degree of voting 'deviance' did occur, especially amongst the so-called 'working class Tories'. Much attention was focused upon this group in order to explain the nature and sources of their cross-class voting: explanations ranged from a misperception of one's objective class position (Runciman, 1966), working class deference (McKenzie and Silver, 1968), a general embourgeoisement of society (Butler and Rose, 1960), the internalisation of the dominant value system which the Conservative Party represented (Parkin 1967, Jessop 1974), and the idea of differential socialisation of political generations, or cohorts[3] (Butler and Stokes, 1974).

Of course, the contradictory class position of these deviant voters (working class Tories as well as middle class Labourites) presented the opinion pollsters with a problem: how to accurately monitor attitudes and opinions and forecast the likely scale and direction of voters' alignments in an election. To do this, pollsters would need to select a sample of the population that was representative of British voters and which included proportionate numbers of class-voters and deviant voters. With random probability samples, such voting deviancy need not necessarily have caused a problem for opinion pollsters, since, by definition, the method seeks to ensure that all voters are given an equal chance of being selected for interview.

With the shift in practice at the start of the 1970s toward more quota-based sampling methods[4] however, pollsters had to address a number of issues which would need to be resolved if they were to measure public opinion effectively. These required that these deviant voter groups be identified and isolated (if they could) from their peers, and consequently that those factors which accounted for their contradictory class behaviour (and the strength of their effect) be determined. Thus, pollsters were required to look beyond occupational status, and identify the range of cleavages which existed (such as housing tenure, unionisation, and life-style) which also influenced voting behaviour and public opinion.

Table 6.2   **Occupational Class and Party Choice 1945-92 (%)**

	1945 Non-Manual	Manual	1950 Non-Manual	Manual	1951 Non-Manual	Manual
Conservative	63	29	68	32	75	34
Labour	28	62	23	59	22	63
Liberal	9	9	9	9	3	3

	1955 Non-Manual	Manual	1959 Non-Manual	Manual	1964 Non-Manual	Manual
Conservative	70	32	67	30	62	28
Labour	23	62	21	57	22	64
Liberal	6	6	12	13	16	8

	1966 Non-Manual	Manual	1970 Non-Manual	Manual	1974 (Feb) Non-Manual	Manual
Conservative	60	25	64	33	53	24
Labour	26	69	25	58	22	57
Liberal	14	6	11	9	25	19

	1974 (Oct) Non-Manual	Manual	1979 Non-Manual	Manual	1983 Non-Manual	Manual
Conservative	51	24	60	35	55	35
Labour	25	57	23	50	17	42
Liberal	24	20	17	15	28*	22*

	1987 Non-Manual	Manual	1992 Non-Manual	Manual
Conservative	49	37	49	35
Labour	20	40	26	45
Liberal	31*	23*	25	20

* SDP-Liberal Alliance 1983-1987

Source: Adapted from Health et al (1985, p.30) for figures 1945-1983, and Crewe (1993a) for figures 1987-1992

With the passing of time, and the increasing heterogeneity of the population, this problem of contacting, including and measuring the myriad of groups and their needs and aspirations has intensified. The consequences of these developments for the polling community will be explored in the next chapter. Suffice it to say that in the early decades after the Second World War, the primacy of social class in shaping voting behaviour was such that the challenges facing the opinion pollsters in Britain were comparatively unproblematic: typically voting loyalties could be estimated by reference to an individual voter's social class position.

This task was made all the easier by a general 'nationalisation' of attitude and opinion change up until the beginning of the 1970s. Swings in party support were remarkable in their uniformity throughout the different regions and localities, and "...to know the swing in Cornwall was to know, within a percentage of two, the swing in the Highlands" (Crewe, 1985, p.103). This relatively stable and uniform situation compares favourably with the situation faced by pollsters today. Here, the polarisation of British politics across a number of geographical dimensions raises technical problems concerning clustering, the number and location of sampling points, the size of the sample itself and the interview method used. These problems will also be discussed in greater length at a later stage in this chapter.

Post-War Performance of The Polls

In the immediate post-war period the pollsters were relatively successful in forecasting electoral outcomes.[5] By looking at the performance of forecast polls over the period up to 1970 (Table 6.3), it is clear that these final pre-election polls have been generally accurate in terms of estimating party shares of the vote, with the mean error per party ranging from 0.7 to 2.2 - that is within the usually quoted acceptable margin of error for sampling of 2.5%.[6]

Since social class was such a strong determinant of party allegiance, and because Britain had a (predominantly) two-party system, psephologists claimed that it was possible to predict the actual size of a parliamentary majority to be gained by the winning party at an election, by reference to the size of its poll lead over the rival party. According to the Cube Law, the ratio of seats gained at an election was in direct proportion to the number of votes secured by a factor of 3. It assumed a two-party model of voting, with relatively even patterns of electoral change and directions of party support across the country (Kendall and Stewart 1950, pp.183-197).

Table 6.3   Accuracy of the Final Day Pre-election Forecast Polls, 1945-97 (%)

Year	Average Sample Size	Expected Mean Error on the Gap (+ or -)	Actual Mean Error Gap	Expected Mean Error Per Party (+ or -)	Actual Mean Error Per Party	No. of Polls
1945	N/A	-	3.5	-	1.5	1
1950	N/A	-	4.6	-	1.7	3
1951	N/A	-	5.3	-	2.2	3
1955	N/A	-	0.2	-	0.9	2
1959	N/A	-	1.1	-	0.8	4
1964	1669*	4.8	0.8	2.4	1.5	4
1966	2645*	3.8	3.9	1.9	1.5	4
1970	2052	4.4	6.6	2.2	2.2	5
1974(F)	2357	4.0	2.4	2.0	1.6	6
1974(O)	1633	4.8	5.0	2.4	1.6	6
1979	1491	5.0	1.7	2.5	0.9	5
1983	1191	5.6	4.3	2.8	1.1	6
1987	1803	4.6	3.2	2.3	1.2	6
1992	2102	4.2	8.5	2.1	2.6	4
1997	1430	5.2	3.0	2.6	1.3	5
Average	1837		3.7		1.5	

*   Based on available data from only 2 of the 4 polls (Worcester, 1991)

Source: Figures for 1945-1987 from Worcester (1991, p.110); 1992 figures based on re-calculating data from Butler and Kavanagh (1992, p.140).

The Cube Law had been fairly reliable in the past (with the exception of the 1950 General Election where, with the redrawing of boundaries, Labour suffered through a wastage of votes in safe seats), but developments since the mid-1970s have meant that the conventional two class-two party model and the Cube Law can no longer be applied to the complex political realities of contemporary Britain.[7] Instead, it will be argued in this chapter that the political landscape has been subject to various tensions and is currently in a state of flux, as the dimensions upon which the party identification model was based have been subject to fundamental changes. Firstly, the British party system has undergone a process of restructuring, which has seen the virtual 'duopoly' of (parliamentary) political power by the Conservative and Labour parties challenged at various times and to differing degrees by the emergence (and re-emergence) of alternative political 'homes' for the electorate in the form of other viable parties. Secondly, at least some sections of the electorate, partly in response to these (and other) political developments, and partly in response to changes in the economic and social structures, has become detached from its class-party bonds, and become instead a volatile and hence unpredictable participant in electoral politics. As a consequence of these recent developments, the challenges facing the opinion pollsters have multiplied. The ability to measure public opinion and voting intentions accurately has become more difficult than it was in earlier decades, requiring careful consideration of polling methodology and techniques.

The following sections will discuss these changes which have taken place in the British political landscape, the extent to which they are either permanent or transient, and the implications which they have for opinion pollsters in contemporary Britain. This analysis will be conducted with specific reference to (i) the party system, and (ii) political culture (in terms of electoral politics).

The Re-Structuring of The British Party System

The two party system which had been a feature of British politics throughout the post-war era was first challenged at the General Election of February 1974, following the rise in electoral support for the previously marginalised Liberal Party (which since 1931 had managed to reach double figures on only one occasion - 11.6% in 1964) to 19.8%. The share of the Conservative vote slumped to 38.8% and then to 36.7% in October, the worst result in its history. Labour were even less fortunate, winning only 38.2% of votes cast, although beating their Conservative rivals by a margin of four seats to win Government office. What was even more politically spectacular about this election however, was the failure of the governing Labour Party to gain a secure majority in the House of Commons. In 1976, the Government were forced to form a working alliance with the Liberals through the Lib-Lab pact. This represented a significant development in British politics, with at least temporary replacement of the traditional two-party system by a multi-party system. Meanwhile, nationalism also made huge political strides. In Scotland, the Scottish Nationalist Party (SNP) pushed the Conservative Party into third place, becoming the 'official' opposition to Labour there. In Wales, Plaid Cymru won two parliamentary seats at Westminster.[8] It was clear from these electoral developments, that British political life had entered a period of far-reaching restructuring:

A thirty year era of majoritarian single party government faced by virtually one-party opposition had, at least temporarily, come to a close (Crewe, Sarlvik and Alt, 1977, p.131).

The Rise of the SDP - Breaking the Mould of British Politics?

This haemorrhaging of the electorate away from the two dominant class-based parties was consolidated at later elections. In 1979, the Liberals won 14.1% of the total vote. However, more significant was the entrance of a new political force at the following General Election in 1983 which threatened to "break the mould" (Bradley, 1981) of British politics, and which represented "... potentially the most important development in British politics since the advent of the Labour Party" (Ingle, 1987, p.165). This political phenomenon was the 'Alliance', comprising the Liberal Party and the newly-formed Social Democrat Party (SDP).

The SDP was established in 1981 by three prominent members of the Labour Party, and the ex-Labour Deputy Leader Roy Jenkins. This right-wing group left the Labour Party in protest following the introduction of a series of reforms at the Party conference in January 1981. These included the adoption of a series of radical policies (including commitments both to withdraw from the EEC, and for unilateral disarmament), and the acceptance of a package of constitutional reforms which ultimately strengthened the power and influence of both the Trades Unions and the left-wing in the constituencies.

The immediate impact of the Alliance on British electoral politics was remarkable. It won a series of parliamentary by-elections (Croydon North-West in October 1981, then at Crosby a month later in November, and Glasgow Hillhead the following March), and at one stage moved into first place in the national opinion polls. By the General Election of 1983, the Alliance had clearly established itself as a major electoral force, winning 26.2% of the national poll, and only narrowly losing second place to the Labour Party (28.5%).

Nationally the British political map was transformed, with what Crewe has described as a new political competition emerging, having the effect of creating two 'two-party systems' (Crewe, 1985) - along both a North/South dimension and an Urban/Rural dimension. In this process, the impact of the Alliance was decisive: while the urban and Northern seats were predominantly Labour/Conservative contests, in the South and in the rural areas the Labour Party was marginalized, with the Alliance providing the challenge to the Conservative Party (Curtice and Steed 1984).

At the General Election of 1987, the Alliance vote diminished somewhat, but levelled out at 23.2%, a drop of 3% from its 1983 figure (see Table 6.4). However, a combination of two key factors, including the operation of the British plurality electoral system as well as the uniform geographic spread of their vote, resulted in the Alliance parties failing to translate this support proportionately across the country into effective political representation. As a consequence, the Alliance parties won only 22 seats out of 651 contested at Westminster. In the post-mortem which followed, criticism from the parties' activists and from the Liberal leader David Steel focused on the 'dual leadership' strategy, which was regarded as having confused and alienated a large potential pool of Alliance voters. The political outcome of the election was that the Alliance of the SDP and the Liberal Party was officially ended. Instead, the conferences of the two parties voted to formally merge into a new single party, the Social and Liberal Democrats (since renamed the Liberal Democrats). However, a renegade section of the old SDP led by David Owen, and the MPs Rosie Barnes and John Cartwright resigned from the party to form a reconstituted SDP.

Following the break-up of the Alliance after the 1987 General Election, the influence of the SDP gradually diminished, culminating in the decision taken in March 1989 to withdraw the party from national electoral politics, and opting instead to continue to exist only as a 'guerrilla force' in British politics. Acknowledging at the September 1989 SDP conference the sharp decline in the Party's political fortunes, the Party MP Barnes argued that the SDP should seek to consolidate its electoral position by contesting only a minority of seats at subsequent General Elections. However, events leading up to the 1992 General Election and the SDP's performance in the election itself combined to finish off the party as a major electoral force in British politics. In June 1990, the national committee suspended the Party's constitution, and the few remaining members of parliament were redefined as 'independents', rather than as SDP members. Furthermore, the SDP's representation in local and national political office receded: the Party failed to win any by-elections during the 1987-92 parliamentary period, suffered a series of disastrous local government elections, and secured only 0.5% of the vote at the European Assembly elections in June 1989 (down 19% from the vote received by the Alliance parties in 1984). At the General Election in April 1992, the SDP vanished from national politics when the two independent (SDP) MPs Barnes and Cartwright narrowly lost their seats to the Labour Party.

Table 6.4 Share of Votes (%) and Seats for the General Elections of 1983, 1987, 1992 and 1997 in Britain[9]

	Conservative	Labour	Liberals etc[10]
1983 vote	43.8	28.5	26.2
1987 vote	43.4	31.7	23.2
Change (%)	(-0.4)	(+3.2)	(-3.0)
1992 vote	42.8	35.2	18.3
Change (%)	(-0.6)	(+3.5)	(-4.9)
1997 vote	31.4	44.4	17.2
Change (%)	(-11.4)	(+9.2)	(-1.1)
1983 seats	397	209	23
1987 seats	376	229	22
Change	-21	+20	-1
1992 seats	336	271	20
Change	-40	+42	-2
1997 seats	165	419	46
Change	-171	+148	+26

As with their erstwhile partners in the SDP, the Liberal Democrats suffered an immediate decline in public support following the decision to dissolve the Alliance. In a number of opinion polls throughout 1989 and at the European Assembly elections of that year, they were displaced as the third force in British politics by the Green Party. Since then however, the Liberal Democrats have re-established themselves as a creditable electoral force, and as the main challenger to the Conservatives in the South of England. Under a new leadership, they have become the obvious political 'home' for the disaffected protest vote in a number of by-elections in former Conservative parliamentary seats (most notably at Eastbourne in October 1990, Ribble Valley in March 1991, and Kincardine and Deeside in November 1991). While all of these gains were recovered by the Conservatives at the 1992 General Election, the Liberal Democrats managed to reverse the slide in party fortunes which had seemed so dramatic in the immediate aftermath of the 1987 Alliance break-up, and secured 20 members of parliament with 18.1% of the British vote. At the 1997 General Election, their share of the vote held up at 17.2%, and they increased their representation in the House of Commons by winning 46 seats.

The Green Party

Political commentators remarked at the June 1989 European elections that "...this election will be remembered for the arrival of the Green Party from almost nowhere to capture an astonishing 14.9% of the vote, taking it in one jump from the lowest to the highest vote anywhere in Europe" (Linton & Curtice, 1989, p.5). In the "...1990 local elections, they averaged 8% in the wards they contested in England" (Butler and Kavanagh, 1992, p.75). The status of the Greens as an electoral force in British politics was acknowledged by the opinion pollsters who began to report their share of votes separately, rather than as part of the "Other" category in polls. Since these elections, the Green Party has failed to build on these successes, gaining only 1.3% of the vote in the 253 seats they contested at the 1992 General Election, although "...in the local elections held just four weeks later their candidates were still able to secure an average of 4% of the vote" (Curtice and Steed, 1992, p.343). This shift in public support reflects a burgeoning expression of greater concern amongst the British electorate with non-traditional, or new postmaterialist values (Inglehart 1981, 1984, 1987, 1990). These changes in the values and orientation of the electorate have been recorded in numerous opinion polls.[11] As a result, we may well see the re-emergence of the Green Party or of alternative environmental and postmaterialist parties as major electoral contenders in the near future.

Challenges to the Scottish Party System

In Scotland the party system has undergone a process of significant change in recent years. Traditionally, the Conservative Party has provided the main opposition to Labour in Scotland, certainly throughout the 1950s and 1960s. However, developments since that time have seen a continued decline in electoral fortunes for the Conservatives. At the 1987 General Election, the Conservatives lost 11 of their 21 seats, while securing only 24% of the vote. Somewhat surprisingly, they gained an extra parliamentary seat and 25.7% of the overall Scottish vote at the 1992 General Election. However, 1997 was a watershed year for Conservative politics in Scotland. The Party under John Major's leadership suffered a heavy defeat across Britain at the General Election; in Scotland however, this defeat turned into a rout. With only 17.5% of the vote, the Party lost all of its sitting Members of Parliament, including three outgoing Cabinet Ministers. The extent of this defeat for the Conservatives was reaffirmed when, as the only major party campaigning against Scottish devolution later that year, its position was rejected by the voters, who opted instead for a Scottish parliament (by 74.3% to 25.7%) with tax-raising powers (by 63.5% to 36.5%). The scale of these defeats at both the General Election and at the referendum was such as to signify a critical diminution of public support for the Conservative Party in Scotland.

The Scottish Nationalist Party (SNP) has provided a major challenge to Labour in Scotland since the mid-1970s. While the SNP has never achieved more than a modest second-placed position to Labour in the opinion polls and in national elections, their decision in 1987 to stand a candidate in every Scottish parliamentary constituency for that and subsequent General Elections has effectively resulted in the creation of a four-party system (Labour, SNP, Conservative, Liberal Democrat).

The SNP continues to represent a potential haven for voters who are disillusioned with the present Parliamentary set-up. In the late 1980s and early 1990s, the Party gained significant support from voters largely because of the increasing centralisation of political power away from the regions and local government in Scotland toward Westminster, together with the introduction of unpopular legislation (including in particular the poll tax, the reorganisation of the NHS, and water privatisation) by large (predominantly 'English') Conservative Party governments. As a consequence of these developments, the SNP has performed relatively well in recent elections. For instance, at the Glasgow Govan by-election in November 1988, Jim Sillars caused a political 'upset', transforming a Labour majority of 19,509 into an SNP victory-margin of 3,554.[12] In subsequent elections, the SNP have continued their successes. At the 1994 European Assembly elections, they gained 32.6% of the Scottish vote, increasing their representation from one to two seats. At the General Elections in 1992 and 1997 they stabilised their support, with 21.5% and 22% of the Scottish votes respectively. However, perhaps their most important breakthrough came with the referendum in 1997 which resulted in large majorities for a Scottish Parliament with tax-raising powers.

It is not surprising then to discover a volatile four-party system in Scotland. Table 6.5 demonstrates how such a complex party system problematises the tasks for opinion pollsters, by focusing on the results of final pre-election polls in Scotland and comparing these to the actual results for the 1992 General Election. What is interesting here is that while Labour is the dominant party and was correctly forecast to win the largest share of voter support, the pollsters consistently under-estimated the Conservative standing, putting them in third place behind the SNP. Indeed, while the average error per party is rather high at 2.8%, the average error on the gap both between the Labour and the Conservatives (7.4%) and between the Conservatives and the SNP (6.9%) are both outside the 6% margin of error (assuming an average sample size of 1000).

Table 6.5   The Record of the Final Polls in Scotland 1992*

	Average Poll Score[13] (%)	Actual Result (%)	Error
Labour	42.0	39.0	+3.0
Conservative	21.3	25.7	-4.4
SNP	24.0	21.5	+2.5
Liberal	12.0	13.1	-1.1

Average error = 2.8
Average error on Labour/Conservative gap = - 7.4
Average error on SNP/Conservative gap = - 6.9
*includes polls conducted by ICM (Scotsman), MORI (Sunday Times Scotland), and System 3 (Herald).

Since the early 1970s then, the British party system has entered a period of significant and accelerating restructuring. Elections themselves can no longer be characterised as two party contests in terms of voter choice (as opposed to chances of winning seats). The Liberal revival in 1974, the formation of the SDP (1981) and the SDP-Liberal Alliance in 1983, the march of the Nationalists in Scotland and Wales, and the (albeit brief) appearance of the Green Party following the European Assembly elections of 1989, all combine to suggest a far more complex party system than that which preceded the early 1970s. All these developments suggest that the two party system is under strain - a process of fundamental political change is under way characterised by new forms of party competition.

This transformation of the party system has long term implications for the opinion pollsters. Their ability to forecast party shares of the vote in elections at the national level, and more especially at the regional and local level, has become a more arduous task. The proliferation of parties offers a degree of choice in terms of potential political 'homes' not previously available to the electorate. This choice makes it psychologically easier for voters to switch from one party to another, not just at General Elections, but at elections which do not result in a change in national government - that is, at constituency by-elections, at local elections, and at European Assembly elections. Voters' alignments to the parties have therefore become less easy to determine, and the outcomes of elections a matter of increasing unpredictability. Once voters have made the psychologically significant decision to break with their 'usual' party there is then the likelihood that they will change again, and the ability to do this will presumably become psychologically easier in subsequent elections. The intergenerational transfer of political loyalties described by Butler and Stokes (1974) will effectively have collapsed as a result of this process for large groups of tactical voters.

Tactical Voting

Compounded with, and an integral part of this problem, is the increasing tendency toward tactical voting which is based upon calculated, rather than committed action. Here, voters take advantage of the relative choice of parties available to them in an election, and a significant minority opt for their second-choice party in order to defeat their least favoured party. This tactical vote may be classed therefore as a superficial action, in that the voter has not been converted to an alternative party.[14] This however does not reduce the problem which tactical voting presents to the pollsters. Norris' (1987a, p.4) conclusions anticipate the potential problems which tactical voting at the local level in marginal constituencies pose for opinion pollsters:

> Tactical voting in key marginal seats, if it materialised, might also undermine conventional seat projections.

Indeed, some opinion polls themselves have indicated that at the individual constituency level (especially in marginal seats where a tactical vote for an alternative party may have produced more politically rewarding results), voters tended to behave differently to the rest of the nation. Thus, a February 1987 MORI poll based on the results from particular marginal seats contradicted national poll trends indicating a hung Parliament, by projecting a General Election outcome of a 94 seat Conservative victory.[15]

In terms of electoral behaviour, marginal constituencies proved to be particularly erratic and consequently difficult to poll in 1987. Special polls in groups of marginals tended to give conflicting pictures of the state of party support:

> Newsnight and Harris suggested that Labour would do better in marginals than in the rest of the country while MORI, NOP and Gallup suggested that it would do worse. The difference between Newsnight and MORI would make a difference of over 100 seats to the parliamentary majority (Butler and Kavanagh, 1988, p.128).

Pollsters are confronted with a very real paradox here: on the one hand, they should include such marginal constituencies in their samples because to omit them may result in their results failing to identify key dimensions of electoral behaviour. However, the extent of electoral volatility which exists in these constituencies and the vigorous swings in voter tactics which occur, may result in a distortion of national poll forecasts if too much weighting is given to them. The scenario being described here is that changes in the party system problematise the forecasting role of the pollsters: the growth in number and in political stature of challenger parties provides the prospect of viable alternatives to the traditional parties for voters, and hence stimulates the development of tactical voting. Final day national pre-election polls may be insensitive to the idiosyncratic nature of voters at the constituency level, especially in those constituencies which have a particularly significant marginal status. The opinion polls may therefore fail to accurately forecast electoral outcomes if they do not identify the direction of voter movement in marginal seats. In fact, at the 1987 General Election, opinion polls only sampled in an average of 95 sampling points, and in 1992, the figure was only 86 (Crewe, 1993b, p.483). This suggests that the opinion pollsters were not taking into account sufficient numbers of marginal seats for their polls to fully account for tactical voting.

As it transpired, Table 6.3 shows that the pollsters were nonetheless able to achieve high levels of accuracy in forecasting the share of support for the different political parties throughout the 1980s. In 1983, the mean error per party measured 1.1, and in 1987, dipped only slightly to 1.2, both well within the expected error of + or - 2.8, and 2.3 respectively. In terms of estimating the margin of Conservative victory, the polls tended to over-estimate the Conservative lead by 4.3% in 1983, and underestimated it by 3.2% in 1987. Where tactical voting did occur, Norris (1987a, p.19) has shown that it did not have the effect locally of invalidating national opinion poll projections:

> There was evidence of limited tactical voting in the marginals but the shift was not in a consistent anti-government direction, and few seats changed hands as a result.

At the 1992 General Election, tactical voting was a continuing feature of voters' behaviour, and in particular, "... one of the most striking features of the results was that the swing to Labour was distinctly higher in Conservative/Labour marginals than in the country as a whole" (Curtice and Steed, 1992, p.332). One potential problem which this situation poses for the opinion pollsters was given by Nick Moon of NOP in his assessment of this election, where he noticed that "...Labour did do better in the marginals as we said they would. The amazing thing is that if Labour had ½% more, it could have won the election" (in Smith, 1992). Consequently, if pollsters do not develop sampling mechanisms and weighting procedures to build these marginals into their polls, then they are unlikely to be able to anticipate the likely winners in a General Election.

Furthermore there was essentially no uniformity in voters' tactical voting in 1992. The logic of tactical voting suggests that supporters of a third- or fourth-placed party may consider switching their vote in circumstances where it will have the greatest impact, that is, where it is likely to result in a defeat for their least-preferred party candidate. For instance, the swing against a candidate of an unpopular first-placed party will be greatest where the gap between him or her and the rival second-placed candidate is relatively small. Supporters of the third- (or fourth- or fifth-) placed candidate will, in such a close contest, consider switching tactically to the second-placed party candidate because this will provide a realistic opportunity for these voters to help defeat an unpopular sitting candidate. Conversely, where the gap is relatively large, voters will be less likely to switch their vote from their preferred party, because doing so will appear to have little effect in terms of reducing the lead of the least-preferred party candidate.

However, the pattern of tactical voting in 1992 did not follow this logic. The average swing to Labour in 1992 (at 4.7%) was greater in those seats where they were relatively far behind the Conservative incumbents (up to 16% behind), than across the nation as a whole (where the swing was only 2.5%). The swing to Labour (3.9%) was actually less where its Party candidates were within closer striking distance of the sitting Conservative MP (that is where they were only 8% behind the Conservative candidate) than in those marginal constituencies where they were between 8 and 16% behind (swing of 5.5%). These figures suggest that the size of the gap between the outgoing Conservative MP and the leading Labour challenger was not a good predictor of tactical voting.

To compound this complexity, Curtice and Steed have concluded that some marginal constituencies are likely to have larger numbers of potential tactical voters than in others, as "... tactical voting may have occurred in some constituencies already" in earlier general elections (1992, p.333). This implies that there is little scope for further squeezing of a third party. As a consequence, the degree of tactical voting which occurs at a general election is not necessarily linked to the distance between the first and second placed parties in a marginal constituency, but may be related to the previous vote achieved by the party in third place.

These complex constituency-voter formulas signal further problems for opinion pollsters which are an extension of the paradox noted above: that is, that not only do they have to consider carefully whether to include marginal constituencies in their samples, they also have to decide which they should be by paying close attention to fine political-historical detail.

The impact of these developments for the opinion pollsters, both in terms of changes to the party system, and the increasing tendency toward tactical voting, is particularly obvious at the local level. Robert Waller of the Harris Research Centre identified the potential problem which exists in sampling individual constituencies in any type of electoral contest. In the run-up to the 1987 General Election, 76 opinion polls were conducted in 52 different constituencies and only 16 of those were found to estimate all the parties' shares of the vote within 3% of the actual result: 14 polls projected the wrong winner; while in 23 polls the error for two or more parties exceeded 5% (Waller, 1987). In by-elections, the problems are particularly pronounced for pollsters. According to Harrop (1988, p.22), "...in the volatile 1980s, organisers of by-election polls face more difficulties than they did 50 years ago". Norris (1987b) maintains that such polls have declined in their accuracy since 1957, and notes for instance that they failed to predict the results of a number of by-elections in the 1980s, including those at Brecon and Radnor[16] (MORI, July 1985), Glasgow Hillhead (Gallup, March 1982), Bermondsey (Audience Selection, February 1983), Chesterfield (Marplan, March 1984), and Tyne and Bridge (BBC Newsnight, December 1985).

The problem does not appear to stem from a diminishing ability on the part of the pollsters. It is more likely that the context within which polls are conducted has become increasingly complex and variable. The changing nature of the party system and the expansion of 'choice' (in terms of the supply of parties which are available to the electorate) has intensified the atmosphere in a by-election campaign, so that even the publication of an opinion poll itself "...can have a decided effect in assisting voters to cast their ballots 'tactically' should they so wish" (Waller, 1987 p.17). Thus, in both Bermondsey and Greenwich (February 1987) it was argued that polls helped the Alliance candidate, indicating as they did a strong possibility that the left-wing Labour candidates (Tatchell and Woods) were vulnerable. And even to some extent, the polls at the Richmond by-election (February 1989) affected the outcome. As the Guardian's editorial (1989, p.22) put it:

> The constituency opinion polls tell the essential story. A government candidate wallowing in heavy mid-term seas; but profound confusion as to who is his tactical challenger. A first poll underlines that confusion. The Democrats and Dr. Owen's SDP are running level. A second poll then shows the doctor's (Dr. Owen - SDP) man ahead. A tactical avalanche follows. The SDP runs the Conservatives amazingly close.

These ideas of the Bandwagon and Squeeze effect have (together with the Underdog effect) been the focus of discussion earlier in this book. Suffice it to say, there is evidence to suggest that the proliferation of parties provides the electorate with a degree of choice which may result in increasing difficulties for the opinion pollsters when they attempt to forecast the outcomes of local level elections. And, insofar as polls may give misleading signals about the state of electoral support for the parties, the results may confuse the final choice if tactical voters take notice of them when deciding how to cast their vote.

The emergence of new parties and greater political competition at elections also presents further potential problems for opinion pollsters. Pollsters have to make a judgment as to whether the electorates' embrace of non-traditional values like environmentalism (as manifest in support for the Green Party) are likely to be long-term or short-term. This has very real implications for the pollsters. They must elect either to instruct interviewers to read out the list of parties to respondents in voting intention questions, or else to leave this effectively as an open-question. If the former practice is chosen, the share of support recorded for such new parties may well be artificially inflated, especially if voters had previously been unaware of that party's existence but may consider it a useful vehicle with which to express a protest vote once prompted to do so. Conversely, if the latter practice is implemented, the respondent may not be in a position to express an informed voting intention, and may fail to consider opting for a new party if this party has been unsuccessful in attracting the levels of media publicity ordinarily secured by established parties. This situation would most likely under-represent new parties if voters have deeply-held value systems and priorities which mirror the policies of these new parties. In Britain, current practice is to ask an unprompted voting intention question.

Electoral Restructuring and Voter Volatility in Contemporary Politics

This growth in party choice may have contributed to the development of another post-1960s phenomenon that has altered the character of British politics: the alleged increase in electoral volatility and the weakening of the voter-party link, described as Class Dealignment and/or Partisan Dealignment. Earlier in this chapter, the stable 'two class-two party' model of British electoral politics in the 1950s and 1960s has been reviewed. In this model, occupational class was widely considered to be the main factor underlying politics in Britain and orienting voters to their natural (class) party. However, since the early 1970s, this virtual duopoly of political power by the two major parties (Conservative and Labour) has receded as a result of a steady decline in class-voting (Heath, Jowell and Curtice 1985; Crewe 1985; Rose and McAllister 1986). Thus, defining the level of class voting as including the number of non-manual Conservatives and manual Labourites as a proportion of total voters, we can see from Table 6.2 that class-voting has fallen from approximately two thirds in the period prior to the 1970s, to less than 50% in the 1980s and 1990s.

On the basis of such statistics it is now generally agreed that there has been a weakening of the voter-party link, and a consequent decay of the two party system (Butler and Stokes 1974; Crewe, Sarlvik and Alt 1977; Sarlvik and Crewe 1983; Dunleavy and Husbands 1985; Franklin 1985). However, there is disagreement as to both the underlying processes governing these developments and the resulting increase in voter volatility, and of the nature and extent to which dealignment has actually occurred. Psephologists have therefore developed models to explain the transformations taking place, and these theories have implications for the opinion pollsters in terms of how best to measure public opinion, forecast electoral outcomes, and identify the changing forces which determine these.

Two major academic interpretations of the changes which began to take shape at the end of the 1960s and 1970s have challenged the Party Identification Model espoused by Butler and Stokes: Class Dealignment and Partisan Dealignment. The class dealignment thesis suggests that various structural changes taking place within the electorate have resulted in a reduction in the association between the occupational class location of voters and their party attachments. The partisan dealignment model suggests that voters have undergone changes in their political attitudes, values and outlooks. Consequently, their views do not automatically correspond with the policies and programmes of the established parties, and this has led to an erosion of their party loyalties.

The class dealignment thesis was explained in terms of a number of important factors, including primarily increased working class affluence, together with the elimination of both poverty and of the glaring class differences and reinforcements which in the past had tended to generate consciousness of shared working class positions (Seabrook, 1978, 1982). Other factors cited to explain this phenomenon included a rapid growth in absolute social mobility (Goldthorpe et al, 1980), and a changing occupational mix in households (Butler and Stokes, 1974). Rose (1976) claimed that traditional notions of class as measured by occupational status, had in part been replaced by 'extended' class effects, including trades union membership, housing tenure, car ownership, and access to a telephone. Other political scientists emphasised the emergence of new cleavages which cut across the old class divisions. Roberts et al (1977) maintained that it was possible to divide the working class along a number of dimensions (union/non-union, public sector employed/private sector employed), while the Radical Model developed by Dunleavy and Husbands (1985, p.19) identified "..a wide variety of production influences (such as social class, economic activity status, sectoral location, unionisation and gender) and consumption influences which are important determinants of alignments" and which underlay class dealignment. Consumption influences here differentiate between "...a commercial commodity mode, and a public service mode...(in such areas) as education and health care" (Dunleavy and Husbands, p.22), and in housing, transport and pensions.

The partisan dealignment approach to explaining the apparent increase in voter volatility and the decay of the two-party system, emphasises a weakening in the intensity of support for the parties and for their programmes:

Whereas the Conservatives and Labour - together used to be able to rely on solid and consistent support from about 40% of the voters, their core support is now much smaller (Denver 1989, p.48).

Thus, voters do not participate in elections on the basis of some abstract, emotive party-loyalty, but on the basis of issue preferences. Franklin (1985) for instance, has identified a 100% increase in the effect of this variable on voting between 1964 and 1983. A Consumer Model of voting has been developed by Himmelweit and colleagues (1985) which builds upon the idea that partisan loyalties have declined as a result of a more rational electorate supporting or opposing political parties on the basis of their programmes, and the extent to which they correspond with their issue-priorities. For instance, Crewe (1985) observed that the decline in fortunes of the Labour Party throughout the 1980s was largely a consequence of the ideological disjunction which existed between its basic principles (the 'collectivist trinity' of public ownership, trade union power and social welfare) and the values and opinions of its (former) supporters.

An additional account of contemporary political restructuring is provided in the form of a Postmodernist model of politics. This focuses on a shift in economic and social organisation and culture, which it is argued has facilitated progressive social differentiation, class decomposition, and the emergence of diverse social constituents; ultimately this process has led to "...the weakening of stable socio-political milieux which were the 'natural' constituencies of traditional parties" in the past (Crook, Pakulski and Waters, 1992, p.142). The electorate is seen now as generationally specific and occupationally diverse, providing a social base for a new form of politics which is based on unconventional, minority, or apparently marginalised political issues and values instead of class. The social forces and movements which this model suggests are emerging in Britain tend to be based on ethnicity, nationalism, feminism as well as various postmaterialist issues, including environmentalism, the extension of civil liberties, overseas aid, and various moral issues (Dunleavy, 1989, pp.205-208). In many respects, Inglehart's work on postmaterialism (1981, 1984, 1987, 1990, 1992) underpins this postmodern model of political and electoral behaviour. Inglehart claims to have identified a changed hierarchy of preferences among voters, which is based both on voters' increasing affluence, and on various historical changes in their formative experiences which favour the development of new postmaterialist values and the growth of new social movements. While the economic recessions of the 1980s and 1990s tended to re-prioritise economic concerns, Dunleavy claims that "...many of the issues associated with the growth of third party voting, such as nationalism in Scotland and Wales, and the role of a few distinctively progressive issues such as civil liberties concerns in boosting Liberal/SDP support, seem to fit the 'postmaterialist' model fairly well" (Dunleavy, 1989, p.208). The performance of the Green Party at the European Assembly elections in 1989, with 14.9% of the popular vote further testifies to the burgeoning relevance of this model.

From a postmodernist perspective (incorporating postmaterialism) these developments have contributed to the erosion of the traditional class/party alliances, and to the emergence of less conventional value systems amongst some sections of the electorate which do not obviously accord with the political programmes of the established mass parties. This has resulted in a corresponding increase in voter volatility at elections. Furthermore, some writers who support this model maintain that a process of radical decoupling has taken place, characterised by widespread social differentiation and an absence of any obvious social referents to bind people together:

> We are moving towards a society without fixed status groups in which the adoption of styles of life ...which are fixed to specific groups have been surpassed. This apparent movement towards a post-modern consumer culture ...would further suggest the irrelevance of social division and ultimately the end of the social as a significant referent point (Featherstone, 1987, pp.55-56).

In this discussion, an attempt has been made not only to demonstrate the extent to which the British electorate is undergoing a process of restructuring in which it is becoming increasingly more volatile and unpredictable than it was in the past, but also to show that there is little agreement as to the cause, nature, and even extent of this volatility. What is clear however, is that the tasks facing the opinion pollsters have become more exacting, because, as has already been discussed, the outcome of elections (which in the past could be estimated largely by reference to the social composition of individuals, groups and communities) are now much more a part of a dynamic 'process', than a mere static 'event', subject to a whole host of independent, inter-related and changing variables.

However, the problems which confront the opinion pollsters amount to more than just the measurement of the beliefs, attitudes and opinions of an increasingly variable electorate: pollsters must also identify what is the cause, nature and extent of this variability before they can develop appropriate techniques to formulate an accurate political profile of the electorate. In essence, the paradox which faces the opinion pollsters is that their ability to measure the political opinions, values and attitudes of a changing electorate depends very much upon their perception and definition of the problem of electoral volatility. Thus, if the pollsters regard class dealignment as the most relevant explanation of electoral volatility, this has implications for their methodological techniques and practices which are likely to differ in a number of respects from those developed if partisan dealignment is accepted.

The Implications for Opinion Pollsters of Class Dealignment

If opinion pollsters accept the class dealignment thesis as their explanation of change within British electoral politics, then this implies that their chief methodological concern lies in how best to select respondents in their polls. Until very recently, opinion pollsters used quota sampling methods, usually based upon class, sex and age. As we have seen, the class dealignment thesis suggests that class is no longer the key determinant of voting, but that other factors need to be included as quota variables. The choice of quota variables should reflect the complex myriad of identifiable electoral groups generated by structural changes in modern society. The design of the polls should ensure that categories based on those social attributes which correlate most strongly with party choice are included. As Crewe (1983) points out, age and sex are only weakly associated with party choice, while the definition and measurement of social class which is traditionally seen as having the principle effect on voting behaviour, are inadequate. He maintains that a more reliable component of a quota frame which would help ensure a fully representative sample, is housing tenure.[17] Using Dunleavy and Husband's Radical Model (1985), any quota system would have to include variables corresponding to both production and consumption patterns, level and degree of state dependency, ethnicity, as well as the orthodox demographic variables, in order to account for the forty-eight structurally-located social groupings which they identify.

Added to these social classifications is a geographical dimension for quotas to include region and neighbourhood which have taken on a more significant role in directing voting behaviour in contemporary elections (Miller 1978; Johnston 1985; Dunleavy and Husbands 1985; Heath, Jowell and Curtice 1985). James has suggested that new variables exist which may help to explain voting behaviour, and which would consequently need introducing into any quota sampling frame: "These may prove to be related to demographics, ownership of key durables, attitudinal positions or life-style changes" (1989, p.19).

However, not only would the pollsters' quotas need to include these wide-ranging social, economic, geographic and cultural variables in order to ensure that the various dimensions of electoral change are not missed, but existing definitions of categories may require review. Heath, Jowell and Curtice maintain that any survey which defines the variable 'social class' according to income and life-style is liable to produce highly unsatisfactory results. They criticise both the traditional manual/non-manual dichotomy as "...wholly inadequate for studying the social basis of politics", as well as the Registrar General's social grade scheme (A, B, C1, C2, D and E) used in market research and in opinion polling which "gives a misleading view of the relation between class and politics" (Heath, Jowell and

Curtice, 1985, p.13). These schemas, by focusing on income levels, and not on economic interests, fail to provide appropriate categories for the self-employed, managers, foremen, apprentices, those not working, and women in work who are usually classified according to their husbands' jobs and not their own.

Goldthorpe (1984, p.31) has argued that a more relevant class schema, reflecting the position of individuals and groups within the economic production process is essential. This would produce a very different picture of political partisanship in Britain portrayed by many political scientists and pollsters, who tend to assign self-employed artisans and manual supervisors to 'working class' categories. Dunleavy describes how contemporary Marxist schemas "...classify people by whether they control other people's Labour or not, and whether they dispose of substantial amounts of 'educational capital' which can form the basis for social class closure practices' (Dunleavy, 1989, p.175). Heath, Jowell and Curtice have attempted to develop a class schema which integrates workplace, occupational and production positions, and which distinguishes between a narrowly defined working class, a large and inclusive upper middle class group (the 'salariat'), a routine non-manual group (four fifths of whom are women), a small group of foremen and technicians, and a petit bourgeois group (Heath, Jowell and Curtice, 1985, pp 13-16).

Thus, if class dealignment is accepted as the relevant contemporary explanation of voting behaviour, pollsters should ensure firstly that they include in their list of quotas relevant explanatory variables which are most associated with voting behaviour, and secondly, that they carefully consider their definitions of these variables. Otherwise they may miss important dimensions of change, or at least misinterpret their findings.

If long-term structural change is taking place within the electorate, this has methodological implications for the opinion pollsters in terms of securing an appropriate sample size. For instance, according to Dunleavy and Husband's formulation of the fragmentation of the electorate, about fifty social groups exist, each with their own unique political profiles. As Scarborough notes, "...such pluralism may well reflect the social complexities of contemporary Britain, but a sample of rather over 1000 is not up to the work of examining the electoral effects of such diversity" (Scarborough, 1986, p.17), because as Hoinville, Jowell et al (1976, p.61) argue, to make inferences about the behaviour, attitudes and opinions of sub-groups of the population, each group must have between fifty and one hundred members within the sample. The paradox here is that while the modern electorate develops a more heterogeneous composition, sample sizes for final pre-election polls have actually declined over time. Thus, sample sizes of over 2000 were typical for elections up until the early 1970s. However, in October 1974 the average sample size for the final pre-election polls was 1,633, 1,491 in 1979, and as low as 1,191 in the General Election of 1983. They have increased since to 1,803 in 1987, 2,102 in 1992, but fell in 1997 to 1,430. However, final day pre-election polls are on average significantly bigger than campaign polls, which were only 1,576 in 1992[18] and 1,236 in 1997.

Finally, a class dealignment interpretation of the nature of electoral change gives rise to a number of other implications for the opinion pollsters. Firstly because of the complex and fragmented character of the contemporary electorate, interviewers would have difficulty using quota sampling methods in actually identifying representatives from each of the numerous social groups, and in filling their quotas for each of these. It is current practice for opinion pollsters (once they have identified which spatial clusters to include in their sample) to refer to appropriate bench-mark data[19] to identify the distribution of variables in these areas, and ensure that interviewers are given proportional quotas to target. Hence, where a polling area comprises 58% women, the interviewer will need to achieve a target quota of 58% women in their interviews and so on. To ensure that interviews are not skewed (where, for instance, all women were drawn from a comparatively young age group, and men from an older age group), pollsters use interlocking quotas.[20]

There are a number of potential problems with quota sampling. Firstly, whether or not the control variables used to set the quotas are appropriate and adequate. Pollsters typically use all, or some of the following variables, including age, gender, housing tenure, occupational class and work status. However some commentators have highlighted the increasing significance of alternative variables related to production and consumption sectors, state dependency (Dunleavy and Husbands, 1985; Marshall, Newby and Rose, 1988; Duke and Edgell, 1987), or indeed, have identified a significant shift away from "...group-based political cleavages to value- and issue-based cleavages that identify only communities of like-minded people" based around postmaterialist value systems (Dalton, Keuchler and Burklin, 1990, p.12). If these developments are taking place, the type of variables employed in quotas need to be re-appraised, and the number significantly increased. However, the interlocking quota control systems imposed on interviewers would be extremely complex, unwieldy, and difficult to fulfil.

Secondly quotas are usually broad categories which leave room for selectivity and subtle bias by interviewers. For instance the very old are slightly under-represented, and ethnic minorities more so in polls. It is likely therefore that their votes will be under-estimated in elections. Pollsters would also be restricted in their use of survey techniques. Alternative methods, such as telephone polls are used by only two of the five leading polling companies (and they have only switched to this method relatively recently), even though research has indicated they have much to contribute in the field of political and social research (Clemens

1983; Walter 1987; Husbands 1987; Miller 1987). Clearly then, an understanding of electoral change which emphasises class dealignment contains a number of methodological implications for opinion pollsters.

The Implications for Opinion Pollsters of Partisan Dealignment

If partisan dealignment is accepted as best explaining the weakening of the class-party link and the demise of the two-party system, then pollsters must develop alternative practices. They should be concerned not so much with the 'demographic' quotas built into their polls, as partisan dealignment implies that voters respond as 'individuals' to issues and events, not according to their social-structural position. Instead, if surveys are to provide election forecasts, questionnaires must be designed in such a way as to estimate both the likelihood of late swing, and the potential for differential turnout.

Partisan dealignment, by its very nature implies that the electorate is increasingly volatile, is more receptive and sensitive to issues and short-term political factors, and is less inclined to form long-lasting attachments to political parties on the basis of social-structural loyalties. As a result, "...opinion polls have been able to trace larger net movements of party support in the election campaigns of the 1970s and 1980s than those of earlier decades" (Crewe, 1983, p.28). Voters are more liable to consider changing their voting intentions in the last few days of a campaign, and thereby confounding the pollsters' estimates of party support in an election. For instance, Crewe identified an increase in the proportion of respondents in post-election surveys who indicated that they had seriously considered switching votes in the short campaign period at elections. Between 1964 and October 1974, this group averaged 22% of voters, but rose to 31% in 1979 (Crewe, 1983, p.28). At the 1992 General Election, Worcester reported that the MORI/Sunday Times panel recall poll "...found that only 63% said they had made up their minds before the election had been called, down nearly 20% from the more usual 80% that we have measured in previous elections ...(and) 8% said they had only made their mind up in the last 24 hours, and 21% during the last week of the campaign" (Worcester, 1992a, p.2). Thus not only is it essential to poll up until the last possible moment in order to increase forecasting accuracy, but also to measure *strength* of beliefs, attitudes and opinions, as well as the *degree* of party loyalty.

Similarly, the effectiveness of an opinion poll depends very much on the ability of the pollsters to estimate the likelihood for differential turnout. This problem occurs either when respondents express support for a political party in an opinion poll and then do not vote, or when those who in polls say they do not intend to vote, actually do so. To compensate for this problem, adjustments for differential turnout must be made to the data produced in an opinion poll, and questions should therefore also be included which measure the commitment and likelihood of each respondent to actually vote.

Another concern which pollsters might also address is the problem of labelling. Changes and confusion within British politics and the transformation in particular of the centre ground, has posed a dilemma for the pollsters in terms of how to actually incorporate these developments into their questionnaires, and how the question-wording itself is to be formulated without under-estimating a new party's presence, or over-emphasising its significance. A case in point concerns the wording used by pollsters in voting intention questions after the break-up of the SDP-Liberal Alliance. MORI's questioning practice was criticised by David Steel of the then newly-formed Social and Liberal Democrats for failing to adequately filter supporters of his party (and of the rival Social Democrat Party) from the group of respondents who reported that they supported the old SDP-Liberal Alliance, the SDP, or the Liberals. In essence, voters in MORI's polls were "...invited to choose between the newly-merged Social and Liberal Democratic Party (SLD) or Owen's Social Democratic Party (SDP)" (Jones, 1988). According to Steel, the phrasing of this follow-up question disadvantaged the Democrats on three counts: firstly it wrongly named his party; secondly, the use of the initials SLD would confuse large sections of respondents whom he claimed would (incorrectly) deduce that the question referred to Northern Ireland's SDLP, rather than the British Democrats; and finally, the voters would be more likely to express support for the SDP whose recognised leader, David Owen was named in the question, than for the Democrats for whom no leading politician was referred to.

Jones (1988) suggests that the confusion was further exacerbated in the follow-up to Gallup's voting intention question which asked "...voters whether or not they support the merger which brought the Democrats into being. If they did, they were allotted to the SLD, if not to the SDP. If they were anti-merger Liberals, however, they were written off". Linked to this is the issue of whether or not you should ask questions prior to such voting intention questions about the party (such as the "Party Leader" question) to prime the respondent, and to help them clarify what parties are available, and who they are.

Summary

How do these developments relate to an analysis of polling in Complex Politics contexts? This chapter has focused on opinion polling in terms of both political culture, and the party system. It has been suggested that, in the post-war period, there are two clearly identifiable phases in the development of these two components. Prior to the 1970 General Election, Britain could be said to be an 'ideal' context for opinion polling. The party system was dominated by the Conservative and Labour parties, and the links between the electorate and the political parties were relatively strong and as far as the opinion pollsters were concerned, relatively predictable. However developments since this time have seen a change in Britain's political landscape to one of more Complex Politics for opinion polling. In the next chapter we will consider the implications of these changes by reviewing how pollsters in Britain and in other late-capitalist countries have performed in forecasting election outcomes in recent years.

Notes

1.   While it is important to consider the variety of functions which political opinion polls assume, this discussion will focus on primarily final-day pre-election forecast polls which provide the only real bench-mark through which to test the performance of polls.

2.   This chapter focuses on the British, rather than the UK political system, as Northern Ireland has dissimilar political and electoral arrangements to those found in England, Scotland and Wales. At the same time, because the differences which exist at a number of political, social, economic and cultural levels are so marked, it does not make sense to include it in the analyses. Therefore all electoral data has been weighted where appropriate to exclude statistics from Northern Ireland.

3.   Here, the phenomena of the working class deviant was perceived as arising from Labour's late entry onto the political scene, which restricted their acceptance by many elderly working class families, and therefore limited their ability to benefit from a generalised transmission of loyalty between generations.

4.   While random probability sampling involves drawing respondents at fixed intervals from lists (usually the electoral register in opinion polls), in quota samples interviewees are selected on the basis of pre-defined characteristics (typically age, sex, and social class in polls).

5.   However, the final polls at the General Elections of 1951 and 1970 failed to predict the outcome of the electoral contests. In 1951, the three final-day polls suggested a Conservative victory of between 2.5 to 7.1%, when in fact Labour secured a larger share of electoral support by a margin of 0.8%: "Were it not for the fact that the Conservatives won 26 more seats than Labour, despite taking fewer votes, the polls' failure would have been regarded at the time more seriously than it was" (Crewe, 1983, p.11). In 1970 however, the pollsters were confounded by an unpredictable electorate who eventually voted the Conservatives into office with a lead of 2.4%; 19 of the 20 pre-election polls had put the Labour Party ahead, and four of the five final polls gave Labour a lead of

between 2 and 8.7%.

6. Probability theory suggests that for random samples, results to particular questions will cluster around the actual 'true' figure in 95% of cases within a defined margin of error. This will be dependent upon the size of the sample, and the variability of the population being studied, usually assuming a maximum possible universe heterogeneity of 50%:50% (Worcester, 1991, p.158). A general rule therefore which applies to the data in Table 6.3, assuming a sample of 1500 randomly drawn electors at each election throughout the period, is that in 19 out of 20 cases, the final day pre-election polls will be accurate within + or - 2.5% for each party's share of the vote. (The margin of error on the gap between the two parties should be twice as large as that for the individual party shares, that is + or -5% in this example). The margin of error is calculated by using the equation:

$$1.96 \times \frac{\text{population variability}}{\sqrt{\text{sample size}}} \text{ or, more precisely } 1.96 \times \frac{\sqrt{\text{Party score} \times (100 - \text{party score})}}{\text{sample size}}$$

Since the early 1970s however, the major pollsters have adopted quota sampling methods, rather than probability samples, and there is some controversy about whether it is possible to estimate sampling error for the former. While it is commonly agreed that the error in quota samples broadly approximates that in random samples, it will often be higher in the former because of the practice of "...clustering within a constituency...(where the) limited range of sampling points would increase the chance of error" (Norris, 1987b, p.5).

7. See Butler (1989) p.50 .

8. Plaid Cymru had previously only ever won one seat in the House of Commons, following their victory at the Carmarthen by-election in 1966.

9. Excludes votes and seats secured in Northern Ireland .

10. Liberal-SDP Alliance 1983 and 1987; Liberal Democrats 1992 and 1997.

11. For instance, see Worcester (1993b) who presents the results of MORI opinion polls tracking the views of the British public towards environmental matters, which show a continued awareness of and concern with such issues over the last two decades.

12. Although the seat was recovered by Labour at the 1992 General Election.

13. However, these are *not* final day forecast polls: the fieldwork dates for MORI are April 2nd, for System 3, April 7th, and for ICM, April 8th. If the polls were conducted nearer to the election day, then they may have traced the shift towards the Conservatives more effectively.

14. For instance, all six of the by-elections which the Conservatives lost to opposition parties in the 1987-1992 Parliament were recovered at the following 1992 General Election.

15. As it happened, the final result some months later in June 1987 was surprisingly close to MORI's forecast, with a Conservative majority in government of 102 seats.

16.   This particular by-election demonstrates the difficulty of sampling in constituencies in predominantly rural areas where it is difficult to contact respondents.

17.   Housing Tenure replaced Social Class as the main quota variable for some of the pollsters at the 1997 General Election.

18.   However, this figure includes one opinion poll conducted by the Press Association with a sample size of 10,460. If this figure is omitted, then the average sample size for the remaining polls of the 1992 General Election campaign period is only 1,394.

19.   Opinion pollsters usually rely on large scale surveys such as the National Readership Survey when deciding the balance between different categories of selected quota variables for interviewers.

20.   Interlocking quota samples take into account different criteria, and interviewers are expected to find respondents displaying a range of characteristics considered important to the study. Hence, if the quota variables are gender and class, the interviewer might be instructed to include particular numbers of respondents from each of the following groups: male working class, male middle class, female working class, female middle class.

7 Polling Performance in Late-Capitalist Societies

Introduction

Having considered the implications that political changes in Britain have for opinion polling, it now remains to focus upon how polls have performed generally in recent elections. This chapter will review the performance of election polls in a number of late-capitalist societies in the context of what we have referred to elsewhere as Complex Politics. It begins with the British General Election of 1992, in which the opinion polls were widely criticised when they failed to accurately forecast the outcome of the election, erring by 8.5% on the Labour-Conservative gap. Elsewhere in Western Europe, the USA, and Australasia, there are a number of election examples in which the pollsters have been unsuccessful in attempting to predict voting intentions. There is a brief discussion of some of these polling examples.

In considering these cases however, it is of course not suggested that all polls are incapable of forecasting electoral outcomes effectively, nor that all elections are unpredictable. Indeed, the examples chosen have been carefully selected precisely *because* they are instances in which the pollsters have largely failed to measure pre-election voting intentions accurately; cases where pollsters have been more successful in this regard have been omitted. This is because the discussion is designed to give an *indication* of the problem which exists for pollsters in these late-capitalist countries so as to demonstrate that polling is a variable and imprecise activity, and that the *potential* for producing inaccurate election predictions exists in all such countries currently.[1]

Opinion Polling in British General Elections

As we have seen, with the exception of the 1951 and 1970 General Elections, the performance of the opinion pollsters has been relatively successful as far as forecasting levels of party support and the margins of victory of the winning party over their nearest rival is concerned. However, in 1992 all this changed as the Conservatives, contrary to all the polling expectations of a hung parliament (with

Labour as the largest party), secured a fourth term in office with a 21-seat government majority.

The 1992 Polling Débâcle

During the 1992 General Election campaign period, there were 50 national opinion polls conducted, which collectively provided a fairly constant pattern of party support,[2] and suggested an average Labour lead over the Conservatives of 1.85%. These findings were usually interpreted by the mass media as indicating that Labour would be the largest party in a hung parliament. The indications from the final pre-election polls themselves were broadly similar, with Labour at 40% + or - 2%, the Conservatives at 38% + or - 1%, and the Liberal Democrats at 18% + or - 2%. These results were largely reinforced by the exit polls, which, when adjusted, suggested between 298 and 305 seats for the Conservatives, and 294 to 307 seats for Labour. However, as Table 7.1 demonstrates, the Conservatives finally secured 42.8% of the vote, a 7.6% lead over their nearest rivals the Labour Party, and were returned to government with 336 seats and an overall majority of 21. The 1992 experience represented the most serious failure on the part of the opinion pollsters in general elections since polling began in Britain (Butler, in MRS, 1994, p.vii). The mean error per party at 2.6% was higher than any recorded in the post-war period, and the mean error on the gap between the Conservatives and Labour at 8.5% was well beyond the threshold of 4.2% which could be explained by sampling error alone with an average sample size of 2102.

Table 7.1   The Record of the Final Day Pre-election Forecast Polls at the 1992 General Election

	Field-work Dates	Sample Size	Con	Lab	Lib Dem	Other	Con Lead	Error on Lead
MORI	7-8.4	1731	38.0	39.0	20.0	2.0	-1.0	8.6
NOP	7-8.4	1746	39.0	42.0	17.0	2.0	-3.0	10.6
Gallup	7-8.4	2748	38.5	38.0	20.0	3.5	0.5	7.1
ICM	8.4	2186	38.0	38.0	20.0	4.0	0.0	7.6
Average	-	2102	38.4	39.3	19.3	2.9	-0.9	8.5
Result	9.4		42.8	35.2	18.3	3.7	7.6	-
Difference			4.4	4.1	1.0	0.8	8.5	

Average error per party = 2.6%   Average error on Conservative Lead = 8.5%

A series of enquiries were set up to try to identify the factors which could account for the discrepancies between the polls and the final election results. Of particular significance were the 1992 and 1994 reports of the Market Research Society, the former of which suggested that there was "...a prima facie case to support the claim that opinion polls are generally likely to slightly over-estimate Labour support and under-estimate Conservative support" (1992, p.15) and had indeed been doing so not only throughout the 1992 campaign, but at most general elections since 1959. Whilst this theory was challenged by most of the major opinion pollsters, many commentators welcomed the report as an opportunity to debate methodology and to suggest possible improvements and technical innovations (see Shrimsley 1992, Kellner 1992, and Riddell, 1992).

These and various other reports provided numerous explanations for the poor performance of the polls, explaining up to two-thirds of the error. The factors outlined include a consideration of the following issues: firstly that the pollsters may have used generally inappropriate methodological approaches and techniques; secondly that the polls were unable to account for differential registration; thirdly, that they were unable to anticipate the extent and direction of voter switching, and of late swing; and finally, that large sections of the electorate may have refused to disclose their voting intentions or indeed have lied to the pollsters. These factors are discussed below.

Issues of methodology and sampling bias The methodology used by the opinion pollsters at the 1992 General Election is based upon a multi-stage cluster-sampling strategy[3] which is used to select between usually 50 and 200 polling areas within which fieldwork is conducted. Approximately 1500 respondents are selected for interview provided they meet certain pre-defined criteria which are presumed to be those variables most closely related to electoral behaviour, and which are consequently set by the opinion pollsters as quota controls. Interviews are conducted in a face-to-face situation, with the majority carried out in the street during working hours. This general approach was common to all the major opinion polling organisations in 1992, and had been so since the early 1970s (Crewe, 1993b, pp.482-483; Worcester, 1989, p.15).

Given that the methods were the same in 1992 as in previous years, this raises the question of why, contrary to the relative success at earlier general elections, the polls of 1992 had performed so poorly. Initial assessments by the pollsters focused upon the margin of error in the polls: Sparrow at ICM maintained that "...normal sampling error (of 3%) probably accounted for at least half the discrepancies" between the final pre-election polls and the actual result in 1992 (see Smith, 1992). However, according to Crewe, the fact that all four final polls were out by over 3% for both parties, and that the error was in the same direction, suggests that sampling error as an explanation for the inaccuracy of the polls "...can be dismissed out of hand" (1993b, p.484). This point was reiterated by Worcester (1992b, p.xx) and by both the 1992 and 1994 MRS reports:

> We are left with a consistent bias which is unrelated to the sampling variability referred to in the usual disclaimers (instead) ...we have to look at factors which are common to all the methodologies (MRS, 1992, p.16).

There are two levels of explanation which consider methodological issues in polling at the 1992 election: polling principles and polling practices. The first level focuses upon general polling principles, chiefly the sampling method employed. At the start of the 1970s, there was a general shift in practice by the opinion pollsters away from random probability samples towards the adoption of quota-based samples. Worcester suggests that this transition took place largely because of the deficiencies of the electoral register as a sampling frame for random samples, as well as declining contact rates and increasing refusal rates where there was no scope for respondent-substitution (Worcester, 1989, p.15).

Furthermore, time-factors virtually rule out the use of random samples for in-home face-to-face interviewing in election polls, where non-contacts may require the use of multiple call-backs. The use of telephone polls may help to resolve this problem in random samples especially where media clients demand 'quickie polls'. However, incomplete telephone penetration together with differential penetration rates amongst electoral sub-groups are alleged to facilitate a pro-Tory bias in such polls which is only partially offset by the use of various weighting procedures which have been developed.[4] A final reason why most pollsters currently rely on quota, as opposed to random, samples is the relative cost of the latter:

> True random sampling would mean taking every nth person from the electoral register, and that is impractical really to do, because it ...becomes prohibitively expensive (Sparrow, 1993a).

Quota samples however are themselves susceptible to a variety of potential sources of bias which may undermine their ability to secure representative cross-sections of the public in opinion polls. Most obvious is that interviewers themselves are responsible for selecting respondents, although the latter must meet certain criteria set as quota controls by the directors of any polling project. However, these quota variables must be closely associated with the subject matter of the opinion polls, and as has been discussed in the previous chapter, there is little agreement amongst psephologists as to the nature of these explanatory variables. Consequently:

Quota sampling is a relatively fragile method of sampling by comparison with probability sampling, simply because they only take certain factors into account in selecting their sample. And it might be other things besides age, sex and class that determine election results (Jowell, 1992).

There is further scope for bias with quota sampling especially in relation to the levels of non-contacts, and refusal rates. Jowell and colleagues report that in the 1992 General Election campaign period, non-response measured between 35% and 47% (Jowell et al., 1993, p.253). The implications are made clear by Crewe (1993a):

> The most serious methodological problem for pollsters is high refusal rates, and the difficulties that pollsters have in trying to find out very much about the people who do refuse. If they are representative of those who cooperate, there is no problem, but if they are unrepresentative of those who cooperate, then there is a very serious problem.

Thus, quota samples tend to under-represent certain groups, especially Conservative supporters, including the very old, the more affluent of the AB's, and those who work the longest hours (Crewe, 1993b, p.491; Waller, 1992a, p.10; MRS, 1992, p.16; MRS, 1994, pp. 43-44). These non-response problems are likely to be most marked for polls that are conducted using street interviews - the approach which was most commonly used during the 1992 General Election by the pollsters.

A second level of explanation which considers possible sample design bias as accounting for the failure of the polls at the 1992 General Election, focuses upon detailed polling practices. Sample size was rejected as a possible explanation. Crewe (1993b, p.491) maintains that polls under 1,100 were on average slightly less likely to underestimate Conservative support (+1.1%), and overestimate Labour support (-0.2%) than samples that were over 2000; the Harris polls of just over 2000 electors for ITN meanwhile "...produced their most pro-Labour results, and may well have suffered, initially at least, from over-hurried interviewers fulfilling quotas of 22 respondents each in little more than a day" (Waller, 1992b, pp.8-9). Furthermore, an ICM Press Association poll of 10,460 gave Labour a 3% advantage over the Conservatives which was broadly in line with the findings of other much smaller polls conducted at the same time (Worcester, 1992a, p.2).

Fieldwork practices may have had an effect on the poll results. However, while pollsters and commentators continue to debate the relative merits of interviewing in the street versus interviewing at respondents' homes, on weekdays as opposed to weekends, and over the number of days necessary to ensure representative samples, "...in the final analysis, the similarity of the aggregated voting intention figures from all the major agencies suggests no clear and consistent lessons concerning technical superiority emanating from these sources" (Waller, 1992a, p.9). However, Harris did conduct a number of polls during the 1992 campaign period which were based on in-house interviewing at the weekends which were markedly more pro-Conservative in comparison to other polls carried out simultaneously.

Crewe (1993b, p.491) found a slight difference between the results of polls conducted in a single day and those carried out over a series of days; the former tended to over-state the reported Labour lead over the Conservatives (Conservative 37.4%, Labour 40.6%; Labour lead 3.2%), whilst the latter was slightly less favourable to Labour (Conservative 38.5%, Labour 39.9%; Labour lead 1.4%). Furthermore, evidence from the 1992 General Election demonstrates that there were very few discrepancies between the results of face-to-face polls and telephone-based polls, although the latter did tend to register "...slightly lower measurements of Labour support" (MRS, 1994, p.66).

Potentially then, there are many different sources of sampling error which may have impacted upon the performance of the polls at the 1992 General Election. However, there is no consensus as to the extent of these effects in terms of actual origin, scale or direction. Consequently, no attempt has been made to measure the proportions of the error on the pre-election estimates of the Labour-Conservative gap, and on the individual party errors which these factors might explain.

Differential registration Many of the reports into the 1992 polling experiences have focused on the failure of the pollsters to design adequate representative samples of the British electorate. This argument maintains that some people who were not eligible to vote were actually included in the pollsters' samples, and these respondents were likely to be disproportionately Labour sympathisers. However, during the campaign period some pollsters did not attempt to screen out these non-registered respondents from their voting intention questions, or to weight the results accordingly.[5]

The 1994 MRS report revealed the extent of this non-registration effect by comparing the size of the 1991 electoral register with OPCS population estimates and identifying a short-fall in the former of 1.93 million persons, 853,000 more than for the 1987 General Election. Having established the size of this residual population, the report estimated its maximum likely impact upon the 8.5% error on the Conservative/Labour gap in the polls by making a number of assumptions. Firstly, that the non-registration was comprised almost entirely of people who were attempting to avoid paying the poll tax. Secondly, that 65% of this group, given the opportunity would have actually casted their vote in an election. Finally, these 'voters' would most likely have been overwhelmingly Labour supporters (Labour

75%, Conservative 10%; SNP, Liberal Democrat and others parties 15%).

As a result, the 1994 MRS report concluded that, at most, non-registration of respondents in pollsters' samples could account for up to 1.2% of the discrepancy in the polls, or one seventh of the 8.5% error on the estimated gap between Labour and the Conservatives (1994, p.83). However, as the 1994 MRS enquiry team note, this estimate is based on extreme assumptions; in reality, Crewe suggests that non-registration accounts for only 0.6% error of the polls (Crewe, 1993b, p.488). He maintains that the reduction in the size of the electoral register is partly based upon the efficiency of local electoral registration officers in improving its accuracy. Furthermore, data from ICM and a Granada Television study suggested that the distribution of estimated support for the Labour Party amongst non-registered voters should be significantly down-graded as this group tended to divide relatively equally between the major parties.

The unrepresentativeness of the pollsters' samples was likely to have been exacerbated by the size of the overseas voting population who were registered to vote, but could not be contacted by the opinion pollsters. This group was extended by the 1989 Representation of the People Act, amounting to 31,942 voters in 1992 (MRS, 1994, p.86), and was estimated to be overwhelmingly Conservative supporting. However, as Jowell and colleagues noted, "...even if they had all voted Conservative, the effect on the overall distribution of the popular vote would have been negligible" (1993, p.251).

The conclusions drawn by the 1992 MRS team suggest that "...poll tax deregistration and the extension of overseas voting were only minor reasons for the discrepancy between the polls and eventual results" (MRS, 1992, p.6). This was reiterated in the 1994 report. However, both reports suggest that opinion pollsters should, as a matter of procedure, filter out those who are not registered to vote in order to help reduce some of the polls' susceptibility to error. Furthermore, Crewe (1993b, p.491) notes that "...the growth in under-registration may have made quotas of the adult population a less reliable basis for a representative sample than the electoral register", which suggests that a conversion back to random sampling may be an appropriate response to eliminate this problem.

Late changers The largest source of polling error identified by the 1994 MRS enquiry was attributed to the volatility of the electorate and the incapacity of large sections of voters to make up their minds before the final moments of the General Election campaign. Evidence from a number of reinterview surveys suggest that three factors accounted for this phenomena, and that together these had a combined effect of between a fifth and a third on the error of the Conservative/Labour gap (MRS, 1994, p.25). These factors included *switching*,[6] *late deciding*[7] and *turnout*.[8] As Worcester notes, snap-shot polls are unable to show the scale or direction of the electorates movement between parties, or in and out of the "don't know" or "won't vote" categories of voters. However, MORI's panel surveys for the Sunday Times suggested that such movement "...was higher than ever before, and ...some 11.1 million electors changed their mind during the campaign out of the 42.58 million in the electorate ...in all, the 'floaters' represented some 38% (of voters)" (Worcester, 1992a, p.2). Advocates of this *switching* explanation for the error in the polls suggest that such late deciders were (ultimately) disproportionately Conservative voters. However, as Crewe (1993b, p.484) asserts, the effects must have been unusually strong and occurred at the earliest, after interviewing had been completed on the Wednesday before actual voting.[9]

According to Crewe (1993b) and Jowell (1993), the reinterview panel surveys conducted suggested that evidence of switching was marginal, amounting to no more than a net Labour-Conservative swing of 0.5% in the MORI and ICM results, and of 0.7% in a similar study by the British General Election Studies (BGES) team. Furthermore, the actual numbers involved were very small. In an ICM recall poll conducted shortly after the election, only 107 respondents declared that they voted differently to the way they had stated in the earlier pre-election poll.

Late deciding appears to have even less influence as switching for explaining the error in the opinion polls. Crewe (1993b, p.484) claims that the context within which the 1992 General Election took place was particularly conducive to late deciding, as "...party identification was weaker than ever, and many voters were cross-pressured by a preference for Labour's policies but the Conservative Party's leader". Yet, results from a Harris-ITN survey suggests that the proportion of voters who remained undecided up until the last week of the campaign was not significantly greater than in previous elections (21% in 1992, 18% in 1987, 20% in 1983, and 18% in 1979). Furthermore, when pressed in recall studies, this group proved not to be disproportionately Conservative-inclined. In the BGES study, 8.2% of voters had previously claimed to be 'don't knows' or 'won't votes', and of these, 26% eventually voted for the Conservatives, and 18% for Labour.

The equivalent figures from MORI and ICM demonstrated even smaller propensities for differential voting among the late deciders. However, by focusing on the difference in the Labour/Conservative gap reported in the final pre-election polls (+0.9%) and in the exit polls (-0.45%), it is possible to identify a large swing towards the Conservatives. However, Crewe warns against the use of such comparisons between data which have been collected using different sample designs (Crewe, 1993a, p.485). Consequently, the 1992 MRS study concludes that the net benefit of this effect to Labour over the Conservatives was approximately 0.3% (1992, p.7).

The final component of late changing in the electorate's voting behaviour is *differential turnout*. The 1994 MRS report notes that turnout was actually higher in 1992 than in 1987 by 2.4%, amounting to 77.9% overall, but that it varied across the regions and across different constituencies. Turnout was highest in the predominantly Conservative regions of the South of England and the Midlands. In constituencies won by the Conservatives in 1987, turnout increased by 3.5%, whilst in equivalent Labour seats, turnout rose by only 0.1% (MRS, 1994, p.18). Butler and Kavanagh (1992, p.143) note how differential turnout may have exacerbated the sampling bias within the polls:

> Pollsters admitted that in drawing their sample of constituencies they had not introduced a weighting for constituency size. Since the electorate in Conservative seats were, on average, 9,000 greater than Labour seats, this could have produced a bias of almost 1% in favour of Labour.

Similarly, Crewe has advocated that pollsters abandon their practice of weighting by region, "...which in 1992 led to the slight over-representation of low turnout Labour regions like Scotland and the Northern region and the slight under-representation of high-turnout and Conservative regions like East Anglia, the South East and South West" (Crewe, 1993b, p.493). According to Curtice and Steed, there was a clear geo-political pattern of turnout with "...typically a 2% to 3% difference in the behaviour of a constituency according to its political complexion" (Curtice and Steed, 1992, p.345). Furthermore, exit polls by NOP and Harris demonstrated that certain traditionally Labour-inclined groups had a lower than average propensity to turnout, including council tenants, semi-skilled and unskilled manual workers, and welfare dependents.

However, the pre-election polls did not indicate the scale of these differential turnouts rates, and neither did they reflect them in the party scores they produced. In response to this, Waller maintains that "...the predictive quality of last minute pre-election polls would presumably be improved by the success of identification of likelihood of turnout and subsequent weighting" (Waller, 1992a, p.11). Nonetheless, as Jowell reports, there is no conclusive evidence of differential party preferences between either those respondents in polls who claimed that they would not vote but who went on to vote on election day, or that group of respondents who, having declared support for a particular political party, stayed away from the polls (Jowell et al, 1993, p.250). Consequently, the MRS enquiry team concluded that this factor accounted for only 0.6% of the discrepancy between the final pre-election polls and the actual voting results of the 1992 General Election (MRS, 1992, p.7).

Nondisclosure effects The various enquiries also considered the extent of two related factors as possible sources of error for the 1992 General Election opinion polls: voters who refused to reveal their voting intentions in the opinion polls, and voters who lied about their party preferences. There is some dispute about the impact of these effects on the polling outcomes,[10] although the MRS report did reveal that both groups are likely to be disproportionately Conservative in orientation, had increased in size from 1987 (by 3% to 5%), and helped to create an underestimation of Conservative support.

Pollsters of course can neither anticipate nor adjust figures for data from respondents who lie, although they can use an incliner question for those interviewees who won't give their voting intention. Furthermore, the bias introduced into polling data by nondisclosures may be partially offset by weighting by other related questions, such as party leader, economic competence and so on (Sparrow, 1993b; Studlar and McAllister, 1992). Thus, pollsters might use responses to such questions to estimate the preferred party of non-disclosure voters. However as Crewe states, consistent lying by a group of respondents, as large as 5% of the sample "...would beg the question of why polls should ever be believed again" (1993b, p.489). For Jowell (1993, p.250), such dissonance between stated intention and actual behaviour "...is as much an occupational hazard for pollsters as it is for forecasters in general". Consequently, it is important to identify the causes of these two elements of nondisclosure at the 1992 General Election, and account for the increase since 1987 if an assessment is to be made of the scale of the problem for pollsters and its likely impact on their data in future elections.

Essentially, three aspects of nondisclosure have been identified by the pollsters and by commentators: a *shame* factor; a *protest* factor; and a *decliner* factor. The first two elements involved a "...systematic deception by a number of Tory-inclined interviewees" (Butler and Kavanagh, 1992, p.142). Voters were allegedly ashamed to admit to the pollsters their support for various unfashionable government policies including for instance, taxation. Instead, they were "...constrained by a 'dominant' political culture to express support for more spending and taxing, because the alternative response was seen as selfish and uncaring" (Kavanagh, 1992). Such an effect is difficult to measure. However, according to Crewe (1993b, pp.489-490) exit poll data under-estimated the Conservative share of electoral support, even though respondents were provided with a secret ballot paper to express their preferred party and did not therefore have to admit publicly if they were Conservative supporters. However, the scale of the error on the exit poll was not as large as that recorded in the pre-election polls, and Crewe does not consider in his report that perhaps the use of this secret ballot technique may have accounted for this less inaccurate estimate of Conservative support.

The second aspect of nondisclosure by some Conservative voters has been defined as the *protest* factor. Here, 'natural' Conservative supporters who had experienced both austere economic policies and unpopular social policies since the 1987 General Election registered their dissatisfaction in the opinion polls in a similar way to tactical and protest voters in by-elections - to punish the government "...knowing that the identity of the government is not actually at stake" (Waller, 1992a, p.6).

The effects of both the *shame* and *protest* factors are nonetheless difficult to quantify. However, the third *decliner* factor can be estimated, and its effect on the error on the 1992 election polls measured as 2 % on the Conservative/Labour gap (MRS, 1992, p.8). This factor takes account of the impact of those voters who refuse to reveal their voting intention in polls. In post-election recall polls, respondents were more likely to reveal their previously secret voting intentions, and were disproportionately Conservative-inclined: in the BGES study the effect amounted to a reduction of the Labour lead in the pre-election polls of 1.3% (Jowell et al, 1993, p.247); ICM results found a Conservative bias amongst former 'won't say' voters of 57%, compared to 29% for Labour, and 14% for the Liberal Democrats (MRS, 1992, p.8).

In a split sample test, ICM (Sparrow, 1993b) focused on a method which was designed both to reduce the levels of non-response to the voting intention question, and to identify the distribution of party support within this group. Half of the respondents were asked the voting intention question in the conventional manner, whilst the other voters were asked to record their party preference on a secret ballot paper. For the second group, the level of refusals for this question fell dramatically from 7% to 1%, and those respondents switched straight over to the Conservative Party (see table 7.2). The overall effect was a change in the Conservative/Labour gap from -5 to +2% (adjusted to +3 when only those mentioning a party are included). However, a similar set of exercises by MORI contradicted these findings by demonstrating a consistent fall in the Conservative levels of support, although, as Worcester (1993c, p.4) notes, "...the size and direction of party effects may, of course, be affected by the political climate"; at different points in the political cycle, the Secret Ballot method may yield different effects and results.

Recommendations for opinion polling after the 1992 experience The net impact of each of these explanations is given in Table 7.3 below. It suggests that over half of the discrepancy between the final pre-election polls and the actual result can be explained by differential registration, late changes of mind, and nondisclosure effects, but that sampling variability does not contribute to an understanding of what went wrong in 1992.

Table 7.2   ICM Secret Ballot Test for Refusers on the Voting Intention Question

	Conventional Poll (%)	Secret Ballot (%)	Difference	Secret Ballot Adjusted (%)
Conservative	28	35	+7	42
Labour	33	33	-	39
Lib Democrats	12	12	-	14
SNP	3	2	-1	] 5
Others	1	3	+2	]
Will Not Vote	12	11	-1	
Unwilling To Say	7	1	-6	
Don't Know	5	4	-1	

Source: ICM figures (Sparrow, 1993b, pp.85-88)

Table 7.3   Error Effects in the 1992 British General Election Polls (%)

Sampling Variability	-
Methodology	?
Differential Registration	1.2
Late Changers	2.5 - 3.3
Nondisclosure	2.0
Total	5.6
Actual Error	8.5
Unexplained Error	2.9

Source: MRS Report, 1994

However, this leaves approximately a 3% margin of discrepancy to explain in the polls, or about 40% of the error. Following the 1992 polling experiences, a number of recommendations were made which advocated various technical and logistical innovations to reduce error in opinion polls. These included:

• If pollsters continue with quota sampling methods they should use as many 'partisan' quota control variables as necessary (MRS, 1994), that they use appropriate indicators as measures of these variables, and that they have access to current and comprehensive base data on which to identify the correct distribution of categories within each variable for every sample point selected.

- The constituencies selected for the pollsters' samples should also be given careful consideration in terms of such factors as: the historical distribution of voting patterns (to check on electoral volatility); marginal status; propensity for tactical voting; charismatic political personalities; strong peripheral party candidates.
- So as to reduce the problems of non-disclosure and *undecideds* in the voting intention question, pollsters should use secret ballots. Such a technique could be developed further by using various weighting procedures to emphasise the views of committed 'core' voters, and reduce the impact in polls of the uncommitted.
- Modelling either with political weighting, or with the use of alternative questions as voting predictors. This may contribute to a clearer understanding amongst the pollsters both of the strength of feeling on political issues and party preferences, and of revealing clues about the likely voting behaviour of the *don't knows* and *won't says*, and estimating and accounting for differential turnout.
- Finally, whether or not quota samples themselves should be replaced, and pollsters revert back to random methods.

British Election Polls since 1992

Since the experience of the British General Election in 1992, the opinion pollsters have had two occasions in which to demonstrate the effectiveness of the performance of their national polls: at the European Assembly Elections of 1994, and at the General Election in 1997.

European Assembly Elections 1994 Apart from local elections, the European Assembly Elections of 1994 provided the first major opportunity for the British pollsters to demonstrate that the 1992 polling débâcle was an isolated incident. Throughout the campaign, pollsters forecast a substantial Labour victory. Final polls suggested that Labour would gain between 44% and 53.5% of the vote, whilst the Tories would be likely to secure a 23% to 28% share of public support. Table 7.4 below compares the actual results with the estimates reported by four of the major pollsters. The data suggest that the polls largely failed to regain the credibility lost from 1992. As Linton (1994b, p.12) commented for the Guardian:

> Opinion pollsters, anxious to restore their reputation after a disastrous performance at the last election, faced fresh criticism yesterday for their failure accurately to predict the outcome of last week's European election.

While the polls correctly forecast a Labour victory, the scale of the Conservative decline was significantly over-estimated. With an average sample size of 1440, the expected average poll error per party would be 2.5%, and 5% on the Labour lead; in reality, the figures were 3.8% and 6.7% respectively - both outside the margin of error for this sample size. The error on the seat projections was also significant. The Conservatives, were widely predicted to lose all but a handful of the 32 seats they were defending from 1989: an initial ICM poll translated into 6 seats, whilst final polls from Gallup projected that they would be reduced to 5, Harris forecast 8, and MORI estimated 9; only NOP and ICM's final estimates came close to the actual result of 18 European Assembly seats with forecasts of 18 and 20. The Market Research Society (1992, p.108) concluded that, far from rectifying the mistakes experienced at the 1992 General Election, the pollsters largely reproduced the error although not on such a huge scale:

The experience of the 1994 European Elections demonstrates that the problems manifested by the polls at the time of the 1992 election still persist.

Table 7.4   Poll Projections at the 1994 European Parliamentary Elections for the British Political Parties (%)

Polling Agency	Fieldwork Dates	Sample Size	Con	Lab	Lib Dem	Other	Lab Lead
Gallup	(25-30.5)	1042	23	53.5	19	4.5	30.5
MORI	(2-6.6)	2669	23	51	20	6	28
NOP	(4-5.6)	c.1000	28	44	19.5	8.5	16
ICM	(6.6)	1050	27	45	22	6	18
Average		c.1440	25.3	48.5	20.1	6.3	23.1
Result			27.8	44.2	16.7	11.2	16.4
Error			-2.5	+4.3	+3.4	-4.9	6.7

Average error per party = 3.8
Source: Mortimore (1994, p.342) and MORI (1994, p.8)

British General Election 1997 Following the polling débâcle in 1992, the opinion pollsters issued warnings about the significance of their performance for their long-term credibility at the 1997 General Election. As Nick Moon of the polling company NOP stated prior to the election:

If we get it wrong, we will have learnt that there is no standard method of polling that can measure support for a party that is regarded as unpopular ...Opinion polls would be totally discredited as far as general elections are concerned (in Smith, 1997).

In the event, the reaction of many commentators to the performance of the 1997 election polls was largely positive, as all the major pollsters[11] correctly predicted a landslide Labour victory. Furthermore, while none of the final pre-election polls managed to forecast the election outcome precisely, all did so within an accepted margin of error[12] (see Table 7.5).

Table 7.5   Poll Projections at the 1997 British General Election (%)

Polling Agency	Fieldwork Dates	Sample Size	Con	Lab	Lib Dem	Other	Lab Lead
Harris	(27-29.4)	1154	31	48	15	6	17
NOP	(29.4)	1093	28	50	14	8	22
ICM	(29-30.4)	1555	33	43	18	6	10
Gallup	(30.4)	1849	33	47	14	6	14
MORI	(30.4)	1501	29	47	19	5	18
Average		1430	31	47	15	7	16.2
Result		-	31.4	44.4	17.2	7	13
Error		-	-0.4	+2.6	-2.2	0	+3.2

Average error per party = 1.3
Source: MORI (1997, p.36)

However, throughout the course of the six-week election campaign, there was significant variation in the opinion polls, and the Labour-Conservative gap reported in the five final polls ranged from 22% to 10%. Indeed, as Nick Sparrow (1997, p.4) of the ICM polling company concluded:

In a closer election, the range of predictions made in 1997 would have led some pollsters to predict the wrong outcome and all of us (pollsters) would have been damned again.

Table 7.6 below summarises this level of variation in support for the Conservative and Labour parties, and in the gap between them.[13] It suggests that during the campaign, the level of Conservative support varied by 10% - between 27% and 37% - with a standard deviation of 1.98, relatively close to the margin of error for these campaign polls (2.79 for an average sample size of 1236). For the

Labour Party, the range of support recorded in the opinion polls was 13%, with a high of 55% and a low of 42%. The standard deviation on its poll scores at 2.96 suggests that there was quite significant variation in its levels of poll support, more than the acceptable margin of error. The gap between the Labour and Conservative parties also showed considerable variation during the campaign period, with a standard deviation of 4.34 (compared to the acceptable margin of error of 5.58), and a range of 22%. Even if the ICM 'rogue' poll which suggested a Labour lead of only 5% in *The Guardian* on 23rd April is omitted, the gap varies from 10% to 27% - a range of 17%.

Table 7.6   Variation in 1997 General Election Campaign Polls for the Party Scores and the Labour-Conservative Gap

	Con	Lab	Con-Lab Gap
Min Score	27	42	5
Max Score	37	55	27
Range	10	13	22
Standard Deviation	1.98	2.9	4.34

O'Muircheartaigh (1997, p.16) notes that while the level of Conservative Party support recorded in the opinion polls was relatively consistent, the polls typically and systematically over-estimated the Labour vote: during the last three weeks of the campaign, four of the five major pollsters forecast Labour at between 48% and 51%, when the actual vote for Blair's Party was only 44.4%.[14] As a consequence of the degree of variation in the polls and of the (mostly) over-estimation of the swing to Labour, O'Muircheartaigh (1997, p.16) claims that the polls did not perform as well in 1997 as some pollsters and commentators have suggested:

> A charitable view of the pollsters' performance would be that they confounded their critics by predicting throughout the campaign a very large Labour victory; that despite the contumely of the commentators and the politicians, the polls were vindicated by the election result and that they need fear criticism no more.
> A jaundiced view would be that the range of predictions offered by the polls in circumstances where Labour was consistently and clearly in the lead meant that they would inevitably be able to point to a successful prediction whatever the result, within a wide range of possible Labour victories.

The issue to be addressed is why was there so much variation in the polls in 1997? In previous general elections, the polls had been marked by their similarity in methodology, however, in 1997 there was no such consensus. Table 7.7 below outlines the variety in research strategy and approach of the pollsters in 1997. In response to their polling experience in 1992, the pollsters made a series of major changes to the way in which they conducted and analysed their polls. Some of these changes were more radical than others. Thus MORI made only three relatively minor changes to its polls[15] in 1997, including:

- the use of smaller, randomly selected sampling areas in which fieldworkers had less discretion over where to interview
- changing and extending the use of quota variables for use in selecting respondents; social class was replaced by housing tenure as a factor in choosing respondents, who were also selected according to car ownership, whether self-employed, and by taking into account regional unemployment
- reviewing the sources of data for weighting quotas, so that proportions of different quota types such as whether a car owner or not are more accurate for interview locations (Worcester, 1997, pp.lxiii-lxv).

Table 7.7   Different Polling Methodologies, General Election 1997

	MORI	Harris	NOP	ICM	Gallup
Sampling	Quota in Home	Quota in Home	Quota Home/street	List-based in home	Random in home
Mode	Face to face	Face to face	Face to face	Phone	Phone
Don't Knows	No	Past Vote	Party ID Economy	Past Vote	Past Vote Best PM Economy
Weight By Past Vote	No	No	Yes	Yes	No

Source: Taken from O'Muircheartaigh (1997, p.14)

Harris also introduced only minor changes to their polling strategies, opting to remain, as with MORI, with the face-to-face quota interview method, but allocating "Don't Know" responses for the voting intention question to political parties on the basis of which party the respondent mentioned they had previously voted for (O'Muircheartaigh, 1997, p.14). NOP were more experimental in their polling than either of these two companies, allocating "Don't Know" responses and refusals to parties by reference to "Party Identification" and "Economic Competence" variables, and also by weighting recorded "Past Vote" to the actual vote in the previous general election[16] (Moon, 1997).

The most radical innovations however were implemented by Gallup and ICM who both switched from interviewing face-to-face to doing so by telephone, as well as reallocating "Don't Know" responses (Gallup and ICM) and weighting by Past Vote (ICM only). There were some important differences in the telephone interviewing strategies used by these companies,[17] but essentially their approaches could be contrasted with those implemented by the other major pollsters (Curtice, 1997b).

It is then, perhaps not surprising that there was such variation in the results found by these different polling companies in 1997, indeed, it might be expected that ICM would produce party scores which differed from the other pollsters because of its very different (telephone-based) sampling approach. However, it might be assumed that both Gallup and ICM would find similar levels of support for the parties as both used telephone polls. However, as Table 7.8 shows, Gallup's findings were typically closer to those companies which used face-to-face quota sampling methods, than with ICM's poll results. The table suggests that ICM recorded higher Liberal Democrat scores and lower Labour scores than the other pollsters. Worcester (1997, p.lvi) and King (1997) both claim that this systematic difference in party support is a function of the questioning method used:

> The explanation for these consistent differences may lie partly in ICM's voting-intention question that begins by reminding respondents of the names of all the main parties - including the Liberal Democrats - that are contesting the election. Gallup merely asks people how they will vote. It may be that reminding voters of the Liberal democrats' existence - and failing to remind them of the smaller parties - has an effect (King, 1997).

Table 7.8   Variation of Party Scores throughout the Campaign by Different Polling Companies, General Election 1997 (%)

	Con	Lab	Lib Dem	Other	Lab Lead
ICM	33	46	16	5	13
Gallup	31	50	13	6	19
Harris	30	50	14	6	20
MORI	30	50	14	6	20
NOP	29	49	14	8	20

Source: Taken from Worcester (1997, p.lvi)

Clearly then, we can see that the scale of the error found in the 1992 General Election polls was not reproduced in the 1997 polls. Indeed, relatively little controversy accompanied the polls in 1997. To some extent, the pollsters appear to have responded positively to many of the recommendations made by the Market Research Society in 1992, and there have been a number of technical and methodological innovations employed. However, this has not been consistent, and there is now no uniform agreed approach to polling in Britain. As a result, the results of the polls themselves are rather volatile, as they have been since the 1992 General Election. The lack of consensus which exists within APOPO about the preferred polling strategy suggests that this will continue, and a revealing conclusion from ICM's managing director suggests that the pollsters should be wary of complacency in the future:

> With hindsight, we are unable to find any other logical techniques that would have provided us with a more accurate prediction. We do not intend, however, to close our minds to further innovation (Sparrow, 1997b, p.20).

Election Polls in Mainland Western Europe

There are a number of recent examples in mainland Europe where the pollsters have failed to anticipate election outcomes. Some of these are discussed below.

Spain 1993 and 1996

At the Spanish General Elections in both 1993 and 1996, the pollsters' forecasts of defeats for the ruling PSOE government under Felipe Gonzales largely failed to transpire. Reporting on the 1993 General Election, *The Times* newspaper commented that, "...for the opinion pollsters, Spain's national election was another night of unmitigated gloom" (1993, p.16).

In the final fortnight of the election campaign, polls predicted (correctly) that no party would win an absolute majority in the *Congreso de los Diputados* (Lower House), but wrongly forecast a slight lead for the opposition Popular Party (PP) in both seats and votes. Furthermore, they over-estimated the electoral support for the left-wing alliance, Izquierda Unida (IU), predicting about 26 seats, 8 more than the 18 actually achieved.[18] In the event, PSOE were returned to government (with the temporary support of the CiU and PNV nationalist parties) with a 3.9% and 18 seat margin of victory over the expected victors, the PP (see Table 7.9 below). The scale of the polls' inaccuracies were such that the leader of the PP, Javier Arenas, was reported as having claimed victory soon after the polling booths closed on the basis of exit poll predictions, before "..he was forced into a humiliating and acrimonious climbdown" (*The Times*, 1993, p.16).

Hooper claimed that an explanation for the error in the 1993 Spanish election polls can be traced partly to the large numbers of voters who withheld their real intentions from the pollsters. He identified two such groups. Firstly, there was a middle class voting group who disguised their support for PSOE because the party had been publicly discredited following wide-spread allegations of corruption in the so-called *Filesa Case*,[19] and also because of its failure to solve persisting inflation and unemployment problems. The second group comprised a large number of poorer, primarily rural, voters. During the campaign Gonzales repeatedly predicted that if a PP government were elected, this would result in a return to the anti-democratic methods of government so typical under the Franco regime. Hooper claimed that this second group of voters were concerned that admitting in an opinion poll that they supported the PSOE might possibly result in some form of punishment by an incoming PP government. He concluded that these developments helped to account for the large numbers of 'undecideds' reported in the polls (about 17%), who were in fact more likely to be PSOE-inclined 'won't say' voters (Hooper, 1993, p.20).

Table 7.9   Election Results for the Spanish Lower House in 1993 and 1996, Percentage of Votes and Number of Seats

	1993 Vote (%)	1996 Vote (%)	1993 Number of Seats	1996 Number of Seats
PSOE-PSC	38.5	37.5	159	141
PP	34.6	39	141	156
Others	26.9	23.5	50	53
Total	100	100	350	350

Source: Valles (1994), Marks (1996)

At the following General Election in March 1996, the polls again forecast a victory for the PP of up to 10%, but their margin of victory over the PSOE was only 1.5%, and Aznar, the party leader, was forced to make concessions to some of the regional nationalist parties after failing to achieve the expected majority in government. The record of the polls during the election campaign was summed up by Hooper (1996):

The unexpected outcome of Sunday's General Election in Spain shows Felipe Gonzales, the country's Prime Minister of the last 13 years, to be not so much a political personality as a political phenomenon ...He lost to be sure, but he lost by so much less than the polls had predicted.

Italy 1995 and 1996

Opinion pollsters came under considerable attack from commentators at the Italian regional elections in April 1995 for their flawed predictions of sweeping gains for Silvio Berlusconi's Freedom Alliance, and a collapse in support for the Democratic Party of the Left (PDS). In one theatrical episode, a pollster apologised on television for his agency's misleading poll predictions before pretending to shoot himself with a fake gun. Another polling agency which forecast a resounding victory for the Freedom Alliance made a public apology to voters and waived its fee (Gumbel, 1995).

In the last two days of the General Election campaign opinion polls and exit polls suggested a right-wing landslide: between 9 and 11 of the 15 regions contested were expected to fall to the Freedom Alliance. In the final exit poll, they were predicted to win 45% of the vote, against 23% for the main opposition, the PDS. The results of the exit poll echoed the trends identified in the earlier tracking polls, and convinced Berlusconi to call for an immediate general election to bring down the Dini government (Phillips, 1995a). In the event however, the PDS won a surprise electoral victory. In contrast to the poll findings, the PDS gained the largest share of the vote at 25%, and won in 9 of the 15 regions. The Freedom Alliance won in only 6 of the regions, with Forza Italia securing only 22% of the vote, and 14% for its electoral partner, the 'post-fascist' National Alliance. Other results included 7% for the Northern League, 8.6% for Communist Refoundation, 7.3% for the Italian Popular Party, and 3% for the right-wing of the former Christian Democrats, the Democrats (Phillips, 1995b).

The opinion pollsters also failed to accurately predict the final outcome of the April 1996 General Election. Hooper reported that the final opinion poll published before the election reinforced earlier general voting intention trends forecasting victory for Berlusconi's right-wing Freedom Alliance with 47% of the vote, and a combined vote of 44% for the centre-left Olive Tree and the left-wing Communist Refoundation (CR) (Hooper, 1996b). The final result however produced the first post-War election victory for the Italian left, with the PDS-led Olive Tree coalition gaining 43% of the vote by itself (284 of the 630 seats in the Chamber of Deputies, 169 of the 315 seats in the Senate), and forming a government with the support of the CR (35 seats). Contrary to polling expectations, the Freedom Alliance gained only 36% of the vote (246 seats in the Chamber of Deputies). A further 59 seats went to the Northern League, with six for the remaining parties (Endean, 1996).

Gumbel (1995) has offered a series of possible explanations as to why electoral opinion in Italy is so difficult to estimate in the opinion polls. Firstly, the public has a deep historical distrust of opinion leaders, and of information they may use which claims to support their position on particular issues:

> Under Italy's old clientistic system, elections were monitored not by opinion pollsters but by local party grandees who would instruct voters on exactly which candidates to pick, and then check the ballot papers to make sure.

The public's scepticism of opinion polling is reinforced by their awareness of the strong links which exist between some of the major polling agencies and the leading political parties. Thus Datamedia, together with the television company for which it conducts polls, is part of the Fininvest company owned by Forza Italia's leader, Berlusconi. Gumbel reports that Datamedia's voting intention polls typically over-estimated public support for Forza Italia and its allies, when compared with other polling agencies. As a consequence of these factors, Gumbel claims that large numbers of polling respondents are deeply suspicious and cynical of opinion polls, and likely to disguise their real views about political affairs if asked to participate in such research (Gumbel, 1995). Furthermore, their reading of the findings of such research will inevitably be tainted by this suspicion of party-pollster relationships. When combined with the newness of the political system in Italy, and the relative absence of stable party-voter alliances of the type which existed there in the past, it is perhaps not surprising that pollsters occasionally experience difficulties in conducting accurate pre-election polls.

France 1995

The multi-party system in France proved to be particularly complex for the opinion pollsters in 1995:

> Voting in the first round of the French presidential election confounded the opinion polls last night [23 April], putting the Socialist candidate Lionel Jospin in first place, and giving Jean-Marie Le Pen's far-right National Front its strongest ever showing, with 15% (Dejevsky and Fenby, 1995).

Throughout the campaign, polls had indicated an increasing hardening of voter support for the leading right-wing candidate and overall front-runner Chirac, and a tight race for the remaining second round election place between Jospin and the centre-right Balladur. The final polls[20] published before the first round election forecast that 26% of the public intended to vote for Chirac, between 19% and 20.5% of voters supported Jospin, and that Balladur would win 16% to 16.5% of the votes. The far-right National Front candidate LePen was forecast to achieve approximately 12 to 13.5% of the votes (Fenby, 1995). In the event, the Socialist Party candidate defied all expectations by achieving a surprising victory over Chirac by a margin of 23% to 21%.

Table 7.10 below compares the final pre-election polls with the actual votes achieved by the candidates. It reports the poll estimates which were closest to the actual result so as to minimise the error on the gap and provide the pollsters with the benefit of the doubt. The data suggest that whilst the poll forecasts were (usually) just within the margin of error, clearly the *consistency* both in the reported lead for Chirac and in the under-estimation of voter support for Jospin, Balladur, and Le Pen, suggests that the polls were misleading.

Table 7.10   Poll Projections at the 1995 French Presidential Elections (%)

Candidate	Election Result	Closest Poll Estimate	Error	Furthest Poll Estimate	Error
Jospin	23.3	20.5	-2.8	19.0	-4.3
Chirac	20.8	25.0	4.2	26.0	5.2
Balladur	18.6	16.5	-2.1	16.0	-2.6
Le Pen	15.0	13.5	-1.5	12.0	-3.0
Others and 'Don't Knows'	22.3	23.5	1.2	28.0	7.7
Jospin Lead	2.5	-5.5	8.0	-6.0	8.5

Average error on the candidates: Closest poll estimate 2.4; Furthest poll estimate 4.6
Source: Fenby (1995), Dejevsky and Fenby (1995), Dejevsky (1995b)

With nine presidential candidates,[21] it is perhaps not surprising that the French voters' preferences were difficult to predict in opinion polls, given the level of choice available to them, and ultimately the degree of political complexity. Furthermore, a large proportion of the electorate remained uncertain about its voting intentions up until the last stages of the election. Between 29% and 34% of the electorate fell into this category (Dejevsky, 1995b; Sage, 1995). To add to this, many voters were frustrated by the established parties' failures to offer strong and convincing leadership on key policies, including unemployment, pay, social security, education and health, and of corruption in public life (Dejevsky, 1995c).

Consequently, these voters were volatile, sceptical, and often attracted to radical alternative parties and candidates. As Rees-Mogg (1995) noted:

> No fewer than 37% of the electorate voted in the first round for Trotskyites, communists, neo-fascists, Greens or the old-fashioned Catholic Right. All these parties advocated radical discontinuity in one form or another, and all reject the French establishment and the supremacy of the officials.

French pollsters generally recognise that the standing of such parties may be under-represented in their findings, largely because voters may be wary of expressing their support to strangers for what society considers to be 'radical' parties (Fenby, 1995). Thus, it is common practice for pollsters to 'factor in' additional votes for such parties (especially the National Front) to compensate for this voter reluctance (Dejevsky, 1995b). This is an imperfect practice which is liable to error. Clearly, the pollsters were unable to achieve precision with this method at the 1995 presidential elections.

Belgium 1995

The difficulty for polls in attempting to forecast election outcomes where radical parties (especially of the Right) exist as significant forces in opposition to the established centre-right and centre-left, can be seen in other countries. In Belgium, the Vlaams Blok had been predicted by opinion polls in 1995 to win at least 15% of the vote across the Flanders region (Lockwood, 1995).

A combination of factors were thought to be at work in assisting the advance of this far-right party. Throughout the campaign period and before, it had been expected that disillusion with the governing parties' leaders (many of whom had been implicated in a scandal over defence contracts), coupled with a combination of rising figures for both unemployment and crime and a general antipathy towards immigration, would result in a collapse of the establishment parties, especially the Flemish Socialist Party. However, with close to 40% of the voters left undecided during the last two days of the election campaign, widespread voter ambivalence about the election, and with a proliferation of small parties creating confusion amongst the electorate,[22] the opinion pollsters were confronted with a particularly complex political landscape to survey (Downs, 1995). Ultimately, by registering only 12.2% of the vote, "...the extreme right-wing Vlaams Blok failed to make the electoral breakthrough widely predicted in the General Election" (Dynes, 1995, p.12), whilst the Christian Democrat and Socialist parties survived the expected electoral meltdown to form a new centre-left coalition government.

Election Polls in the USA

In the USA, no recent polls have erred as significantly as those conducted during the presidential contest in 1948, where Truman's unexpected victory over Dewey "...created a crisis that some feared would threaten the existence not only of public opinion polls but of all applications of the survey method" (Crespi, 1990, p.15). However, as Worcester reports, whilst the *final* pre-election polls generally have a good record in forecasting shares of support within the margin of error, there is often significant variation across polls during the *earlier* election campaign periods. This was particularly the case in 1992, where the poll ratings for Bush and Clinton, complicated by the addition of the Perot factor as a third option for voters, were especially volatile.

Worcester notes that this is partly due to the methodological short-comings of the polls conducted in the USA. Typically, pollsters there do not conduct interviews in the last 24 hours of an election campaign, and consequently fail to include the voting intentions of those who switch party and candidate loyalties at the final moment. National samples are often significantly less than 1000 (and are often only 400 in state-wide polls), and are considered too small for pre-election polls because the associated margin of error will be too great for meaningful vote projections. Furthermore, interviews are usually conducted over the telephone, and consequently, the results exclude non-phone owners (this would be particularly significant if the latter group were disproportionately supporters of one party or one candidate over another). In addition, these polls contain neither absentee nor overseas voters. Finally, no attempt is made to weight or compensate for non-respondents and 'refuseniks', who comprise approximately 50% of interview attempts.

These methodological weaknesses within the polls are compounded by inadequacies in the way that the data are reported. There is little consistency between polling agencies both in terms of which universe is set as the base of the report (all respondents, all registered voters, or just those likely to vote) and in the reallocation of "don't knows". This issue is of particular importance given the significant differentiation of voting registration across groups with strong party loyalties. Ethnic minority groups (predominantly Democrat-inclined)[23] have a large proportion of non-registered persons, and tend to have a lower election turn-out rate than white voters. As Walker reports, "usually only 21% of Hispanics and 39 per cent of blacks vote in elections, compared with 49% of whites" (Walker, 1994, p.1). With these issues in mind, Worcester (1992, p.3) concludes that "...its a miracle that the polls did as well as they did (in the USA in 1992)".

In elections in the USA since 1992, polling forecasts have often been variable and misleading. At the mid-term elections in November 1994, seats were contested for the House of Representatives, the Senate, and state governorships. Throughout the campaign, most polls suggested major gains for the Republicans, although a minority of leading pollsters forecast narrow Democrat victories.[24] However, the landslide victory actually achieved by the Republicans was not revealed by the polls:

> Most pollsters think it unlikely the Republican's will bag the 40-odd seats they need to win control (of the House of Representatives) for the first time in 40 years (Freedland, 1994, p.26).

In the event, the Republicans won significantly more seats than expected, with a net gain of 53[25] in the House of Representatives, taking their total from 178 to 231, a majority of 27 overall. In the Senate, they gained 9[26] seats, with a 53 to 47 seat victory over the Democrats, and won 30 of the 50 state governors. Some high profile state governor contests were also subject to intensive polling, much of which failed to predict accurately the final outcome. For instance, poll predictions for the incumbent Democrat New York state governor, Mario Cuomo, varied throughout the campaign, suggesting both a landslide victory and a narrow win (Walker, 1994; Freedland, 1994, and 1994b). Eventually Cuomo lost the seat by a margin of 49% to 45% to his challenger, George Pataki (Muir, 1994, p.15).

At the US Republican primaries in 1996, there were some notable pre-election poll failures. In the New Hampshire primary, polls were especially variable. Only four days before the vote, three polls were released simultaneously, all with differing forecasts: a CNN poll predicted a Buchanan win, with 26% of the votes, compared to 23% for Dole, 18% for Alexander, and Forbes in last place with 15%; the figures for the Boston Globe were 22%, 25%, 14%, and 14% for Buchanan, Dole, Alexander, and Forbes respectively, with corresponding figures of 21%, 21%, 15%, and 15% from the New York Post (Fletcher, 1996). In the event Buchanan won by the narrowest of margins, with 27%, to Dole's 26% (see Table 7.11). In Arizona, the polls reported the primary as too close to call, with a narrow win predicted for Buchanan with 24% of the vote, Dole and Forbes both at 23%, and Alexander trailing at 10%. Contrary to all polling expectations however, Buchanan was pushed into third place, with a comfortable win for the outsider Forbes.

These examples confirm the predictions made by Worcester above, that the polling industry in the USA is not immune to failure, and indeed, as in other countries has produced misleading voting intention data in a number of important elections.

Table 7.11   Republican Primary Election Results 1996 (%)

Primary	Dole	Buchanan	Forbes	Alexander
Iowa	26	23	10	18
New Hampshire	26	27	12	23
Arizona	30	27	34	7

Election Polls in Australasia

Pollsters in both New Zealand and Australia have found recent elections difficult to forecast.

Australia 1993

In March 1993, all indications suggested that the Labour Party would lose governmental power in Australia to the conservative Liberal-National coalition after 10 years and 4 terms in office. Under Paul Keating, the government was presiding over record levels of unemployment and a generalised economic recession, and struggled to regain the support of the public following the ousting of the former Prime Minister, Bob Hawke, 12 months earlier. In the early stages of the campaign, opinion polls gave the opposition a convincing 12% lead over Labour, with only a 0.9% swing need to attain control of the House of Representatives. At no stage did commentators seriously expect Labour to recover the deficit, and it was widely predicted that John Hewson's opposition coalition would form the next Australian government:

> The opposition entered the election campaign ahead in the opinion polls and remained in front until close to the election. Although Labour appeared to be closing the gap as the campaign wore on, until the last day or two the trend looked to be not quite strong enough to save the government from defeat (Bean and Marks, 1993, p.254).

The final day polls reinforced this message, forecasting the opposition to win between 45% and 46% of the popular vote, a lead over Labour of between 3% and 5% (1% after the redistribution of second preference votes). As a consequence, it was reported that "...pollsters predict a (Liberal and National) coalition majority of between 5 and 10 seats" (John, 1993, p.16).

However, as Cockburn (1993) notes, even by election day party support had not hardened, and there was a considerable degree of indecision amongst Australia's voters, particularly given their concerns over the opposition's post-election plans. These included a A$10 billion reduction in public spending, industrial relations reforms, health-care and family-support changes, and the introduction of the GST, a 15% consumer tax on goods and services.

The final election results underlined the extent to which the pollsters' predictions had misjudged the mood of the voters. Against all expectations, the Labour Party increased their 9 seat majority in the 147-member lower chamber to 13 with 80 seats, 15 seats more than the Liberal-National coalition. In terms of votes, Keating's party actually gained a larger share of public support than achieved in 1990, with 44.9%, a swing of 2% (see Table 7.12).

Table 7.12   Election Results for the Australian House of Representatives in 1993

	1st Preference votes % (Previous election 1990)	Seats (Previous election 1990)
Australian Labor Party	44.9 (39.4)	80 (78)
Liberal Party	37.1 (35.0)	49 (55)
National party	7.2 (8.4)	16 (14)
Australian Democrats	3.8 (11.3)	- (-)
Others	7.1 (5.9)	2 (1)

New Zealand 1993

At the General Election in New Zealand in November 1993, the ruling National Party was widely expected to achieve a second consecutive victory over the opposition Labour Party, albeit with a slight fall in the size of its 34 seat parliamentary majority. Throughout the campaign period, polls had shown a steady National Party lead over their main rivals of between 4% and 6%, and the outcome of the election was widely considered a formality (Table 7.9). However, the initial results indicated an unexpected collapse in support for Prime Minister Bolger's Party:

> Despite polls predicting a comfortable win for the prime minister Jim Bolger, there was an 8% swing against the National Party, which lost 20 seats and held on to 49 (Zinn, 1993).

At first, commentators claimed the electoral outcome was a hung parliament. The Prime Minister was forced to announce publicly that political compromise could be achieved, and that there would be no parliamentary deadlock following the election results: "...there is, I can emphatically say, no political crisis in New Zealand" (in Verdon, 1993, p.1). In fact, a recount at the South Island seat of Waitaki, one of many marginal seats, reversed the initial National defeat by Labour when postal votes came in to give the government 50 seats, and the smallest of majorities in the 99-member parliament.

Nonetheless, the election outcome represented a significant failure on the part of the opinion pollsters to forecast the electorate's voting intentions. As Table 7.13 demonstrates, the final three polls all over-estimated National's share of the vote, with a very high average error of 4.7%, and under-scored Labour by 1%. The error on National's lead was of 5.7%, which would be considered by most pollsters and commentators as unacceptably high.[27] An explanation for the National Party's loss of votes was given as the stronger than expected showing for the left-wing Alliance, whose 18.2% share of support was significantly higher than the 11% forecast in the polls during the campaign period (Zinn, 1993b):

Last minute gains by the Alliance and a poor turnout among National loyalists disrupted poll-driven media expectations (Levine and Roberts, 1994, p.246).

Table 7.13   Poll Projections at the 1993 New Zealand Parliamentary Election (%)

Polling Agency	National	Labour	Alliance[28]	New Zealand First	National Lead
Heylen	39	32	*	*	7
Gallup	40	36	*	*	4
Time Magazine	40	33	*	*	7
Average	39.7	33.7	11†	11†	6
Result (Votes)	35	34.7	18.2	8.4	0.3
Result (Seats)	50	45	2	2	
Error on Vote	4.7	-1	*	*	5.7

Average error per party (National and Labour) = 2.9
*Data not available
†Approximate only
Source: Levine and Roberts (1994, p.247) and Munro (1993, p.15)

In fact, Levine and Roberts' (1994) analysis of the election results and pre-election polls concludes that, contrary to earlier elections where voters had shown considerable loyalty to their preferred parties, the 1993 election demonstrated significant volatility within the electorate throughout the campaign. There was no obvious pattern to this movement amongst the voters, except to say that there was a considerable shift to the Alliance and to New Zealand First. These parties seemed to gain votes from both National and Labour (randomly) from new voters, and former 'non-voters'. Clearly the pollsters were unable to estimate the extent and nature of this voter volatility, and its direction.

This voter volatility was largely a result of the electorate's frustration with an inflexible political system. Furthermore, the electorate grew increasingly wary about the policies of Labour and the National Party. While the National Party in government had achieved significant success in lowering inflation, securing a national budget surplus, and improving export receipts, it was criticised for creating a climate of economic insecurity with increasing unemployment rates and a widening divide between the relatively wealthy and the poor. However, while such social developments undermined public support for the governing party, voters grew increasingly suspicious of the Labour Party's taxation policies. As a consequence, large numbers of voters considered looking beyond the traditional parties for political representation.

A further issue for pollsters in New Zealand concerns the result of a national referendum which was held simultaneously with the election. The results showed 54% of voters in favour of a change in the nature of the electoral system to one based on proportional representation. This is likely to increase the complexity of the political landscape for pollsters, particularly in terms of the party system: it may strengthen the national profile and standing of the Alliance and New Zealand First, and encourage the establishment of newer parties; in so doing it may facilitate wider voter choice, and encourage tactical voting and increased voter volatility. Such changes may have an increasingly adverse effect on the opinion polls in the future.

Summary

This chapter has attempted to demonstrate that throughout the late-capitalist world, opinion pollsters have experienced some major difficulties in forecasting party support at elections. There are a number of reasons for this, but essentially they appear to correspond with, and indeed to be a result of various structural changes in both the nature of the electorates in these countries, and of the party systems which exist. There has been a shift towards what has been referred to elsewhere in this book as a Complex Politics context for opinion polling, in which the various processes of transformation which are taking place have had the effect of unsettling the political landscapes. These changes appear to be ongoing. As a consequence, opinion pollsters in late-capitalist societies face a much more volatile situation than they did in the early decades of the post-Second World War period. The performance of the opinion polls in a number of recent elections in these countries suggests that, at the very least, pollsters should continue to re-appraise their methodologies and practices to meet the challenge of political and social restructuring and change which characterises contemporary societies in late-capitalist countries.

Notes

1.   It goes without saying however, that not all cases where pre-election polls have effectively 'failed' in their endeavours have been included.

2.   However, on two occasions Harris produced results which apparently contradicted these trends. Firstly on March 24th, their poll for the *Daily Express* gave the Conservatives a 5 point lead, while polls published simultaneously elsewhere gave Labour leads of 3% (MORI in the *Times*), 1% (ICM in *The Guardian*) and, most unusually, of 4% by Harris themselves for ITN. Secondly, on April 1st, Harris again put the Conservatives ahead (by 1%) whilst other pollsters continued to track Labour leads of between 7% and 4%. At the time, these apparent differences were put down to sampling error (Crewe, 1992), fieldwork dates, interview timing, and whether interviews were conducted in-house, or in the street (Waller, 1992b).

3.   Pollsters tend to divide the country into strata, which are geo-politically based. Thus, parliamentary constituencies are grouped into regional order, and then, for each region, ranked by the political results of the previous General Election. The required number of constituency sampling points are then selected randomly using a fixed interval sampling method. Variants of this method are used by all the major polling companies in Britain (Waller, 1994; Worcester, 1994; Moon, 1994; Wybrow, 1994). However, once these sampling points are selected, various strategies are available to the pollsters to create their pool of respondents, including selecting voters randomly from the electoral register, via a random walk process, or by using a quota method.

4.   For example see Miller, 1987.

5.   Gallup and NOP had experimented with questions which sought to identify whether or not respondents were on the electoral register prior to the 1992 election campaign, but this resulted in only a negligible difference to their results. Consequently, the question was dropped by the pollsters (Moon, 1994, Wybrow, 1994). MORI and ICM did try to identify those not on the electoral register, but as the 1994 MRS report states, "...this procedure is not infallible in that respondents may not always be aware that they are not on the register" (MRS, 1994, pp.83-84).

6.   Switching involved respondents voting differently from the way they stated in the final day pre-election polls.

7.   Late deciding occurred on election day amongst people who actually voted for a party, but told pollsters that they were undecided.

8.   Turnout effects emerged either when respondents told pollsters they would not vote but at the last minute did go to the ballot box, or else when they expressed a preference for a party in an opinion poll but then later decided not to vote.

9.   Although Worcester notes that results from the Tuesday night sample of MORI's final pre-election poll was significantly more Labour-oriented than the findings revealed by the fieldwork conducted on Wednesday. This suggests that voters were moving away from Labour in the final moments of the election campaign before voting took place on the Thursday.

10. See for instance Harris (1992), Murray (1992) and Kavanagh (1992).

11. These include the five full members of APOPO (Association of Professional Opinion Polling Organisations).

12. For an average sample size of 1,430 people, the margin of error (+/-) for each political party is 2.6%, while for the Conservative-Labour gap it is double this at 5.2%.

13. However, the findings include what has come to be described as a 'rogue' poll conducted by ICM for The Guardian newspaper on 23rd April, which reported a Labour lead of only 5% while the polls published directly before and after showed this as 16% and 21% respectively (Gallup for the Daily Telegraph, and MORI for the Times). This 'rogue' poll may skew the level of variation, but as only one of 47 polls conducted during the course of the campaign, the impact is likely to be only negligible.

14. In contrast, only ICM forecast Labour support at less than the final vote during the election campaign.

15. See for instance Curtice (1997a) who provides a detailed overview of how the polls have changed since 1992.

16. For instance, if a poll finds too few people saying they voted for the Labour Party at the last election, the pollsters adjust their findings as a whole to try to increase the support for that party in its poll. Thus, the recorded level of support for Labour in the "Past Vote" question becomes the same as its actual vote in that previous election.

17. Thus, Gallup selected households by random-digit dialling, and then individual respondents by nearest birthday. In contrast, ICM used a directory with a final random number, and then selected individuals by quotas (O'Muircheartaigh, 1997, p.14).

18. Although the sudden withdrawal of the IU's leader, Julio Anguita, with a heart attack one week before the election is likely to have had a detrimental effect on the alliance's fortunes (Valles, 1994, p.89).

19. This concerned charges of irregular funding of the PSOE and of self-enrichment of leading members of the Party. Ultimately it led to significant splits and public wrangling within the Party (Valles, 1994, p.87).

20.   A seven day moratorium on the publication of pre-election polls in France, in place since 1977, was largely broken with a series of polls published in the last 48 hours of the campaign. Shortly after the outcome of the first round of the election was announced, calls were made to lift the ban on polls. Mancel, deputy leader of Chirac's RPR party claimed that "...polls don't make opinion, and the argument that the ban allows voters to choose completely freely without being influenced by the polls is not tenable" especially when voters could read the poll estimates in the foreign press (in Dejevsky, 1995, p.8).

21.   'Other' candidates included Hue, Laguiller, De Villiers, Voynet, and Cheminade.

22.   As Downs notes: "A host of opposition and protest parties attacked from the fringes. In addition to the parties of the extreme far-right, ballots would offer voters alternatives from among the ecologists (Agalev in Flanders, Ecolo in Wallonia), the Flemish nationalist Volksunie, and a variety of minor lists. Communists, anti-fascists, neo-nazis, unionists, anti-royalists, youth advocates, seniors' advocates, anarchists, and a party calling for the return of Wallonia to France were among those competing for the pool of uncommitted voters" (Downs, 1995, p. 339).

23.   For instance, at the USA mid-term elections in 1994, the Republicans gained the largest share of support from white voters by a margin of 58% to 42% over the Democrats, whilst 60% of Hispanics, and 91% of blacks voted for the Democrats (Walker, 1994b).

24.   A CNN/ USA Today poll taken 10 days before the elections forecast 49% for the Democrats, with the Republicans nationally at 46% (Freedland, 1994).

25.   This includes one House Democrat who defected to the 52 newly-elected Republican members (Hames, 1995).

26.   The Democrat senator from Colorado crossed the floor to increase the number of Republican gains from eight (Hames, 1995).

27.   Data on the sample size of the polls is unavailable. However, if we assume sample sizes of 1500, the margin of error for National's individual vote, and for its lead over Labour would be 2.5% and 5% respectively. Corresponding poll estimates for both these scores are beyond such assumed margins of error.

28.   The Alliance is a broadly left-wing coalition, comprising Green, New Labour, Democrat, and Mana Matuhake parties and movements. It was established by a former senior Labour Party member, Jim Anderton in 1989, who left the Party after its conversion to monetarist policies (Zinn, 1993).

8 Opinion Polling in Central and Eastern Europe under Communism

Introduction

While political opinion polling is well-entrenched in contemporary capitalist political systems, the same cannot be said for the countries of Central and Eastern Europe. This chapter focuses primarily on the development of political opinion polling in these countries in the period prior to the collapse of communist regimes there at the end of 1989. Polling was a feature of these communist-led societies, although it was limited in terms of its activities, the scope of issue coverage, and its ability to measure public opinion effectively. The major focus of the discussion concentrates on the methodological issues and problems confronting opinion pollsters in these societies during this time.

The Development of Opinion Polling under Communism

Although it is generally thought that public opinion polls were not carried out in the Soviet Union and other East European countries until the 1950s (Kwiatkowski, P., 1992, p.359), there is evidence to suggest that polling activities can be traced as far back as 1945 in both Hungary (Hungary News Agency, 1947) and in Czechoslovakia (Adamec and Viden, 1947/48). For instance, the Hungarian Institute of Public Opinion Research (HIPOR) was set up in August 1945, as a branch of the Hungarian Press Agency, "...organised after the manner of the American Institute of Public Opinion" (HIPOR, 1947). It conducted research into how public opinion reacted to a variety of political events and issues, and how it perceived political parties, leaders, policies and programmes. At the General Election in 1945, it accurately forecast the levels of support for the five main parties with an average error of less than 2% per party (see Table 8.1).

151

Table 8.1   Accuracy of the Pre-election Polls at the Hungarian General Election in 1945

Political Party	Polling Estimate (%)	Election Results (%)	Error
Social Democrats	17.6	18.0	0.4
Communists	19.9	17.5	2.4
Smallholders	53.2	56.0	2.8
Peasant Party	7.2	7.0	0.2
Democrats	2.1	1.5	0.6

Average error per party = 1.3%

Error on Smallholders lead over second placed party = 4.7
Source: Hungarian News Agency, (1947), p.6.

In the immediate aftermath of the Second-World War, the liberation from Nazi occupation in Czechoslovakia ushered in a series of conditions necessary for the establishment of opinion polling in any country. These conditions were:

- the emergence of an open and competitive party system;
- the freedom to express opinions without fear of retribution;
- relatively unobstructed information diffusion within society;
- and a necessity for political elites to establish lines of communication with the mass citizenry.

As a consequence of these developments, the Czechoslovak Institute of Public Opinion Research (Ceskoslovensky Ustav Pro Vyzkum Verejneho Mineni, hereafter UVVM), was set up at the end of 1945 as an independent research organisation. The formal operating policy of UVVM was that it should monitor public opinion on political, social and economic issues, to provide data so that policy-makers could identify the needs and aspirations of the citizenry, and legislate accordingly. Furthermore, all surveys were to be conducted in the public interest, rather than for any sectional or partisan advantage. As its founder members explained, one key objective of the polling institute was that there should "...be no alliance with any particular political party, and no propaganda for any particular ideology" (Adamec and Viden, 1947/48, p.550).

In this early period, the opinion pollsters in Czechoslovakia operated with a fair degree of autonomy from the state and their (predominantly governmental) sponsors. There was little governmental intervention in or censure of UVVM's polling activities, and the polling institute was relatively free to conduct research into any area of politics, economics, society or culture. Furthermore, the data were publicly available in the monthly journal *Verejne Mineni* (Public Opinion).

In its first year, UVVM conducted polls which were designed to help the reconstruction of political structures after the period of repression and the suspension of democracy which had characterised German occupation between 1939 and 1945. The public was asked to consider the most effective methods for reorganising the administrative mechanisms at local, district and provincial level, and their reactions to plans for curbing the influence of the traditional state structures, and for broadening the powers of elected representatives in the newly established National Committees. Furthermore, the polls considered which further reforms could be implemented to democratise the political system. The leaders of the Czechoslovak resistance movement had agreed upon a joint Government Programme at Kosice during the final phase of the country's liberation which formalised the political structure of the new state and guaranteed representation in government of all political parties. This programme for political reconstruction was accompanied by the *Two Year Plan*, a blue-print for economic rehabilitation. The polls monitored the public's awareness of, and reactions to these programmes, together with their perception of the government's performance, and the popularity of ministers and party leaders (Adamec, Pospisil and Tesar, 1947).

UVVM also conducted a pre-election poll for the May 1946 General Election. During this period, there was 'limited' political pluralism. Before the German invasion, there were approximately thirty political parties in Czechoslovakia, but after the war, there were only eight (four in Bohemia and Moravia-Silesia, and four in Slovakia). The union of five of these parties formed the National Front, a grand coalition government with no legitimate opposition. At the election, the Communist Party gained 40% of the votes and 114 of the 300 seats. With the support of the Social Democrats, they mustered a majority in Parliament and were invited by President Benes to form a government. The performance of UVVM in accurately forecasting the outcome of the election to within 1.1% of the final results was an indication to the public and to policy-makers alike of the ability, effectiveness and validity of polls in measuring public opinion (see Table 8.2). The success of UVVM at the election led to a proliferation of political opinion polling by the institute.

In February 1948, the coalition government was replaced by a government composed of members of the Communist Party and its supporters from other parties. Elections were then proposed for May of that year, and Party leader Gottwald pronounced that the communists would secure the largest share of votes, and that this would signal majority support for their plans to revolutionise Czechoslovakian life. UVVM organised three pre-election polls to test the levels of support for the parties and to forecast the likely outcome of the election.

However, after the questionnaires from the first wave of the survey were collected, they were confiscated by government officials. Nonetheless, they had already been processed by hand, and a visiting American journalist learned that the results suggested that the Communist Party would gain only about 30% of the votes cast at the forthcoming election, much less than the 40% achieved at the election in 1946 (Adams-Schmidt, 1952). Such a finding might have had a damaging effect on the Communist Party, calling into question their claims to represent the majority of citizens, and undermining their ambitions for constructing a new state and society based on the Stalinist-model which had developed in the Soviet Union.

Table 8.2   Accuracy of the Pre-election Polls at the Czechoslovakian Constituent National Assembly Elections May 26th, 1946

Political Party	Polling Estimate (%)	Election Results (%)	Error
Communist Party	39.6	40.2	0.6
People's Party	19.2	20.2	1.0
Social Democratic Party	16.0	15.6	0.4
National Socialist Party	22.5	23.7	1.2
Blank Voting Slips	2.7	0.4	2.3

Average error per party = 1.1%, Error on Communist lead = 0.4%
Source: Adamec, Pospisil and Tesar, 1947, p.13

The view of polling held by the new communist-led government was one of suspicion: the prospect of an independent opinion polling institution publishing findings which ran contrary to the propaganda of the Party, and which denied the alleged consensus of public support for the values and aims of Marxism-Leninism was perceived by the party leadership as intolerable (Adamec, 1991, pp.1-2). Furthermore, the polling methodologies had been imported by Adamec and Viden from the USA when they visited Albert Cantrill and George Gallup shortly after the war. The methodologies they used when they returned were a direct reflection of those employed by the pollsters in capitalist countries. Samples were generated using a quota method (based on gender, age, social class, community size and geographical distribution), and personal interviews were conducted with structured questionnaires (Adamec and Viden, 1947/48). In a period of mutual suspicion between the Western capitalist bloc and the new communist-led countries, it was perhaps not surprising that the authorities were critical of opinion polling activities.

As a consequence, the period after the rise to political power of the Communist

Party in February 1948 was one of repression for opinion polling in Czechoslovakia. UVVM was permitted to continue its activities for a further two years but only after it had been reorganised, and only in the context of enquiring into non-political issues. The chief editor of *Verejne Mineni* was forced to leave the building as soon as the Communist Party had assumed control of the government, and the journal was closed down. The institute's entire personnel, none of them members of the Communist Party, were sacked; one founder-member, Cenek Adamec, was imprisoned and later forced to work in a factory. As a result of these events, opinion polling gradually disappeared in Czechoslovakia (Adamec, 1991, pp.1-2).

Public opinion research was largely perceived as an irrelevant activity in the communist-led countries. For instance, the Soviet Communist Party under Stalin's leadership had their own methods for measuring public opinion: "...the instruments by which public opinion was discovered included the secret police, the party apparatus...letters to the mass media, and 'self-criticism'" (Gitelman, 1977, p.2). Worcester observes that, between "...1930 and the mid-1950s, the Soviet leadership tended to assume that party cadres, aided by KGB sources and informants, knew what needed to be known about the citizenry's needs, attitudes and preferences" (Worcester, 1987a, p.S82). Furthermore, independent opinion polls which were geared towards reporting the publics' rating of the performance of the Party, and of the Party leaderships, and which sought to measure satisfaction levels with policy proposals and outcomes, were viewed by the party hierarchies as unnecessary. Stanislaw Kwiatkowski, former Central Committee member of the Polish Communist Party and chief political (and polling) advisor to General Jaruzelski in the 1980s comments that:

> The picture of a differentiated society that emerged from the public opinion research did not fit the thesis on the moral and political unity of the nation obligatory at that time (Kwiatkowski, S. 1989, p.4).

Communist governments throughout Central and Eastern Europe took a rather dim view of Social Science generally, and of social research methods and opinion polling. As a leading Polish opinion pollster during the communist reign in Poland during the 1980s, Piotr Kwiatkowski (Kwiatkowski, P. 1992, p.358) notes:

> During the Stalinist period, every attempt to express independent opinion on social or political issues was brutally suppressed. The notion of public opinion was officially condemned and sociology was banned from the universities of all communist countries as a Western 'pseudo-science'.

However, a large number of Central and East European countries had strong, established traditions in sociology that pre-dated the communist era. In Poland, Bulgaria, Yugoslavia, Russia, Czechoslovakia and Romania, sociology emerged in the latter half of the 1800s as a social protest, rather than a purely academic discipline. Many early prominent sociologists in the region were progressive, often socialist activists, who "...combined their sociological studies with an active engagement in various struggles for social justice, democratic freedom and national independence" (Wiatr, 1971, p.4). After the victory of the October revolution in Russia in 1917, sociology in the USSR became concerned with the study of the emerging socialist society and consequently, it was officially perceived as a method for understanding and contributing to the human condition; this was considered as serving a more useful purpose than the objectives of those who held a more traditional, humanistic view of sociology as the accumulation of knowledge for knowledge's sake. In this latter context, objective, empirical sociological research was seen as alienated from the problems of human society by communist leaderships, and was irrelevant in the struggle for constructing an international socialist community (Wiatr, 1971).

With the political ascendancy of the Stalinist bureaucracies, sociological research, with the exception of the official Marxist-Leninist approach, was virtually non-existent up until the end of the 1950s. Empirical-quantitative studies of society and politics were criticised because they were identified with a broadly Western, chiefly American orientation to the study of society. Attila (1990, p.3) notes that, as a consequence:

> Political science did not simply disappear after a small period of emergence and early successes in democratization (1944-48) but it was banned as a pseudo-science of the bourgeoisie - an autocratic rule does not need the science of Democracy.

The suppression of sociology then, in the period up until the end of the 1950s in Central and East European communist political systems was a function of the political leaderships' view of it as 'bourgeois politology', and 'reactionary political science', and as a threat to communist hegemony (Ivanian, 1990, p.2).

In the light of these discussions, it is not surprising that the early communist regimes demonstrated little enthusiasm for opinion polling. However, there is some evidence of polling taking place in communist-led societies, although these polling institutes were usually set up, financed, controlled, and accountable to the ruling Party. When attempts were made to reassess the nature of society, and encourage political debate, sociology and ultimately opinion polls were endorsed.

Shlapentokh characterises this relationship between the State, Party and social science-based research as one in which political-environmental factors were paramount. Thus, in periods of Stalinist ascendancy, sociology and hence social and political research were largely repressed, and in reform periods, such as the 'golden age' of Soviet sociology (1965-72) and later, at the end of the 1980s, controls and censorship were relaxed, and in many communist political systems, institutions were set up to explore sensitive, often 'political' issues.

Thus, when Nikita Khrushchev assumed the leadership of the Soviet Union, sociology was rehabilitated; in 1960, Boris Grushin, one of the founders of Soviet sociology established the Institute of Public Opinion based at the newspaper *Komsomol'skaia pravda*, and in 1961 the Party leadership endorsed the founding of a section for sociological research at the USSR Academy of Sciences Institute of Philosophy. Generally, the areas for research were largely restricted to social and economic issues concerned with work, family life and living standards. However, between 1965 and 1972, the research began to investigate political and current affairs issues - an unprecedented development in the direction of Soviet sociology. In 1968, the Institute for Concrete Social Research was endorsed by the Politburo of the CPSU, and was involved in conducting a series of 'political' projects concerning Soviet life. However, the political repercussions of the Czechoslovak *Prague Spring* had a significant impact on the activities of this and other social and political research centres. It led to a crisis of confidence amongst the Soviet leadership, which then embarked upon a generalised campaign of political repression aimed at 'intellectuals', and their most visible manifestation, empirical sociologists. In 1971, the CPSU sanctioned a large scale purge of the Institute for Concrete Social Research, and its polling branch the Centre for the Study of Public Opinion was closed.[1]

However, during the 1980s, the communist leaderships in the Soviet Union gradually warmed to the idea of conducting and publishing opinion polls, although early studies were limited in scope of issues covered: in 1983, the Soviet leader Yuri Andropov announced that a national institute of public opinion would be formed to cover the entire USSR (White, Gill, and Slider, 1993, pp.180-183). Slider observes that the rationale was based upon the experiences of a public opinion centre created by the Georgian Communist Party. There, the reform-minded Shevardnadze frequently cited polls as an aid to policy-making and agenda-setting (Slider, 1985). As a result of Mikhail Gorbachev's 'Glasnost' and 'Perestroika' programmes, such centres were actually established the following year (Kwiatkowski, P. 1992, pp.359-360).

The development of these polling centres is explained by Valery Korobeinikov in terms of the role that they could take for the government for initiating and extending the processes of political democratisation. In the first instance, he observes that the spirit of public opinion research was written into the Soviet constitution of 1977, which stated that the extension of socialist democracy is closely connected with "...greater openness and publicity, and constant responsiveness to public opinion" (Korobeinikov, 1988, p.160). Secondly, in a more concrete sense polls assisted politicians by identifying public attitudes to reform; they provided feedback from citizens in terms of their views about government plans, and assisted policy-formulation and implementation. On political reform, public opinion polls were conducted to help clarify voters' attitudes to innovations in the electoral system (particularly the secret ballot) and the nomination of party candidates (Korobeinikov, 1988, pp.161-162).

Finally, Korobeinikov comments that polls were used by the ruling Communist Party "...to improve the work of the various party committees". Thus, two republic-wide polls were conducted in Georgia in late 1986 where "...respondents were given the opportunity to evaluate the activities of all governing bodies in the republic...[and to] indicate problems caused by Cadre policies simply seen as incorrect" (Korobeinikov, 1988, p.161). Polling institutes were established in many other Central and East European countries during the communist era, including for instance Hungary, Poland, Czechoslovakia, Yugoslavia, Romania, and Bulgaria (Piekalkiewicz, 1972; Connor and Gitelman, 1977; Klein and Krejci, 1981; Welsh, 1981; Worcester, 1987a; Kwiatkowski, 1989; Kwiatkowski, 1992).

Many of these polls were limited in terms of their ability to provide accurate representations of public opinion. White et al for instance describe the nation-wide network of polling centres established by Zaslavskaya in 1988 across the Soviet Union (VtsIOM) and comment upon their general unreliability, and large margins of error. Sample sizes were not sufficient to account for the population diversity, and extreme regional variation undermined the efficacy of polls in providing typical national pictures of public opinion. Furthermore, certain groups were over-represented - including ethnic Russians, urban respondents, and those in the larger settlements - which inevitably reinforced the sample bias. Data were usually aggregated, so that differences in response across key variables such as gender, age, nationality and social group could not be identified, and temporal comparisons were unachievable because of the lack of question-wording consistency across polls (White, Gill and Slider, 1993, pp.182-183). This raises a key issue when describing the development of polling in communist societies: methodological limitations of polling organisations in seeking to measure public opinion. This is discussed below in relation to Polish polling experiences which, it is assumed, raises general issues which can be applied to other communist contexts.

Methods and Issues in Polling Communist Political Systems

Political opinion polls conducted in the countries of Central and Eastern Europe had their methodological origins in the USA and Western Europe (Shlapentokh, 1987, pp.21-22). Prior to the Second World War, most sociological research was qualitative-based (Lutynska, 1991), but the new techniques imported from the West employed the sample-survey method. The following discussion focuses on various issues which emerged as researchers under the direction of Stephen Nowak and Zygmunt Gostkowski attempted to apply American political science techniques to Poland. It suggests that there are certain key methodological problems in polling public opinion which are common in all communist political systems,[2] and which are linked to the social and political context of questionnaire interviewing. These include: the levels of non-response in such political surveys; the problems associated with 'don't know' responses; and the influence of third parties in the interview process, together with the context of the interview.

The Interview Situation and Non-response

It is possible to differentiate two dominant models of the interview situation and the role of the respondent for capitalist and communist societies (Przybylowska and Kistelski, 1986). The first model assumes that in countries like America and Britain, the respondent is strongly motivated towards providing 'true' answers, and this derives from a belief in the usefulness of social studies and of the expression of one's own opinions. We have challenged this model in the light of recent empirical evidence, especially in relation to the British General Election polls in 1992.[3] A second model, developed by various sociologists in communist-led countries, assumes that the respondent has a positive attitude towards the interview, and is prepared to express his or her 'real' opinions, since social research contributes to the solution of social problems. It is claimed that the interview unites both the researcher and the respondent as partners in their efforts to improve social life. Both of these approaches focus on the attitudes of a 'model citizen', and assume that social research has a positive role to perform in society.

However, the findings of researchers at The Polish Academy of Sciences Institute of Philosophy and Sociology (hereafter IFiS) suggest that neither model is applicable to Poland under conditions of communist rule. They maintain that the public closely associated "...sociology, and social and political research within the state, its institutions, and the system of political power" (Przybylowska and Kistelski, 1986, p.22). Social surveys and political opinion polls were perceived to be linked to governments' propaganda strategies - part of a process whereby public opinion data were collected, and then manipulated and reported in such a way as to give the impression of universal support for the government and for the principles and programme of Marxism-Leninism (Kwiatkowski, P. 1992, p.363). There was little sense that polls could help either to facilitate beneficial changes within society and for individuals generally, or that such data were taken into account in formulating and implementing policies. Such polls were therefore observed with a large degree of ambivalence and scepticism by the public (Przybylowska and Kistelski, 1986, p.24).

A common view held by the public was that polling research was state-sponsored, and sought to monitor citizens' loyalty to the government and control their consciousness. As such, many people were reported by IFiS to be afraid of revealing any opinions which might in some way incriminate them, or else lead to some form of retribution by the state. The granting of an interview therefore often required a suppression of fear and apprehension. On the basis of these findings, it is surprising that people took part in opinion polls at all in communist political systems. Indeed, Lutynska reports that at the end of the 1970s, the refusal rate in surveys conducted by OBOP in Poland was only about 12% (Lutynska, 1987, p.47). This apparent contradiction is explained in terms of two major factors. Firstly, respondents' behaviour was governed by a traditional and deeply internalised cultural norm requiring them to be hospitable to people, including strangers. This accounted both for people inviting interviewers into their homes, and for volunteering to take part in political surveys. Secondly, the interviewer was usually treated as a representative of a state agency which formed part of the dominant power system. It was thus possible that "...fear of running into troubles or of being called to account for a refusal of interview dominates over the feeling of apprehension resulting from participation in the interview" (Przybylowska and Kistelski, 1986, p.25).

The public's reaction to opinion polling was however dependent on the political climate at the time of interview. Przybylowska and Kistelski (1986, p.26) observe that during the relatively liberal October 1956 period:

> A hope for changes in the execution of political power and prospects for gradual democratisation of social life and for free expression contributed to, and facilitated the introduction of opinion polls.

However, the introduction of Martial Law in December 1981 effectively stifled spontaneous and open expression of social and political opinions. Indeed, by 1982 "...the question was even raised whether it made any sense to conduct questionnaire surveys in Poland... [because of] concern about refusal to take part in questionnaire surveys" (Lutynska, 1987, p.44). Refusal rates were often recorded between 40% and 50% during this period, and these varied according to socio-economic and demographic status, and between regions and cities. Ultimately, sample-surveys were often biased under Martial Law conditions.

A number of factors have been identified which help to explain both these low levels of response, and of response variation. Lutynska claims that sponsorship of the research tended to make a significant impact here. The highest rate of refusals occurred in polls conducted by state-controlled organisations (OBP 28-50%, CBOS 23-44%, OBOP 16-28), while in academic surveys non-response ranged between only 3% and 4%. Furthermore, the name of the research centre may also have influenced respondents' willingness to take part in such research. A common problem for the Centre for Press Research (OBP) was that they were associated with newspapers which had a low credibility rating amongst large sections of the public:

> People do not want to speak with representatives of the press, since they fear that their answers will be twisted, passed on to non-academic centres, or may be used for propaganda purposes contrary with their own beliefs (Lutynska, 1987, p.48).

The subject of the research also played a significant role in reducing the levels of public participation in polls - especially politically sensitive topics. When combined with the effects of other factors such as the sponsor of the poll, the political context in which it was conducted, and generalised public concern for lack of anonymity in such surveys, this was seen as a major impediment to the achievement of representative polls. Finally, interviewers were often associated with government officials, the police and the security services, and activists of the ruling PUWP; during the period of Martial Law, the fear of retribution from the state for criticising the authorities and the principles of Marxism-Leninism in polls was greater than in other periods of communist rule (Lutynska, 1987, pp.48-50).

The Incidence of "Don't Know" Responses

During the Martial Law period, respondents in opinion polls were likely to exercise some discretion in answering questions on politically sensitive topics by registering "don't know" responses where they felt that the expression of their views might lead to some punitive action by the authorities. The use of such replies were therefore a means through which people could disguise their non-response in polls. Lutynska's research has found that during the period 1980-1985, the number of such replies trebled for questions which were 'easy but sensitive'; she claims that question sensitivity was a more important factor than question complexity, or lack of knowledge about the issue polled.[4] Kwiatkowski reports that the incidence of such responses were variable, particularly marked in terms of educational level, and influenced by the 'sponsorship' factor: respondents were more likely to answer "don't know" to politically-sensitive questions polled by the state-controlled institute CBOS, than by the academic IFiS (Kwiatkowski, P. 1992, p.367). This suggests that the reliability of many political opinion polls (particularly those conducted by state-owned and controlled agencies) and the validity of the data collected were extremely limited in communist political systems.

The Presence of Third Persons in Interviews

Research at IFiS has also revealed that the presence or absence of third parties in the course of an opinion poll interview will have a major impact on the reliability of the data collected. This will be further complicated by the context in which the interview is conducted (Lutynska, J.,[5] Lutynska, K., 1969). In the first instance, Lutynska reports that in a series of survey-experiments between 1966 and 1968, the percentage of interviews in which third persons took part ranged between 27.4% and 63.7%, depending on the research topic; the average rate was 46.1%. This factor was accountable for a difference in respondents' expressed answers by up to a margin of 20.1%. Third persons were also likely to participate as 'active respondents', rather than as passive listeners in the polls:

> The respondents may be reminded of certain facts or prompted, the strangers may present their views and opinions on the subject in question, they may make remarks referring to the questions, the interviews or the respondent, they may even begin discussions and quarrels in connection with some of the problems taken up in the interview (Lutynska, 1969, p.140).

This poses the question of how to interpret the findings: whose opinions were the subject of research - the individual, or the group?

Jan Lutynska observes that in later studies conducted by IFiS in the 1970s, researchers found that different answers were given by respondents according to where the interviews were conducted. He concludes that in general, interviews in the home were relatively more conducive for the expression of private opinions (especially on political issues), whereas in a work environment participants were likely to express views which they considered supported the 'official' positions on various topics and issues.

Summary

This chapter has demonstrated that the main methodological issues confronting the opinion pollsters in communist political systems were directly related to the political atmosphere which existed. That is, that people often avoided expressing their views on political issues in polls for fear of punishment by the authorities. Either they refused to take part in the opinion polls or else they answered "don't know" at strategic points within the interview. Generally, respondents attached a low value to the efficacy of political opinion polls, and the motivation to take part was low, especially during periods where traditionalist-Marxist-Leninists were in power. This lack of public co-operation in polls was summarised by Lutynska (1987, pp 50-51):

> They are afraid, do not believe in the anonymity of the survey, believe that this is a 'waste of time', 'makes no sense', 'will change nothing', 'is of use to nobody'…(or) would be doctored-up and used for propaganda purposes.

Furthermore, the lack of formal rights of free expression inclined many respondents to avoid making public utterances about the political set-up, government leadership, and current affairs for fear of retribution by the state. Instead, where citizens felt compelled to take part in political surveys, they were likely to disguise their real opinions if they felt that these did not correspond with the official issue-positions, or else they stated that they did not have an opinion. This was particularly likely in polling institutions associated with the state. Response rates were also variable. As a result, those who did participate in polls were unlikely to be representative of the full population, and the polls themselves to be unreliable indicators of the state of public opinion. As a consequence of these issues, opinion polling was a rather undeveloped activity in European communist political systems: the distribution of political power, and the nature of those both in government and in key positions within the state ensured that there was minimal scope and demand for polls; furthermore, where political opinion polls were conducted, the results were usually biased and/ or flawed in many ways.

Notes

1.   For a complete overview of the influence of political factors in Soviet society, see Shlapentokh (1987) chapters 1 to 4, and chapter 13.

2.   Of course, considerable differences in terms of the development of sociology and sociological research did exist between these countries, especially between the Soviet Union and other Central and East European communist states. For instance, Jones (1989) claims that while in countries like Poland, Yugoslavia and Hungary sociologists were often involved in subversive activities and organisations, the same could not be said for those in the Soviet Union. Other differences in polling developments, practices and conditions across these communist political systems occurred in terms of: the degree of state interference and decentralisation of planning, co-ordination and funding of the research; the extent of formal empirical sociology training amongst the practitioners; quality of methodological approaches and techniques, particularly in terms of sampling

procedures and data analysis; the actual frequency with which such polls were conducted; and the role of polling data in policy development and review (see for instance Welsh, 1981, pp.9-11).   However, if compared to their counterparts in western liberal-capitalist societies, it is possible to see significant similarities in the experiences of pollsters in Central and Eastern Europe to make such generalisations meaningful for analytical purposes.

3.   See for instance, Crewe (1993b), Jowell et al (1993), Sparrow (1993).

4.   These findings are reported by Krystyna Lutynska in 'Replies of the Type "It is Hard to say" in the 80s and their Determinants' from an un-dated collection of essays on survey methodology by Gostkowski presented to the author.

5.   Year unknown. Paper presented to the author on a research visit to the Institute of Philosophy and Sociology, Lodz in May 1991.

9 Complex Politics and Opinion Polling in Post-Communist Societies

This chapter focuses on polling in Central and Eastern Europe during the post-communist period, and considers parallel issues for late-capitalist societies which have been addressed in chapter 5. In the first section, there is a brief review of some of the political changes which have taken place since the collapse of communism. This discussion is designed to describe the Complex Politics environment in which polling operates. There then follows an analysis of the use of polls by post-communist governments, parties and mass media organisations, as well as the role of polls within the general processes of transition.

Political Change in Post-Communist Countries

The overthrow of the old communist order at the end of the 1980s was a remarkably quick and peaceful process, given the usually repressive, and often violent way in which civil revolts and reform movements had been quashed in the past (such as the 1956 Hungarian uprising, and the Czechoslovakian Prague Spring of 1968). Although the pressures toward reform and political liberalisation had been mounting in Poland, Hungary and the Soviet Union for a number of years, when the actual transition came in the form of popular elections, they were widely perceived as dramatic events. In East Germany, (former) Czechoslovakia and Bulgaria, the victory of popular front movements over their respective communist governments occurred within the space of months and weeks, while in Romania, the revolution ushered in a new regime within a matter of days. However, the transfer of political power from the ruling Marxist-Leninist parties to the new political forces has not led to the establishment of consolidated capitalist market economies, nor to stable western-style parliamentary systems. The processes of transformation at both these levels have become long, drawn-out affairs. The economic prospects of virtually all the successor states in the region are extremely uncertain, with structural unemployment, rising prices, and only halting privatisation typical; furthermore, while "...hopes for a democratic development are running high, seasoned political scientists have good reason not to exclude the possibility of a new kind of authoritarianism in Eastern Europe" (Berglund and Dellenbrant, 1994, p.10).

In this discussion there is an overview of the changes which are taking place in post-communist societies which provides an insight into the uncertain and unpredictable political environments which pollsters survey. This will help to gain an understanding as to the scale of the problems faced by pollsters in both acquiring a role within the political processes of these countries, and in attempting to measure public opinion effectively.

The Unfinished Transformations in Central and East Europe

One of the major areas of dispute within the literature on post-communist systemic change in Central and Eastern Europe concerns the *direction* of change, and the extent to which there has been a *consolidation* of 'democratic' political systems. Park for instance alerts us to the need to be sensitive to different 'schemes' of transition. It is suggested that Turkmenistan has undergone practically no change in the nature of its regime, whereas Kazakhstan's transition has been from "communist totalitarianism" to "post-communist authoritarianism". Meanwhile, Estonia's transition can be characterised as a shift from totalitarianism to a democratic political regime (Park, 1994, p.406). Smith claims that any definition of *transition* needs to consider both *fast-track* and *slow-track* cases, and concludes that there is no 'normal' post-communist society; countries within the region have arrived at a post-communist 'state' in different ways and over different periods. Furthermore, the process is reversible, and the outcomes will not be identical (Smith, 1994, pp.116-117).

However, one central issue which emerges from the literature, is that of the problems of "democratic consolidation" (Mainwaring, O'Donnell and Valenzuela, 1992; Baumann, 1994; Bryant and Mokrzycki, 1994; Pridham, Herring and Sanford, 1994; Pridham and Vanhanen, 1994; Welsh, 1994). This 'constructive' phase of systemic change (Terry, 1993, p.333) can be distinguished from an initial 'democratic transition' process (a 'destructive' phase which is concerned with the overthrowing of a nondemocratic regime), and entails instead the "...institutionalisation of a new, democratic set of rules for political life" (Munck, 1994, p.356). Thus, 'democratisation' should be seen as an overall process not only of the *dismantling* of the former nondemocratic regime, but also the *aggregation* of what the comparative literature calls a liberal or constitutional democracy (Baumann, 1994, p.17). This involves the establishment of new pluralistic structures, procedures and practices, the internalisation of a democratic ethos by citizens and key political actors alike, and their 'habituation' to the new political rules (Rustow, 1970; Schmitter, 1988; Mainwaring, O'Donnell and Valenzuela, 1992).

Much of the literature concerned with the prospects for democratic consolidation in post-communist countries is markedly pessimistic, and suggests that transition periods are characterised by great uncertainty with regard to both the process and the results (Munck, 1994, p.362), and that the collapse of hegemonic regimes may in fact usher in a variety of alternative outcomes. The establishment of a Western model of liberal democracy is only one of a number of differing scenarios that may emerge from the ruins of the old regime. An alternative version of the future for the post-communist societies suggests that "...an authoritarian relapse in one form or another cannot at this stage be excluded in some cases" (Pridham and Vanhanen, 1994, p.5). Indeed, as Welsh (1994, p.381) notes:

> Disturbing signs of governmental instability, stalemates in decision making, the emergence of violent protests, and war involving different ethnic groups, as in the former Yugoslavia, reinforce the notion that the outcome of transitions from different forms of authoritarianism are not linear and are often marred by insecurity and uncertainty.

Von Beyme (1996) maintains that for many of the post-communist countries, the future is likely to be one of 'anocracy', a mixture between democracy and authoritarian regimes. Ekiert envisages three possible nondemocratic outcomes of the transition process. These include: firstly, the reversal of the current process, and a return to communism, together with all that that entails (the establishment of a one-party or hegemonic political system, and state monopoly of the economy); a prolonged period of 'Lebanonization' of political, social and economic life, characterised by anarchy and instability; and finally, the possibility of the emergence of a new radically transformative, nondemocratic regime. The explanation for these pessimistic scenarios are given in the rapid collapse of the former communist regimes, that was superseded by the creation of a 'power vacuum' that "..was hastily permeated by highly fragmented political forces ...(unable) to form an effective political alliance" (Ekiert, 1991, p.288). As a consequence, many post-communist governments have been incapable of implementing programmes geared toward the alleviation of the acute economic and social crises which have beset their countries, and have as a result, alienated large sections of the public from the democratic process. The possible implications of such developments impeding progress toward 'democratic consolidation' are summarised by Schöpflin (1994, p.145):

After the initial rather naive democratic euphoria, the obstacles to democratic transformation became evident and the attendant social problems came to provide fertile ground for extremist movements of both right and left.

The lack of a generalised democratic political culture within the post-communist generation, together with the relative social rootlessness of the electorate discussed in chapter 4 of this book, makes the public particularly susceptible to the appeals of such extremist and nondemocratic forces.

Uncertain Post-communist Futures

This uncertainty in progressing toward 'democratic consolidation' has led Bryant and Mokrzycki to conceptualise the restructuring as 'transformation' rather than 'transition'. Their reasoning is that the latter term suggests an outcome can be predicted, but as the discussion above implies, the shape of the political systems in Central and Eastern Europe is opaque, and the transition to liberal democracy and capitalism far from assured (Bryant and Mokrzycki, 1994, p.7). Indeed, as Circautas claims, the very dismantling of the communist institutions without a carefully worked out plan of what to erect in their place has led to a political *vacuum,* ". . . in which uncertainty about the rules of the game has come to represent the only certainty . . . this vacuum is one of the most significant aspects, if not *the* most significant aspect, of the transformations underway in Eastern Europe" (Circautas, 1994, p.36). Baumann uses the concept of *liminality* to describe the situation in the post-communist countries. Liminality suggests that there is no clear unilinear path that connects the stage of democratic transition to democratic consolidation. Between these two phases lies the terrain of liminality, into which the post-communist countries have entered. For Baumann (1994, p.16), this is an unstructured, formless condition in which the future cannot be predicted:

> Liminality is not determined; neither is it determining. It is rather a break in determination; a locale of unbound possibility; not a crossroad but a desert where routes are yet to be drawn - marked out by the footprints of the travellers.

Absence both of strong governments and of established and agreed principles of democratic practice suggests that there are various competing scenarios which might evolve in these countries in the future, and not all of them necessarily entail the consolidation of democracy. As Baumann concludes, the prospects facing post-communist societies in Central and Eastern Europe are such that "...everything may happen, yet little can be done" (1994, p. 32).

Complexity and Party Systems in Central and Eastern Europe

As an indication of the extent to which the restructuring process currently underway in Central and Eastern Europe falls short of 'democratic consolidation', it is useful to look at the nascent party systems which are emerging there, for, as Cotta (1994, p.100) notes:

> The party system and its stabilisation seem to play an important role in the consolidation of a new democracy.

However, the party systems that are emerging are often highly complex and volatile, and consequently far from stable. For instance, Pridham notes that there has been a generalised fragmentation of the broad umbrella movements which had been prominent in the collapse of the former communist regimes,[1] together with a proliferation of new political parties and organisations (Pridham, 1994, p.34). The scale of this tendency toward party 'overload' can be established by reference to some of the elections which have taken place since 1989. In Poland for instance Ekiert reports that 240 political organisations, including 80 parties, contested the May 1990 local election (1991, p.312). At the first fully free General Election in October 1991, 29 of the 70 political groups that put forward candidates won entry to the *Sejm*, and reorganised themselves into 18 parliamentary clubs. However, as Grzybowski notes, only a short time was to pass after the election before these 'alliances' began to fragment and disintegrate (1994, p.63).

The Czechoslovakian General Election of June 1990 can be characterised as one of overloaded party pluralism. Bankowicz notes that, "there were literally hundreds of parties competing for the favour of the voters and the party system was becoming more and more fragmented as time went by" (1994, p.162). The seven political parties that finally secured parliamentary seats then underwent a series of restructurings, which transformed them into nineteen parties by the eve of the General Election of 1992. In Hungary, over 50 parties contested the General Election in March 1990, while the Romanian parliamentary elections of September 1992 saw 79 parties and alliances compete for entrance to the Chamber of Deputies, and 65 for the Senate (Datculescu, 1993, p2).

The formation of these new parties is bound up with "...a broader process of political aggregation, which has been untidy, remarkably varied, and faces a future that remains opaque" (Waller, 1994, p.38). Thus, Cotta explains the complexity of the nascent party systems in the absence of pre-communist pluralistic electoral legacies. Drawing on Rokkan's conceptualisation of the development of party systems, Cotta distinguishes between 'continuous' systems (such as Britain) and 'discontinuous' systems (including post-communist systems). In the latter, there are periods of democratic 'breakdown', but in Central and Eastern Europe, this period of discontinuity has been such that pre-breakdown (that is, pre-communist) parties are often unable to reassert themselves as dominant forces. As a consequence, the weak thrust of continuity from the past democratic experience (which was only relevant for a small number of these countries) provides significant scope and opportunity for new parties to fill the vacuum within the party systems. However, the lack of stable electoral cleavages makes it very difficult for these new parties to develop sustained links with sections of voters, which results in significant levels of party instability, party breakdown, and party replacement. Where parties are able to survive, it is likely that they will be weak and compelled to embark upon a process of coalition building (which often results in coalition breakdown).

Another problem facing parties in attempting to secure stable bases of support, is their frequent inability to develop distinctive identities. White, Gill and Slider for instance claim that in post-Soviet Russia, a plurality of parties have failed to articulate and communicate to the electorate coherent and detailed political-legislative programmes, opting instead to champion broad and generic commitments which demonstrate their acceptance of the rules of 'democratic' politics, and advocacy of the 'free market'. As a result, such parties can usually only be differentiated by the personalities of their leaders.

The fusion of these two factors - convergence politics with strong party leaders - tends to lead to the formation of weak parties. Consequently, such parties will be encouraged toward building political alliances as survival strategies. However, there is likely to be intense rivalry between party leaders, many of whom would be unwilling to accept what would be perceived as secondary positions to another in alliance, when they are dominant within their own parties. An example of this can be seen from Bulgaria, where the Democratic Party under Stephan Saevov, left the umbrella grouping, the Union of Democratic Forces (UDF) shortly before the General Election of December 1994. The reason is given as due to the outcome of a leadership crisis between Saevov and the leader of the UDF, Dimitrov, rather than as the result of any substantive policy conflicts (Gjuzelev, 1995). The implications of this issue for progress toward the establishment of a stable party system and more generally of 'democratic consolidation', are summarised by White et al (1994, p.159):

> The result is likely to be heightened conflict, ostensibly focused upon ideological nuances. Such conflict has been responsible for the splitting of many parties and the debilitation of the democratic movement.

An additional dimension of the party formation process in post-communist societies that is providing further impediments to the progress toward 'democratic consolidation' can be traced to the development of 'nondemocratic' parties. Lewis,

Lomax and Wightman note that the consequences of capitalistic-style reforms - recession, unemployment, inflation, and growing social inequalities - have had the effect of unleashing "...forces (parties) which sit uneasily with the progress of democratisation processes" (1994, p.152). The electoral advances of the ultra-nationalist Zhirinovsky in Russian elections throughout the early 1990s is a case in point, but similar movements have gained the support of large numbers of people throughout Central and Eastern Europe.

The complexity and volatility of these party systems combine to make for an uncertainty in their future shape and form. As Cotta states (1994, p. 123):

> We can reasonably expect that in many of these countries further significant transformations of the party systems will take place in the next years. Any conclusion about these party systems has necessarily to be tentative.

As we have already seen, the party system performs a key role in the 'democratic consolidation' of any post-communist society. Consequently, these conclusions suggest that the advance toward democratisation is far from assured in Central and Eastern Europe.

Implications for Opinion Polling of the Uncertainties of Democratic Consolidation in Central and Eastern Europe

The newly-emerging post-communist political systems must be seen therefore as in a state of considerable flux, undergoing processes of protracted and profound restructuring. For opinion polling, the context can be defined as one of Complex Politics. The future development of societies, and in particular, their political orientation and form at the *macro*-level, is difficult to judge and particularly volatile. This is mirrored at the *micro*-level on a number of dimensions. Firstly, as we saw in chapters 3 and 4, there is significant diversity of values, cultures, traditions and identities which had been suppressed under communism, but which have come once more to the fore. When these are combined with the general social rootlessness of the publics in post-communist contexts, the result is the creation of fragmented and atomised publics. As a result, there is plenty of 'raw material' for the polls to survey, but this public opinion is highly volatile, and the variety of cross-group cleavages results in often contradictory and spontaneous attitude, opinion and behaviour changes. Such conditions are not conducive for generating accurate assessments of public opinion in polls. Secondly, the establishment of political pluralism provides an additional dimension of public opinion for the polls to measure - electoral politics. However, these burgeoning competitive multi-party systems are particularly complex and usually unstable with a large number of new, as well as re-emerging parties, often forming shifting alliances and coalitions, based on a variety of historical, spatial, political, social, economic and cultural factors. This complexity is likely to reinforce the volatility of public opinion and behaviour in respect of electoral politics, and place significant obstacles to pollsters in achieving good quality data. The next chapter will consider issues confronting opinion polling in post-communist societies in which these developments play significant roles.

Opinion polling is also largely dependent upon both the changing modes and tendencies of citizens' participation in political affairs, as well as the nature of the policy process. Issues relating to both these aspects of post-communist societies will also be considered. Thus, in terms of the former, the overthrow of regimented and highly centralised Stalinist regimes has led to the development of a relatively confident and expectant citizenry, who were initially eager to take advantage of their newly-gained rights of free expression to take part in activities aimed at re-shaping society and the political system. Such activities resulted originally in high levels of citizen participation in opinion polls which, as we shall see in the next chapter, has declined with the more recent alienation of the public from political affairs. Furthermore, the public took a keen interest in the reporting of political affairs in the news-media; however, private ownership of newspapers in particular, has resulted in fierce competition and a reduction in the quality of news-stories. As we shall see in this and the next chapter, the decentralisation and deregulation of the information media has led to a drop in the quality and professionalism of journalism in the reporting of current affairs and of polls, and has led to a decline in the public's perceptions of polls, and of a reduction in poll response rates.

Polls and the Political Process

The remainder of this chapter will focus on the changing policy process in post-communist societies, and how this impacts upon the scope for, and development of opinion polling there. As was seen in chapter 8, prior to the collapse of communist regimes throughout the region, polling was limited in terms of its activities, the scope of issue coverage, and its ability to measure public opinion effectively.[2] In the period immediately following the collapse of the old communist regimes, the new and often inexperienced governments and parties were initially quite receptive to public opinion, and considered that polls were a useful tool in gauging the needs, interests, and aspirations of the citizenry, and of obtaining feedback on their proposals for building new societies. This section focuses primarily on the use made of opinion polls in post-communist societies by a range of political agents, including governments, political parties, and mass media organisations, in order to provide an account of the role of polls within the general processes of transition currently underway in these newly democratising countries. It is based almost entirely upon semi-structured in-depth interviews with both opinion polling companies, and with users of the polls.[3] The interviews were designed to help identify the rationale for opinion poll usage by these political agencies, how the information was built into policy and programmes, and the degree of importance attached to polls in general activities. It became clear during the course of the interviews that while opinion polls provided the opportunity for these political actors to articulate the views, needs and aspirations of the citizenry on political matters, ultimately polls were used not to establish some form of participatory 'direct democracy', but instead primarily to help political elites gain competitive advantage over their rivals and maximise their political power.

Governments and Polls

As is the case in late-capitalist societies, governments in post-communist countries find great value in using opinion polling data (particularly for policy development) and in fact are major sponsors of such research there. For example, in Hungary, polls have in the past been used regularly to ask the public how they rate the various government and state institutions, and to ascertain the level of confidence that people have in these. In addition, governments are interested in identifying citizens' satisfaction with the new political system, and what steps they would like decision-makers to take in order to improve the current political arrangements (Kiss-Schaeffer, 1991; Somogyi, 1991). Polls are also used to help define the shape and direction of individual policies. For example, according to Somogyi (an opinion pollster), the government polled the public on the issue of land reform in 1991 in order to gauge the level of support for the proposed legislation, and the form that it should take (either as shares, or in terms of returning the actual land to its previous owner-families).

Polls have been used extensively in this way by governments in Romania, Bulgaria, (the former) Czechoslovakia and Poland (Dohnalik, 1991; Strzeszewski 1991; Hoscalet, 1991; Datculescu, 1995; Popov, 1995). Opinion pollster Datculescu claims that polls perform a significant range of functions for government in post-communist Romania. Here, they are often utilised as a means of auditing public opinion, and particularly the main concerns of, and problems confronting, the public. Thus, his own company, IRSOP, was commissioned by Prime Minister Roman in 1990 to identify the extent to which the government's plans for economic and market reform had the support of the public, and indeed, the final programme drew heavily on the results of these polls. Furthermore, polls were sponsored by the government in 1995 as part of the general debate concerning the type of electoral system (majoritarian- or proportional-based) that should be devised for the next election. Datculescu also notes that governments place significant emphasis on opinion polls in the more general area of policy-development, including for instance: the technical aspects of privatisation policies; the development of social policies to soften the effects of national transition programmes on the elderly; and rural/urban migration policies.

One early example of the intervention of polling in the general processes of government in Romania, is cited by Datculescu as following a series of demonstrations in January 1990, outside the headquarters of Petre Roman's provisional government. The main demands of the demonstrators were for the Communist Party to be banned, and for its leading members under Ceausescu to be executed. The government, which had recently outlawed the death penalty, were unsure as to how representative of public opinion the demonstrators and their demands actually were. IRSOP conducted an opinion poll which concluded that in fact the demonstrators' demands were regarded by the general public as anathema to democracy, and more in line with the methods of the former Ceausescu regime. By the time the data were available however, the issue had lost much of its salience, and the demonstration largely dissipated. Nonetheless, following discussions with Prime Minister Roman, Datculescu claims that the polls performed a significant role in confirming in government circles, that they had the support of public opinion behind them in their refusal to cede to the demonstrators' demands (Datculescu, 1995).

A series of polls were conducted by the Bulgarian Socialist Party government during the water crisis of 1995. Polls had suggested that the situation was considered as particularly acute by the public, but the government were faced with a dilemma in resolving the water shortages: a solution seemed to lie with the development of a new water pipeline, but these plans were thought likely to entail negative ecological consequences for particularly the mountain region adjacent to Sofia; furthermore, a similar programme begun in 1990 had been met with citizens' demonstrations and riots organised by Eko-Glasnost, and the government were concerned not to provoke copy-cat actions. Polls however, suggested that mass opinion prioritised the solution of the water crisis over environmental concerns. The issue for the government remained as how best to action the public's demands without compromising both their environmental agenda, and the ecological system itself. In this, polls may perform a *problem-identification* role, by informing the government of mass sentiment on the matter, but the issue of *problem-solution* is too complex a process for polls by themselves to solve (Popov, 1995).

In (former) Czechoslovakia, Herzmann reports that his institution's polls

(UVVM) were commissioned by the Presidential Office for a variety of reasons between 1990 and 1991. In the first place, polls enabled the president's advisory team to maintain close contact with the public, and develop legislation from a position which is informed by public opinion. Thus, in the early months after the Velvet Revolution, polls were conducted with the specific objective of developing democratic mechanisms (such as the electoral system) on the basis of consulting the public via the polls. Secondly, polls are frequently used in parliamentary debate to legitimise policy positions, set the political agenda, or else to de-sensitise issues (Herzmann, 1991). Hartl (1991), of polling agency STEM, claims that the Czech Parliament commissioned a series of opinion polls on the Bohemian, Moravian and Slovak national questions prior to a vote on the issue in February 1991 which influenced the outcome of the debate:

> We prepared the results of the surveys before Parliament's plenary session on these topics. We prepared a report for all MPs two weeks before. Debate until that time was very emotional. Survey results de-sensitised the debate, and showed that the population were relaxed and calm about these issues. The topic then became pushed aside from the political agenda because of our survey. It showed Nationalism was not really backed by the population.

Polls are sometimes used in an equivalent way in Poland. In early 1991, proposals were raised in Parliament which were designed to outlaw abortion. In the interim period before the issue was brought to a vote, the government decided to hold a series of consultations with the public, in order to gauge the mood on the issue. However, according to one opinion pollster, the process was "...not a 'real' consultation because a lot of priests imposed letters against abortion upon their parishes, and a lot of pressure was put upon congregations" (Kwiatkowski, P. 1991b). The results of an opinion poll however published on the day of the parliamentary vote, contradicted the findings of these 'consultations', and suggested that the majority of the public did not agree with the anti-abortion lobby. As a result, the Polish Parliament voted not to allow a change in the law at that time. However, opinion pollster Nowotny (Demoskop, 1991) points out the problems of using polls in this way:

> On the question of the law against abortion, the danger is that the poll results are taken as an absolute, and the poll will be taken as a 'surrogate' for a referendum, and as an argument in the political dispute.

Some pollsters then are clearly wary that politicians in the new post-communist societies often place too heavy a reliance on opinion polls, using them as a tool for developing and implementing policy, rather than as a feedback mechanism to monitor the electorates' views.

This discussion has demonstrated the ways in which polls feed directly into the process of defining democratic structures and institutions in post-communist societies, and also help to ensure that political elites are kept in touch with people's views, needs and aspirations. It also suggests that polls may be used in governmental and parliamentary debate to influence the course of policy-making and legislation.

Polls and the Political Parties

Political parties are also important users of the polls. However, the nature of the party system is such, that it largely impedes the development of strong and sustained party-pollster links of the kind that are noticeable in countries like Britain. In Poland for instance, the proliferation of parties results in a situation where demand for the polls as a source of political intelligence to help market the parties cannot be satisfied because "...there are thousands of parties, and they are usually too poor to buy polls" (Kwiatkowski, P. 1991a). The same is the case in Romania, Bulgaria, and in Hungary, where there are relatively few political parties with sufficient financial resources to commission their own polls (Datculescu, 1995; Muscetescu, 1995; Kivu, 1995; Ivanov, 1995; Moser, 1995). This is a major fetter on the development of the industry, although the larger parties do frequently sponsor such opinion research especially on poll omnibuses[4] (Somogyi, 1991; Dohnalik, 1991; Hoscalet, 1991). Indeed, over 50% of respondents in the survey for this research reported that they had been commissioned by political parties within the previous twelve month period. Furthermore, the parties often make substantial use of secondary polling data. Hoscalet notes that the election campaign team for the Civic Forum in (former) Czechoslovakia conducted a detailed analysis of the polling results generated by his company, AISA, in order to develop a campaign strategy for the General Election in June 1990 (Hoscalet, 1991). Moser (1995), president of the Agrarian Union, states that in Bulgaria, it is common practice for smaller parties like her own to rely on secondary polling data because of the prohibitive costs of commissioning their own primary data. Ironically, she claims that at the December 1994 General Election, her party, along with many others, utilised polling data reported in a campaign document produced by rivals, the Bulgarian Socialist Party.

The uses to which polls are put by the parties in these post-communist societies largely reflect those for parties in late-capitalist societies. These include monitoring the dynamics of electoral opinion, targeting specific voter groups, and helping to build electoral strategies. Kivu recalls that from the time of Ceausescu's fall, to the middle of 1992, almost all of his company IMAS' work in Romania focused on political issues, and much of it was for political parties (although since that time, the balance has been more toward market research). This political polling research involves measuring general voting intentions, the reactions of the public to specific political events, the authority of individual party spokespersons, together with the values and demographics of different voter groups to try to identify electoral constituencies for party clients. Furthermore, prior to the General Election in Romania in 1992, polls were commissioned to ascertain the issue priorities of the electorate and of targeted groups, with the intention of modifying and shaping the *image* of these parties (Kivu, 1995). Polls are used in similar ways in Bulgaria. Gjuzelev maintains that polls have been used by his Democratic Party to assist the establishment of an identity amongst the electorate. Regarding itself as a naturally right-wing party, it found itself largely devoid of any social base within the electorate because of the relatively small size of the Bulgarian middle class (only about 3% of the population), and the virtual absence of any large, *private* industrial enterprises. Consequently, polls were undertaken in an attempt to solve this identity crisis, and revealed that it would be electorally beneficial to target small land-holders, and those voters whose ancestors had lost their land, industry and dwellings during the communist period (Gjuzelev, 1995).

Another major area of polling research undertaken by the parties is geared toward developing electoral strategies. For instance, prior to the 1992 Romanian General Election, the polling agency CIS were asked by the Democratic Convention to gauge the distribution of votes between its member parties. The data were to be used in preparatory dialogue to organise the number of places that each party should have on the coalition's electoral list, as well as their rankings on this list. CIS negotiated only with the dominant Peasant Party, which largely ignored the data because the results did not reflect their interests. Consequently, the final list was significantly more favourable to the Peasant Party than their position in the poll actually warranted, and led to intense argument between the party and its coalition partners (Campeanu, 1995). These developments helped to inform the Liberals within the Democratic Convention in 1993 that they should consider possibly leaving the coalition. Polls conducted by IMAS played a significant role in this reasoning, and ultimately in the fragmentation of the National Liberal Party (Kivu, 1995). The majority within the leadership of the Liberals decided to leave the Democratic Convention after studying IMAS' polling data which suggested that it would be politically expedient to do so, although one wing of the party opted to remain within the coalition. The National Liberal Party then split, with one of the groupings deciding to re-join the Convention coalition. Meanwhile, the group which had originally stayed in the Convention then decided to leave, and form its own independent Liberal Party. Later, in January 1995, the

Liberal PL93 commissioned IMAS to assess the impact of their possibly leaving the then 4-party Liberal Coalition platform within the Democratic Convention, and standing instead as an independent party. Polls suggested that this strategy would gain the party a 20% share of the vote, and consequently, PL93 left the Democratic Convention later that year (Kivu, 1995).

In Bulgaria, secondary polling data has been utilised by the Popular Union (an alliance of the Democratic Party and the Agrarian Union) to aid the focusing of their general campaigning strategy, after results showed that the public had little awareness of who the Union was, which parties comprised it, and what it stood for. Furthermore, polling data suggested that crime was of crucial concern to voters, and consequently, in the final 48 hours of the 1992 General Election, this issue became the primary campaign theme for the Popular Union (Moser, 1995). The Popular Union also organised a special strategy conference for the municipal and mayoral elections in April 1995, which had a specific focus on the electoral importance of opinion polling, and how to use its results in campaigning. A number of West European and North American electoral consultants and opinion pollsters addressed the conference, including the "Westminster Foundation" (a right-wing organisation), political advisors to the German CDU, and others (Gjuzelev, 1995; Moser, 1995).

For the Bulgarian Socialist Party (BSP), polls played a significant role in guiding their perception of, and orientation to, the government of technocrats which replaced the UDF administration in December 1992. Initially, the BSP had given qualified support to the government, but National Committee member, Miroslav Popov claims that their position changed dramatically following a series of opinion polls which suggested that the public were in favour of a strong, single-party-based government. Consequently, the BSP decided to withdraw their support in parliament for the government, which led to the elections in December 1994. As Popov concludes, in this process, "...polls assist (the) formulation of political strategy as an important tool" (1995). During the 1994 General Election campaign, the BSP made substantial use of their long-standing relationship with the polling company British-Balkan Social Surveys (BBSS), and commissioned a series of large-scale polling studies, the results of which were compiled into a campaigning document and sent out to activists three weeks before the election. The report identified 100 key geographic areas for focused campaigning, as well as which target groups should be singled out for special consideration (such as highly educated workers, and women working at home), and how best to win their support (including for instance which themes and policies to prioritise, and how to present them). As Popov explains, the campaign was not dictated by the polls, but the data performed a significant role in its development and focus (1995).

However, while polls provide obvious benefits to the political parties in their general campaigning strategies and political marketing, their usage for these purposes is often a source of significant controversy, usually because it is typically only the larger parties which have the resources to commission them. Consequently, smaller parties often attempt to discredit political opinion polls on the grounds that they facilitate unfair electoral competition, and help contribute to the continued dominance of the larger parties. In countries where the electoral system sets a minimum percentage threshold of voter support before a party can gain representation in parliament, this is a particularly contentious area for polling. Thus, Gjuzelev claims that theoretically, in countries like Bulgaria where such electoral rules apply, polls could perform a useful function for smaller parties: where there are for instance 120 parties vying for parliamentary representation at an election (Bulgaria 1994), polls can help create a bandwagon for a party if the data demonstrate that it has more support than the minimum electoral threshold (4% in this case), by suggesting to voters that their support for that party would not result in a *wasted vote*. While opinion polls reported publicly in the media might assist some smaller parties in this way, their lack of resources implies that they are unable to commission their own polls in an attempt to generate such bandwagons. Meanwhile, Gjuzelev claims that the larger Union of Democratic Forces (UDF) is able to sponsor and then manipulate its own polls for electoral gain as it attempted at the General Election in 1994; the UDF claimed on a number of occasions that its polls indicated that the Peoples Union (PU) and other small, anti-BSP parties would achieve less votes than that required to cross the 4% electoral threshold, and that voters should therefore support the UDF if they wanted to help defeat the BSP. In the event (and contrary to the claims of the UDF), three such parties and coalitions (including the PU) gained sufficient votes to enter the parliament independently of both the dominant UDF and BSP parties (Gjuzelev, 1995).

In a similar example, Anastassia Moser, president of the Agrarian Union, suggests that there is widespread evidence of collusion between the former communist BSP, and the polling agency BBSS in trying to disorientate their rivals. This party-pollster *alliance* has a historical basis to it, in that the BBSS is the reorganised, former state-polling institute National Public Opinion Centre, which operated under the command of the communist regime during Zhivkov's era - consequently there are significant and long-standing links between the leading personnel in both organisations. Moser claims that BBSS was engaged in a propaganda-based campaign to create uncertainty and divisions within the Popular Union of which her Party was a member. BBBS released a series of poll results in the run-up to the 1994 Bulgarian General Election which indicated that, in coalition with the Democratic Party, the Agrarian Union would achieve only 3% of the vote, but on their own, they would pass the 4% electoral threshold with 5%

support. These results from BBSS contradicted other opinion poll findings. In the event, her party stayed with the coalition, which ultimately gained 6.5% of the votes, and 18 seats in parliament (Moser, 1995).

Allied to these problems is the criticism and scepticism that both political parties and the public have of any close associations that pollsters may have with the political parties. According to Somogyi (1991), this is a hang-over from the communist era, where polling institutes were usually seen as an information-gathering appendage of the state, and as such a propaganda instrument of the Marxist-Leninist parties:

> Pollsters which are associated with a particular party are distrusted. For instance, the Meridian polling organisation are accused of being in contact with the biggest opposition party, the Free Democrats. So people don't believe their results. And (the) state-owned organisation is still accused of being associated with the old Communist Party. This company is the Hungarian Institute for Public Opinion. Their leaders were members of the Party. And if they had resigned, it was only to change direction with the way the wind blows. So they are still perceived as Party members.

In (former) Czechoslovakia, the polling company Demoskopy was criticised for similar reasons. Its founder was a former director of the state-owned polling institute UVVM, as well as a candidate for the Socialist Party at the June 1990 elections. The share of public support recorded for the Socialist Party was consistently higher in Demoskopy's polls than in any other institute's polls. Opinion pollster Herzmann claims that this is due to the biased nature of Demoskopy's field-interview force, which was recruited through the Socialist Party's newspaper.

Similar problems arise in Romania, where "...the election returns (in 1992) baffled the expectations of most analysts and contradicted the forecasts of all but one Romanian pollster" (Datculescu, 1993, p.1). Only IRSOP correctly predicted victory for both Iliescu and for his National Democratic Salvation Front - all the other pollsters' forecasts were that Constantinescu and the Democratic Convention would be the likely winners (Datculescu, 1993, p.29). However, Sandu notes that even IRSOP's record was inconsistent: of the two polls they conducted, only the second correctly identified the eventual presidential and parliamentary victors, although the poll results were significantly different statistically from the final voting results (Sandu, 1995). Furthermore, throughout the campaign period, there was significant variation recorded in the results of individual pollsters, as well as across polling agencies (see Carey, 1995). Sandu claims that one source of blame for these polling failures lies in the nature of the interview teams employed.[5] IRSOP, for instance recruited its fieldworkers from the Research Institute for

Youth Problems, which had been established by, and was accountable to, the Central Committee of the communist youth organisation under Ceausescu's reign. Sandu, vice-president of the Romanian Sociological Association, claims that it was therefore generally acknowledged to be left-wing (hence the strong showing for the NSDF in its polls). However, IMAS' interviewers were recruited through the right-wing weekly "22", the journal of the *Group for Social Dialogue*, which was active within the Democratic Convention. Both polling agencies have replaced their fieldwork teams since the 1992 General Election, following criticism from the general sociological community in Romania and from the media there (Sandu, 1995).

One of the most critically received party-pollster associations reported during the various research visits conducted for this study is that between the Bulgarian Socialist Party (BSP), and the polling agency British-Balkan Social Surveys (BBSS).[6] However, it is not entirely clear whether or not there is any direct collusion between the two in terms of massaging and manipulating poll results to create a bandwagon for the BSP in elections. Certainly, at the 1991 General Election, BBSS were the only polling agency to predict (incorrectly) a victory for the former communists, and in 1994, their forecast of the final BSP margin of victory was both higher than other pollsters' pre-election polls, and than that actually achieved by the Party[7]. Furthermore, there is intensive criticism of this relationship by opposition parties, and anti-socialist newspapers. Gjuzelev, for instance claims there is a triangular network of deception on behalf of the BSP, which includes the party, pollsters, and some media organisations: the largest circulation daily newspaper, "24 Hours" is a supporter of the BSP and arch-critic of the UDF, reporting only polls conducted by BBSS; and a subsidiary of BBSS, Mediana, again with a largely pro-BSP executive, has an exclusive polling contract with the state television company (which has a virtual monopoly over this media form) (Gjuzelev, 1995). As a consequence, many opposition parties, commentators, and political activists allege that the BSP, BBSS, Mediana, and a number of media organisations have between them a virtual monopoly of the processes of polling information diffusion within Bulgaria, and significant scope therefore to manipulate the public through 'fake' or massaged polls (Gjuzelev, 1995; Ivanov, 1995; Moser, 1995). The criticism which the party, pollsters and media receive, whether warranted or not, has the effect of undermining the credibility of polls generally, as far as the public is concerned. In Romania, IRSOP has in the past been condemned on similar grounds for the polling research they have conducted for the ruling NSF in 1990 and 1991, and later, for the NDSF-dominated government, and Iliescu's presidential team.

The electorates' scepticism of party-polling is further undermined by the proliferation of (largely unknown) ad hoc *ghost* pollsters during election campaign periods. This is a significant problem in Romania, where more established pollsters often claim that these ghost agencies (which are usually linked to various political parties) have as their sole purpose to manipulate electoral outcomes and the general political process. Furthermore, they often place little store in the need for adopting rigorous scientific methods, largely because they claim that polls are inherently limited. Such ghost agencies justify their polling methods (and any differences in their results from mainstream polls) by reference to the failures of polls to accurately predict elections in countries with established polling track-records - for instance, in Britain, Italy, and France in the early 1990s (Abraham, 1995). Thus, Kivu reports that in the 1992 Romanian General Election period, there were about 10 such 'fake' polls produced by ghost polling institutes, all using non-rigorous methods (such as sample sizes of 100 respondents). One such poll suggested that the Greater Romania Party, scoring about 4% in most polls (and achieving 3.9% in the election), had the support of 30% of the voters (Kivu, 1995).

State regulation of polling provides a further example of the publics' scepticism of opinion polling; in Bulgaria for instance, electoral law prohibits the publication of polls 14 days prior to an election, and a government ban on exit polls has remained in place since the BSP election victory in 1990. In relation to the latter, the action was brought about when the opposition UDF mounted a campaign alleging procedural irregularities and fraud during the election, including a charge that the German polling institute INFAS had manipulated their findings in order to generate a bandwagon for the BSP, and falsify the elections. Ultimately, the UDF campaign culminated in a mass demonstration against electoral fraud, which won the support of President Zhelev. As part of the government's response to this campaign, exit polls were banned (Gjuzelev, 1995; Stoyanov, 1995).

Polls and the Media

A further way in which the development of polling in these new societies is mirroring late-capitalist political systems is in terms of the quantity (and as we shall see, the quality) of media-polling activities. In Hungary, media-pollster activities are particularly vigorous:

> Each newspaper has their own poll, and nearly everyday an opinion poll is reported, [conducted] by different companies. There are five companies producing polls for newspapers regularly, and about one hundred small ones (Kiss-Schaeffer, 1991).

Somogyi reports that television polling and secondary reporting of polls were common activities during the May 1990 General Election in Hungary, where "...polls became a popular source of information" (Somogyi, 1991). However, in

Poland, the restructuring of the media industry in 1990 led to the collapse of the RSW, a huge state-owned media group previously organised under the Communist Party, and a potential major investor in polls. The replacement of a state-controlled industry by a privatised industry, guided by the free-market has led to a situation whereby a proliferation of small media companies, engaged in fierce competition with their rivals, and in a weak and vulnerable economic position, do not have the available resources to sponsor more than the occasional ad hoc public opinion poll (Kwiatkowski, P. 1991b).

Nonetheless, the media-interest in, and reporting of opinion polls is substantial in these countries. Where there are formal associations with the media as sponsors of the polls, the pollsters themselves report that they are usually able to exert control over how the polls are devised, conducted, analysed and reported. Evidence suggests that there is significant pollster autonomy from their media clients. Pollsters are usually confident that they are able to ensure that acceptable scientific standards of reliability are met in Hungary, Poland, (former) Czechoslovakia, Bulgaria and Romania for instance. There is close collaboration and negotiation with the clients on sample size and question-wording, and basic technical details are usually reported (sample size, number of sampling points, fieldwork dates and method, and size of the sampling error). This enables readers to judge the reliability of such polls.

One major area of concern with media polls however, is the organisational and budgetary restrictions which the media impose on the pollsters. When combined, these impede the performance and accuracy of the polls, and ultimately undermine their credibility amongst the public. Nowotny (1991) claims for instance that it is usual practice in Poland for "...regular newspaper polls to be made very quickly - one day interviewing, and the next day the results. This type of survey is only possible with quota samples, not random samples. So the statistical parameters are not very strict". A further key problem is the lack of polling expertise amongst journalists in many of these countries. As a consequence, they often misinterpret, exaggerate or even distort the poll findings. In Romania, as in other post-communist countries, journalists typically have no training in (nor inclination to find out about) the usage and reporting of poll findings (Abraham 1995; Kivu, 1995). They tend to have little understanding of social science empirical research, nor of the need for precision reporting, including the differences in findings from 'open' and 'closed' questions, question bias, and statistical significance; it is not uncommon for journalists to make what might appear to be merely basic typographical errors which in fact have significant statistical interpretation implications (such as the reporting of an *800* sample size poll as *8000*).

Often, the press will conduct their own polls. Muscetescu (1995) claims that there were many such polls in Romania during 1990, which tended to ignore basic social science research convention. Problems arising from this included for instance, the use of double-barrelled and poorly structured questions,[8] the over-sampling of easy-to-contact groups like intellectuals, and the under-sampling of groups which are more difficult to contact, such as peasants. Datculescu (1995) criticises the press for using *coupon polls*,[9] where there is no control over sample selection, and which are both voluntary and subject to self-selection. These results are later reported in other newspapers, often as if they had been conducted by established opinion pollsters using methodical and rigorous scientific techniques.

Another major issue in the media's usage of opinion polls, is the tendency to publish only findings which support a particular political inclination, or ideological outlook. This is especially noticeable in the press. According to Herzmann (1991), in (former) Czechoslovakia:

> Certain newspapers with a party bias or inclination, look for the data that fit their orientations.

This practice is common elsewhere in Central and Eastern Europe. Muscetescu claims for instance that in Romania, the media often use poll stories to strengthen their partisan positions; media output of polls depends more on what the data actually say, than on how professionally polls have been conducted. Consequently, there is overt political manipulation by the media (especially the press) of opinion polls (Muscetescu, 1995). However, there is a growing tendency for pollsters to assert their professionalism and independence vis-à-vis their media clients, and they often assist in the drafting of press reports. Nonetheless, the most important (and influential) aspect of media poll stories - the headline - is usually written by the journalist, with no input by the pollster.

The implications of selection, interpretation, and reporting of poll stories by the media on *ideological* grounds is given by Ivanov (1995). He suggests that there are two important aspects of contemporary Bulgarian society which have the effect of making the public susceptible to media-poll bias. The essence of these is likely to apply to other post-communist countries. Firstly, he proposes that one important legacy of communism is that of 'paternalism', one aspect of which includes the public having 'politics' explained to them by leaders. In the post-communist societies, this is reflected in the publics' tendency to look for opinion 'leaders' (politicians, the mass media, opinion pollsters) to help them make sense of politics. Consequently, in countries like Bulgaria, there is an absence of any completely independent opinion-*making* by the public - people are relatively easily influenced therefore by any poll they read. The second aspect of contemporary society therefore which contributes to the vulnerability of the public to manipulation is the misrepresentation or distortion of polling data by media organisations. This is likely to have a significant effect on public opinion formation, and as we have seen, is as common in post-communist societies as it is in late-capitalist societies. The mass media organisations tend to present data in specific ways in order to promote their ideological positions and the parties which best represent them, and to encourage the salience of preferred political agendas. In Bulgaria, virtually all the newspapers have at least informal links with political parties, and this is common throughout Central and Eastern Europe (Ivanov, 1995). The scope for media-polls to influence the public, regardless of how objectively and professionally they were conducted, is therefore significant in post-communist countries.

Furthermore, as is often the case in countries like Britain, journalists are often poorly trained in polling and psephology, tending to focus on headline polling data such as voting intention levels while ignoring other results. There is a tendency to sensationalise small changes in party support, without referring to, or publishing the technical details (such as sampling error) which might help to point-up the minimalist nature of such findings, or bring to the readers' attention the qualifications which pollsters attach to the raw figures. Thus, in countries like Bulgaria, Romania, Poland, Hungary and (former) Czechoslovakia where the electorates' support is distributed amongst a multitude of competing parties, a one or two point change in a particular party's poll ratings is often reported by the media as indicating a significant development. It also tends to suggest to journalists and the public that there is major variation amongst the pollsters, demonstrating that the polls are unreliable. Where this is the case, Herzmann (1991) claims that:

> The public doubts if the polls present a 'real' picture of society. They wonder if we are lying, cheating or helping a political party.

This public scepticism of polls is reinforced by the tendency in some post-communist countries to treat poll issues as headline stories themselves, rather than as illustration of current affairs issues. As one example, the Romanian popular daily newspaper *Ziua (Today)* reported a study which cast doubt on the credibility of the polling industry, and received significant air-time on national state-television. On a front-page top-headline story, *Ziua* (1995) reported that a North American consultancy, Rowlands Research Team had produced a 124-page report on the credibility and political independence of four of the leading polling agencies, and concluded that there was clear evidence of political complicity between IRSOP and the presidency. The headlines[10] read:

> Ziua Succeeded To Find Out Some Secrets From Washington. American Experts Demonstrated:
> Iliescu Succeeded To Manipulate Us By IRSOP For Five Years

Datculescu's Company (IRSOP) Has The Lowest Degree Of Credibility, And The Highest Level of Political Dependency Among Romanian Public Opinion Institutions.

According to Romanian opinion pollsters, such stories are not untypical, and reflect a preoccupation with, and often discrediting of pollsters by the media, especially if they have conducted work for political parties, movements or institutions anathema to that media organisation. For instance, both Sandu (1995, vice-president of the Romanian Sociological Association) and Campeanu (1995, Director of the polling agency CIS) claim that the editor of *Ziua* is a former leading member of the Romanian Securitate, whose paper has formal links with the anti-Iliescu right-wing UDF. The newspaper article fails to consider basic questions with which to assess the validity of the study's findings, including: who Rowlands Research Team are; why they conducted the research; on whose behalf the research was undertaken; how the study was conducted; and what criteria were used to measure both *credibility*, and *political independence*.

As a consequence of such developments in the use of polls by media organisations, the public has become increasingly sceptical of political opinion polls in many post-communist countries, because of the way they are used, and occasionally abused by the media and journalists.

Summary

In this chapter, we have seen that, in contrast to communist societies, there is significant demand for opinion polls in post-communist societies by governments, political parties and the mass media organisations. However, these polls are used predominantly to manipulate the public and the political process, rather than to devolve power to citizens. Thus polls are used by elites not to extend democracy in post-communist countries, but for their own political ends, and to help achieve their own ideological goals. These general issues will be pursued in the final chapter.

Notes

1.   See chapter 4 for a discussion of the general processes involved.
2.   See also Kwiatkowski, P. (1992), Piekalkiewicz (1972), Welsh (1981), Connor and Gitelman (1977).
3.   The intention was to gain a sense of the changing conditions for opinion polling, and of the development of the industry in post-communist countries. Specifically, the objective was to add depth and clarity to issues which had

emerged from a questionnaire survey of opinion pollsters conducted by the author between the end of 1990 and the beginning of 1993. The interviews took place during a series of field trips carried out in Poland, Hungary, and (former) Czechoslovakia in 1991, and later in Bulgaria and Romania (1995). See Appendix for a critical account of the methodology used.

4.　An omnibus is a regular poll conducted by an institute, where clients pay to have particular questions put to the public.

5.　Other problems cited include: IMAS' reliance on postal surveys, which had a very low response rate; and the high percentage of "undecideds" in all polls, whose demographics suggest they were likely to be Iliescu sympathisers (the polls by CIS were particularly sensitive to this problem, as they failed both to prompt this group, and to screen them out from the reported results).

6.　The historical roots of this relationship have been mentioned above.

7.　Data received from Ognian Shentov, Director of the Centre for the Study of Democracy, Sofia, May 1995.

8.　Double-barrelled questions appear to ask only one question, but actually ask two or more questions (such as "How did you vote in the election?". Here the respondent may be unsure as to *which* election is actually being referred to, and of course, they may have changed their vote at different elections).

9.　Coupon polls are questions written into the newspapers themselves which readers are invited to complete, and then send back to the newspaper for analysis.

10.　Literal translation by Dumitru Sandu, and verified by Pavel Campeanu.

10 Methods and Issues in Polling Post-Communist Societies

Introduction

As has been seen, during the communist era sociology, and in particular opinion polling, were perceived by the ruling forces as both largely irrelevant, and also reactionary. In contrast, polls play a significant role in contemporary politics in Central and Eastern Europe. The analysis of the development of opinion polling considered here concerns the methodological issues posed for pollsters in these societies. This will enable us to identify similarities with late-capitalist political systems in terms of the effectiveness and limitations of political opinion polling in Complex Politics contexts. As in chapter 9, much of the discussion is informed by results from interviews with, and a survey of, the pollsters and with users of the polls carried out during the early 1990s.[1]

General Polling Approaches Used in Post-Communist Societies

In terms of general approach, organisation, sampling methods, and interview procedures, opinion polling in post-communist countries is remarkably similar to polling carried out in the USA and Western Europe. The principles of polling are such that they are concerned with contacting representative samples of citizens so as to infer the political opinions, attitudes and beliefs of the total population. As for organisation, again there is a comparability with the Western approach. The survey results for this study indicate that only 20% of respondents conducted polls with a sample size of less than 1000 persons; over 6 in 10 of the respondents (64%) used sample sizes of between 1000-2000, which compares with Britain where the average sample size for polls is about 1500.

Interestingly enough, there was no clear overall pattern with regard to the preference for sampling methodology. Table 10.1 describes the sampling methods used by opinion pollsters in these post-communist countries. For each country, it shows the number of pollsters who use a particular method regularly, and indicates which is the most commonly used. It demonstrates that pollsters in most countries surveyed adopted random sampling methods, although in some countries (notably the former Czechoslovakia, and Estonia) quota sampling was more popular than random sampling, and it is likely that this popularity might spread to the other countries of the region in the future. This can be attributed to a number of factors. In the first place, while random sampling was seen as scientifically *superior* to quota sampling, the latter, because of its relative organisational and logistical simplicity, was quicker and cheaper than random sampling. Interviewers do not have to visit particular named persons, nor do they have to make multiple call-backs if they are initially unable to make contact. Furthermore, if a respondent refused to take part, interviewers using the quota sampling method could make a substitution, providing the *replacement* respondent met certain criteria as set out in the quota system. Secondly there was perceived to be a negative trade-off when using random samples in that, while they are often required by foreign clients (Hoscalet, 1991; Somogyi, 1991), there were often response problems involved in polling certain minority groups which might be included within a random sample, but which lived in areas which could be defined as *no-go areas* for the field-workers. As Somogyi explains (1991):

> Sometimes interviewers will not want to go to places where it is clearly too dangerous to conduct an interview. This is a problem with random samples, where you have no choice but to go to the named house.

This problem may be partially compensated for by the use of carefully selected interviewers who are familiar with such territories, or who are able to gain acceptance within a particular sub-culture under investigation.

A third limitation of random samples is the lack of available up-to-date sample lists, or *sampling frames*, from which to select respondents in polls. In Hungary, for instance, the main sampling frame used by pollsters is the national census which was over 10 years out of date by October 1991. There was also a problem concerning the accuracy of the sampling lists in Hungary, where it was estimated that addresses were wrong in up to 30% of cases (Somogyi, 1991). In the former Czechoslovakia, the central register of addresses available for random samples was inaccurate in 40% of cases (Hoscalet, 1991). To compensate for a similar problem in Poland the state-owned polling organisation CBOS used a substitute strategy in the form of a "random route" sample, where at each address, the interviewer selected a person in a targeted household according to a particular random procedure, such as which resident had their birthday most recently (Kwiatkowski, P. 1991b).

Table 10.1   Sampling Method Used Most Regularly in Central and Eastern Europe

Country	Proportion of pollsters using random sampling methods regularly	Proportion of pollsters using quota sampling methods regularly	Proportion of pollsters using a combination of both sampling methods regularly
Bulgaria	+6/6	1/6	1/6
Hungary	1/2	1/2	
Poland	+5/5		
USSR	+8/10	3/10	3/10
Lithuania	+2/3	1/3	1/3
Yugoslavia	1/1	1/1	
Czechoslovakia	2/13	+10/13	
Estonia		+2/2	
Latvia			+1/1

+ Most common sampling method

In Romania, similar problems occurred with the available sample frames, where the deficiencies in voter coverage, together with the drawn out bureaucratic procedures involved in acquiring the electoral register, made most political opinion polls (where speed is often an important factor) very difficult. Furthermore, the electoral lists were not usually available at constituency (or lower) level, so interviewers would be compelled to work very large spatial areas (Muscetescu, 1995). Consequently, there was a tendency toward employing random-route sampling approaches as in many of the other post-communist countries. However, as Sandu reports, a project is currently underway, with support from the European Community, to computerise the Romanian electoral register which will improve significantly its efficacy as a source for pure random samples (Sandu, 1995).

Another limitation of random sampling methods has been identified by Swafford, and has been intimated already. That is, that many respondents contacted at home would feel uncomfortable if asked to reveal their opinions on sensitive political issues. This is a particular problem in the former Soviet Union:

> The sample design employed by most survey organisations in the CIS draws names from housing or voting lists. Consequently, interviewers seek their assigned respondents by name. This introduces a measure of difficulty in convincing respondents that their replies will in fact be kept confidential (Swafford, 1992, p.354).

Finally the re-emergence of group differences, or *cleavages*, in the post-1989 period (based on class, ethnicity, religion, territory and so on), is steering the pollsters toward considering the use of quota samples in order to 'catch' these dimensions through the quotas set (Herzmann, 1991). As Slomczynski and Wesolowski explain, whereas in communist political systems there was (diminishing) social stratification, in post-communist contexts, the socio-economic and political transformations that have taken place are facilitating conflicts, and the differentiation of the public along a number of quite complex dimensions (Slomczynski and Wesolowski, 1990); while the group interests and value systems are as yet relatively incoherent, they are nonetheless beginning to take shape in many countries of the region, including Poland, Hungary and the former Czechoslovakia (Kwiatkowski, P. 1991b; Somogyi, 1991; Hartl, 1991; Hoscalet, 1991; Herzmann, 1991). Quota samples aim to ensure that interviewers are able to secure a representative sub-sample of each of these key groups, so that the final poll results comprise an appropriate mix of the various value systems which exist.

In terms of interviewing method, there was a marked preference amongst the pollsters in Central and Eastern Europe reported in this survey. Table 10.2 provides an indication of the numbers of pollsters who use different types of data collection methods for each country surveyed. Face-to-face interviewing is by far the most popular mode, used frequently (that is, between 50% and 100% of the time) by 8 out of 10 respondents (82%). For British companies conducting polls in the region (Gallup and MAI Information East Europe) this method was used in all cases. In comparison, telephone interviewing was not used at all by half of the pollsters in the region (51%), and of those who did use this method, virtually all (91%) used it less than 40% of the time. However, telephone polling in the former Soviet Union was comparatively more widespread; there, six of the ten polling organisations surveyed used telephones at least sometimes in the interview process. However, this might be more a necessity than choice, due to the huge geographic expanse of the former Soviet Union which must make face-to-face interviewing very problematic. This latter point may help to explain the fact that 60% of the pollsters in the former Soviet Union conducted postal surveys (although five out of these six respondents used them in less than 20% of their polls - only one polling agency used postal surveys in all their polls). Generally however, this method was not used by the pollsters in the region - nearly half (47%) conducted no postal surveys at all.

Table 10.2   Most Frequent* Interview Method Used by Pollsters Throughout Central and Eastern Europe

Country	Number of pollsters using face-to-face interviews primarily	Number of pollsters using telephone interviews primarily	Number of pollsters using mail interviews primarily
Bulgaria	+6/6		1/6
Czechoslovakia	+11/13		2/13
Estonia	+2/2		
Lithuania	+3/3		
Poland	+5/5		
USSR	+6/10	1/10	1/10
Yugoslavia	+1/1		
Hungary	+2/2		
Latvia			+1/1

* Most frequently is defined here as use of the method in over 50% of cases
+ Most common interviewing method

The Context of Political Opinion Polling - Problems and Issues

The context within which pollsters conduct their operations is particularly complex, resulting in greater methodological and technical problems than exist in late-capitalist societies. In an open question for this survey, respondents were asked "What problems, if any, logistical or organisational, (eg. geographic, communication, demographic, literacy) make polling in your country particularly challenging?". The survey suggests that the major problems are concerned with communication issues, demographic restructuring, spatial issues, and political change.

Communication Issues

In terms of problems with the interview process, face-to-face interviewing was mentioned by 8 of the 45 respondents for this survey, with telephone interviewing (7), and postal surveys (2) also cited as sources of difficulty. This of course is a fundamental issue for pollsters, and was mentioned by (British) Gallup for all the countries in the region which it polls. These communication problems were compounded by various other issues which were cited by the pollsters. Respondents claimed that basic infrastructure - the resources (particularly financial), facilities, and technology (such as telecommunications and fax-machines) - are not yet adequately advanced for intensive opinion polling. A major issue here concerns fieldwork. Although some of the larger polling organisations employed their own interviewer teams, smaller companies needed to sub-contract this aspect of the research to other organisations. However, in some countries such as Romania, no such fieldwork organisations were available (Sandu, 1995). Where they did exist, they were usually restricted to the major cities only. Furthermore, such fieldwork sub-contracting raised a general issue for the pollsters - it made control and supervision of the interviewing problematic. It also raised questions about the commitment of the fieldworkers to the polling institute and to the research project (Somogyi, 1991; Hoscalet, 1991; Nowotny, 1991).

Demographic Restructuring Issues

Another issue confronting the pollsters was *demographic restructuring*. Respondents in the survey suggested that the new electorates were too heterogeneous to enable effective aggregatable statistical analysis, and furthermore that they had little sustainable social identification. As we have seen, the populations are undergoing a process of relative social fragmentation, with a range of new groups and classes slowly crystallising, such as entrepreneurs, middle classes, unemployed and homeless groups, and various other underclasses. However, membership of these groups is often short-term, and as such their value systems are unlikely to be fixed.[2] Furthermore, the decomposition of the old social stratification system poses other problems beyond just volatility in attitudes. Herzmann claimed that in (former) Czechoslovakia, the basis upon which such groups were emerging need to be identified by the pollsters. These factors could then be built into the survey design as quota control variables. However, a problem remained in that there were no reliable statistics upon which to measure the profile of the population, and how these variables were distributed. It became difficult therefore to identify the proportions of the sample that should have been included for each category of these variables in samples (Herzmann, 1991).

These demographic changes also present logistical issues such as language and cultural complexities for the pollsters. The problems are particularly acute in research which is commissioned and designed by clients from Western Europe or the USA. In the countries of the former Soviet Union, individual questions may be culturally meaningless to some respondents because they have been designed to address issues or use languages which are appropriate for audiences of the sponsors' home countries, but alien to the respondent (Swafford, 1992). In Romania, Sandu claimed that many such questions were too long for respondents to understand. However, reorganising the questions may cause changes in their meanings, and consequently, invalidate any cross-national comparisons. The only means of solving this dilemma may be to involve the indigenous pollsters in the initial research and design stages of the study to ensure cultural relevance and appropriateness, although many international sponsors are reluctant to do this (Sandu, 1995).

Related issues can be found in many of the former Soviet Union countries which have very heterogeneous populations, each with their own language. Interviewers may need to be fluent in a number of such languages, and there may also be a need to have alternative translations of questions available for different respondents. There may also be various cultural norms which prevent some people from taking part in opinion polls; for instance, Muslim women in some Central Asian areas of the former Soviet Union may be unwilling or unable to participate in polls without the permission and presence of partners, husbands or fathers. This renders the use of random polling which is designed to contact specific individuals, virtually impossible (Swafford, 1992, pp. 354-355).

Spatial Issues

Geography and population density are other issues impeding the development of the polling industry in Central and Eastern Europe. The physical size of some territories means that the practicalities of actually conducting a set number of interviews in situations where the population is widely spread, is particularly difficult for individual field-workers. This is most pronounced in the region comprising the former Soviet Union, where the population density is very low (12.8 persons per Km^2) when compared with the other countries of the region, and with West European countries like Britain where it is 233.3 per Km^2 (European Marketing and Data Statistics, 1990). This field-work problem is compounded by deteriorating regional and cultural relations within national boundaries, which have been a feature of many post-communist political systems. It may be of course that there will emerge polling *no-go* zones, which are too dangerous for interviewers to work in (such as has been the case throughout various countries of the former Soviet Union as well as the former Yugoslav Republics).

Allied to these problems is the question of *telephone penetration*, which restricts the options available to pollsters for conducting interviews, given that the context within which these take place are so complex, and require methodological innovation. The dilemma for pollsters in Central and Eastern Europe is that the low percentages of household telephone incidence is more marked than in countries of the West. While in Britain it is 80-85%, the rate throughout Central and Eastern Europe varies, and was reported in the survey as at its lowest in Hungary at 17%. In countries like Bulgaria, Romania, Poland, Hungary and the former Czechoslovakia, the use of telephone polls was virtually impossible. Even where phones were available to the public, the phone system and quality of communication was often very poor, and the logistics of conducting interviews with named persons extremely problematic. Furthermore, there was no *telephone culture*, and "...many people would be surprised to be interviewed by phone" (Kwiatkowski, P. 1991b). The situation is compounded because of the unequal distribution of telephones. In Britain, the major variation in telephone ownership is between classes, and sophisticated weighting schemes have been developed in an attempt to compensate for the bias. However, in the countries included in the survey, there are many dimensions of variation, primarily geographical, but also social and political.

In Poland, one of the chief dimensions of telephone ownership bias was reported as between urban and rural areas (with higher penetration in the latter). However, even in large cities there were districts which were practically without telephones, such as Ursynow in Warsaw, which is inhabited by predominantly young people. Thus, telephone ownership was also skewed by age. Furthermore, the percentage of ABC1's on the phone was much higher in Poland than in the corresponding C2DE groups. This social class bias was linked to educational background (Kwiatkowski, P. 1991b). Spatial biases were also significant in (former) Czechoslovakia. Herzmann reported that only two attempts had been made to conduct telephone polls by the middle of 1991, and these were restricted to Prague, because smaller cities and rural towns and villages were not usually linked in any significant way by phone. However the experiments were a failure because both the penetration rates and ownership variation in Prague were severely distorted; it was typical for some areas of the city to have only one phone per block of residential flats (Herzmann, 1991). As Hoscalet (1991) concludes:

> Of course telephone penetration (in the former Czechoslovakia) will change, but it might take ten years.

In Hungary, disproportionate telephone ownership ruled out the possibility of pollsters drawing representative samples in telephone polls. Telephone ownership differed according to social class (workers and intellectuals), membership of political parties (while most people did not have access to a telephone, former Communist Party members as a rule usually did), and spatial location. As Somogyi (1991) explains:

In Budapest, telephone ownership is bad; in the rural areas it is worse. Recently I needed to phone two companies in a village with five telephones. It was a large village with many factories, but still only five phones between them. It would be impossible to interview individual people in that village.

Telephone penetration in Romania was reported as very limited (at 20% nationally), and markedly differentiated (70% in the larger cities like Bucharest, Timisoara and Cluj, and significantly less than 20% in small rural towns and villages). Furthermore, there was significant ownership variation across key groups such as social class (Kivu, 1995; Sandu, 1995; Muscetescu, 1995). In fact, only one company by 1995 had experimented with phone polls (CURS for the newspaper, *Libertada*) and these polls were restricted to Bucharest (Abraham, 1995).

Consequently, the use of telephones in interviewing the general public is ruled out for many of the pollsters in Central and Eastern Europe, and this would help to explain the extremely small number conducted there. This is a significant limitation for polling, especially in situations where it is necessary to complete a political opinion poll quickly in order to get an immediate response of the public to a particular political event. Thus the polling institute Meridian conducted a phone poll to analyse the impact of a taxi and truck drivers strike in Budapest, during October 1990. However, while they were able to produce their findings more rapidly than had they had done so using a face-to-face interviewing method, rival pollsters expressed little confidence in the results because of the alleged over-sampling of (telephone-owning) Communist Party members, which was likely to skew the data toward support for the strikers (Somogyi, 1991).

Problems of Political Change for Opinion Polling

The general processes of political change currently taking place throughout Central and Eastern Europe present a number of issues and problems for the pollsters. In the immediate aftermath of the collapse of communism, the party systems which emerged were noticeable for their complexity and general instability. As we have seen, for many countries of the region, these characteristics still exist. Often there is a proliferation of political parties, with high levels of party replacement, and shifting party coalitions and alliances. Furthermore, there is a generalised lack of voter-party alignments. Partly, this is because there are various social and demographic changes that are taking place within the electorate causing considerable voter volatility. The cleavages which underlie the party system are also complex, and in most cases particularly weak, and this prevents many parties from devising programmes and ideologies which match the interests of particular socio-economic and cultural groups and classes. Furthermore, the newness of many of the political parties makes it difficult to establish a high profile within the electorate. Finally, the electorate is particularly volatile, and typically lacks any sense of political identity - the recent successes of former communists in a large number of these countries suggest that even the anti-communist value system which tended to bind people together appears to have lost its salience.

So, how do these developments affect opinion polling in post-communist political systems, and what lessons do they have for late-capitalist countries? With the 'pluralisation' of the party systems, the standard "If there was a General Election tomorrow, which party would you vote for?" question takes on a new political meaning, with very important implications for the pollsters. Firstly, the emergence of new political parties, and the ending of the Communist Parties' political hegemony provides an array of potential homes for the new electorates. The party political landscapes have undergone a number of shifts and changes. In Poland for instance, Solidarity, which gained a landslide victory at the 'restricted' elections in June 1989, has subsequently disintegrated. The anti-system consensus which previously bound together a heterogeneous coalition of disparate anti-communist forces (socialists, conservatives, liberals, the Catholic Church and so on) fractured in the face of continued economic recession and social decline. By the beginning of 1991, Solidarity had split into three political movements, each with their own parties and factions. Many of these have since undergone further splits and mergers. Furthermore, the Polish Peasant Party underwent a process of reorganisation and then fragmentation, while the parties of the Left passed through a process of alignment, dealignment and realignment.

The party system in Poland still has all the makings of a *party overload* system. Indeed at the 1993 parliamentary elections, the winning left-wing coalition, the Democratic Left Alliance (SLD) comprised 28 groups, including descendants of the former ruling communists, the PZPR, trade union organisations, women's movements, socialists and others (Lewis, 1993, p.31). Although the new electoral law set a 5% threshold for parliamentary representation designed to decelerate the process of party fragmentation and political instability (Lewis, 1993, p.29), some commentators are sceptical of the effectiveness of such a measure:

> Some of the parties gaining representation, including the winning Alliance of the Democratic Left, were broad coalitions of a variety of political groups, and it is yet too early to say whether or not the new electoral system will have a lasting impact on the political map in Poland (Grzybowsky, 1994, p.69).

Such complexity is a common feature for the party systems throughout the post-communist countries.[3] Datculescu argues that there is a general pattern of complexity in the party systems of Central and Eastern Europe, in which the "inflationary number of parties and candidates makes it almost impossible for voters to decide on the basis of differentiation between individual merits and assets" (Datculescu, 1992, p.7). Such a pattern can be very confusing for voters in these new societies - it will affect how well a candidate is known, the salience and visibility of an election, and the degree of crystallisation of voter attitudes.

The ability of the pollsters to trace voting alignments, especially in election periods, is made more arduous by these political developments. The range of political parties as potential homes for voters is such that monitoring party shares of electoral support, and forecasting electoral outcomes is extremely problematic. Somogyi (1991) of Mareco in Hungary explains the concern amongst pollsters:

> We have ten or so major parties, and many smaller parties . . . we will not do pre-election polls because the party system is so complex. If you get it (the election forecast) wrong, you can get a very bad image, so we must get it right to convince our major clients that we are good at our work.

Furthermore, the huge number of parties competing for votes inevitably results in a situation where typically, many will fail to achieve a share of public support above the typical margin of error of 3%. The problem for the opinion pollsters here is that it is generally taken that if a party achieves a percentage share of electoral support that is smaller than the margin of error in an opinion poll, then the result will not be meaningful in any real way. Consequently, forecasting the electoral performance of these parties is extremely problematic (Kwiatkowski, P., 1991b).

However it is not just increased electoral choice which complicates the tasks for pollsters when trying to forecast general election outcomes. Citizens often find it difficult to differentiate their preferred party from other parties because of the similarity of party names. Hence it is not surprising to note that in (former) Czechoslovakia, poll interviewers complained that respondents at the 1990 General Election often got confused when asked to choose their favourite party from a list which included (amongst others) the Civic Democratic Party, the Civic Democratic Alliance, and Civic Movement (Herzmann, 1991). In Romania in 1995, for instance, there were five 'Liberal' parties, and opinion pollster Kivu maintains that much of the supposed 'volatility' in polls can be accounted for by voter confusion when presented with a show-card which lists numerous parties with similar names. The proliferation of Nationalist parties also contributes to this labelling complexity in polls, where the names of these parties are typically very similar.

The problem is further reinforced by the virtually continual reorganisation of party coalitions and alliances. The Romanian opposition UDF for instance, has a very volatile party composition, and consequently, when voters attempt to express their support or not for this umbrella movement, it is difficult to recall whether or not it contains their preferred party (Kivu, 1995). Related to this issue is the tendency toward the *personalisation* of politics which was mentioned earlier. Muscetescu (1995) at the CSOP polling agency, notes that, as a consequence of this phenomenon, even where respondents do identify with a particular party, this may lead to problems in opinion polls. What he defines as *inertia voting* for instance, had the result of benefiting the NSF in the 1992 Romanian General Election, because many voters thought that it was still the party of President Iliescu (who in fact had joined the breakaway NDSF). A combination of these factors emerged as a major issue for the pollsters in Poland following the break-up of Solidarity at the beginning of the 1990s:

> The parliamentary elections this Autumn (October 1991) will be extremely difficult for polling institutes because political life is so volatile, and the names of the parties are 'empty songs' for many people. We have hundreds of parties, and people will answer the question 'which candidate will you support?' without really knowing who they are, or what they are talking about (Strzeszewski, 1991).

These problems have their origins partly in the absence of any political identity amongst the majority of the electorate. The lack of attachments between the multitude of parties and the new electorates serve to further complicate the pollsters' tasks. This is not surprising, bearing in mind the relative newness of the political parties and coalitions in these post-communist societies, as well as the lack of any clear programme or ideology being promoted:

> The situation is made complex because the parties do not know their political 'place'. So how should the voter know who the parties are if the parties themselves don't know. Therefore they (voters) cannot say who they will vote for, because the parties have not clearly defined themselves and their policies. So the problem of course for pollsters is that it is difficult to say that, if your opinion is this, then you will vote for that party, because that party's position on that issue is likely to change (Somogyi, 1991).

This is further reinforced by (and underpins) the volatility of the newly enfranchised electorate. Pollsters surveyed as part of this research reported that, firstly there were few signs of any emerging alliances between groups of voters and the parties, and that secondly, trends in political views were generally unstable. Finally, they reported that there were large numbers of voters who were unable to decide upon their preferred political parties and candidates in opinion polls. Herzmann reports for instance that at the 1990 Czechoslovak parliamentary elections, only 15% of voters remained undecided up until the last week before voting (this compares with 21% in Britain in 1992). However, by the end of 1991, the percentage of 'undecided' voters had increased to 17% in the Slovak region, and 29% in the Czech Republic:

If you add the instability of the electorate - the 'changers' - to the 'don't knows', this leaves a great amount of problems for pollsters to forecast the election, especially as there are not really any parties with a large share of support (Herzmann, 1991).

This voter volatility is also apparent in other countries. Somogyi claims that in Hungary "...there is a big majority of people who do not know how they will vote, and they are not used to having an opinion about political issues" (Somogyi, 1991), while in Poland, Dohnalik notes that there is substantial variation in the trends of public support for the government and political institutions (Dohnalik, 1991). In Romania, Datculescu reports that late decision-making by the newly-enfranchised electorate makes it particularly difficult for pollsters to forecast the likely share of support for parties at elections. He claims that a common feature in all post-communist elections is that "...many voters did not have voting intentions in any meaningful sense of the word until the final days before elections and even then, their intentions were not firm" (Datculescu, 1992, p.7). Perhaps, the volatility of public opinion in the post-communist systems is best summarised by Zaslavskaya, who mentions that in the region comprising the former Soviet Union "...the main generalising characteristics of public consciousness today are its marginal, or transient character, its instability, morbid sensibility and explosiveness" (Zaslavskaya, 1990, p.25).

The final problem for opinion pollsters caused by political restructuring in post-communist societies is concerned with response rates in polls. People's unwillingness to participate in polls was cited by respondents in the survey as a major obstacle to providing accurate measures of public opinion, and particularly voters' party preferences. The situation can be illustrated by reference to the East German experience of the British On-Line Telephone Services polling agency, which reported that "... the main reason for refusals was that some people were worried about answering questions over the phone ... some just hung up, others explained that they were anxious or hesitant to talk to strangers" (Schulz, 1989, p.3). This fear of personal expression was still evident during the General Election there in March 1990, when The Guardian reported that "... Voters who are used to keeping their opinions to themselves after living in a Communist state might be reluctant to talk freely to the pollsters" (Reuter, 1990, p.14).

There is no doubt however, that the situation was far more acute under the old communist regimes, and that there are historical precedents which suggest that in periods of political reform, the public's willingness to respond does improve. Thus, in 1968-69, one of the ways that Czechoslovakian citizens felt they could influence the pace and direction of reform was through participating in polls.[4] Supporting this idea, Gitelman observed that "... the universal experience has been that following a period of 'acculturisation' to opinion research, East European publics respond very favourably (to opinion pollsters)" (Gitelman, 1977, p.11).

Indeed according to the survey carried out as part of this research, although there were major problems involved in organising face-to-face interviews for polls, the refusal rate was typically within acceptable limits: 30 of the 45 respondents reported it as 10% or less. This is generally because people felt more confident in post-communist societies that they could speak openly about political affairs than had been the case in the past:

> People are now more willing to take part because they know nothing can happen to them if they express their views (Hoscalet, 1991).

However, there are significant numbers of *refuseniks* who remain unconvinced about the confidentiality of opinion poll interviews, and either refuse to participate entirely, or else falsify their answers in order to express what they feel is the socially or politically acceptable answer. Both Campeanu (CIS) and Kivu (IMAS) report that a common problem confronting polling agencies in Romania, is that many potential respondents ". . . still have reflexes of times when you had to give the 'right' answer to a question" (Kivu, 1995). They claim that this is most serious in small rural and provincial communities where the local administration has significant power and strong information networks. Thus, respondents may be wary of expressing negative views about the party in office, or of revealing their genuine voting preference, either because to do so may incur a withdrawal of privileges, or else some negative sanctions (Campeanu, 1995; Kivu, 1995).

An additional problem for the opinion pollsters concerns the alienation from political life which many citizens are experiencing, fuelled by the failure of the new political regimes to solve immediate economic and social problems. Consequently, the initial euphoria which greeted the collapse of communist rule throughout the region, and which was reflected in the high levels of public participation in opinion polls, has been replaced by scepticism and apathy and, importantly for the pollsters, a corresponding increase in the rate of refusals in polls. As Somogyi (1991) reports:

> Now the situation is changing. People are fed up with politics which does not put bread on the table, and the non-response level has increased to between 10% and 20%.

A similar situation exists in (the former) Czechoslovakia, Romania, Bulgaria, and in Poland, where the impact of economic restructuring has resulted in a mood of pessimism and political suspicion amongst the public:

> Many are frustrated with the economic problems, and hate all politicians and political elites, especially the working class and peasants, so anything is possible . . . Many

want to withdraw from politics and any form of political participation. This is made worse, because many candidates promise everything, and are not able to do anything" (Kwiatkowski, P. 1991b).

Members of the new socially, economically, and culturally disadvantaged groups are most likely to retreat from political life in this way, and to avoid or refuse to participate in opinion polls. (Herzmann, 1991). Furthermore, people are unsure about the future pulse of democratisation. In Hungary for instance, the reaction of the public to the attempted coup in the former Soviet Union in September 1991 was one of fear; many people thought that the events might lead to a reversal of the internal political democratisation process by external forces. As a consequence, the refusal rate in Hungarian political opinion polls increased at that time (Somogyi, 1991). This suggests that the public's participation in polls may be partially linked to the sense of internal and external political stability or instability which pervades.

Summary

The political environment is particularly volatile in post-communist societies, and subsequently difficult for the pollsters to assess. We have seen that the publics which have emerged are heterogeneous, and as yet relatively undefined. There are no obvious characteristics which tie these groups to the political parties or help to shape stable political priorities and orientations which the pollsters could otherwise simply monitor and estimate over time. The volatility which emerges through this is compounded by the restructuring of the political landscape. The growth of pluralistic political systems often snowballs into *party overload* systems, which are characterised by high levels of party replacement, and an ongoing process of party coalition and/or fragmentation.

Allied to these problems is the general absence of any coherent programmes or political ideologies put forward by the majority of the parties. This ultimately results in a failure both to develop political identities and to appeal to specific groups of the electorate. Consequently, the parties are often unable to form political bases amongst the public, and their support tends to come from an amorphous mass of the citizenry rather than any clearly identifiable groups. The general absence of stable party-voter relationships which emerges from the combined impact of these situations is likely to create problems for the pollsters in their efforts to monitor the development of the unfolding party system, and to estimate the likely share of party support in elections. The tasks of the pollsters throughout the region are likely to be made all the more arduous by the potential decline in the publics' participation in opinion polls (particularly those covering political issues) caused by a pervading sense of alienation which people in the region feel from political life. It also appears that there are many methodological issues facing the pollsters which may impose limitations on the nascent industry. Consequently, opinion polling will have to undergo rigorous reassessment if it is to assert itself as a 'democratising force' in these new post-communist societies, and contribute to an understanding of the emerging electoral processes there.

Notes

1.   See Appendix for full details of the research strategy used.
2.   See Chapters 3 and 4 for a full discussion of these developments.
3.   See the section on *Complexity and Party Systems in Central and Eastern Europe* in Chapter 9 for further examples of such overdeveloped party pluralism.
4.   See for instance Piekalkiewicz (1972) for a discussion of the role of opinion polls during the *Prague Spring* in Czechoslovakia, 1968.

11 Conclusion

For polls to strengthen democracy, they must function in the service of the
community at large and not become the exclusive property of entrenched interest
groups (Crespi, 1989, p.133).

Introduction

The purpose of this chapter is to compare the Complex Politics situations currently
facing pollsters in different European countries. The first section considers the role
and functions of polling in late-capitalist and post-communist societies. This will
enable an examination of the democratic credentials and potential of polls. The
second section focuses upon the various political contexts in which polling takes
place in countries across contemporary Europe, and how these impact upon the
performance of polls. The discussion will conclude that the conditions are likely
to be more problematic in post-communist societies than in late-capitalist societies,
although the processes of political restructuring that are gaining momentum in the
latter are combining to blur the distinctions in terms of polling public opinion
effectively. From this, there follows a review of the major practical issues which
Complex Politics political conditions present for opinion pollsters in both late-
capitalist and post-communist societies. Finally, new areas for research are
suggested to complement the findings of this study.

Polls and the Democratic Process

Developments in post-war Europe suggest that Gallup's hopes that polls might
help to improve the democratic process, whereby they would give the public
greater access to the centres of political power in societies, have been largely
unfounded. The evidence derived from the experiences of polling in post-
communist and (particularly *late-*) capitalist political systems suggests that polls
have contributed to the establishment of lines of communication between policy-
makers and the public, and this has improved the process whereby the needs,
interests, and aspirations of ordinary citizens can be articulated and monitored. In
this way, polls do have a value in terms of establishing linkages between citizens

and governments. However, the discussion in this book so far suggests that these bonds are only *virtual*, and that polls have failed to address in any concrete way the imbalance in which political power is largely monopolised and exercised by dominant elites. In fact polls, to varying degrees, have been used by these same dominant interests and groups to reinforce their political hegemony and control. This is the case for both late-capitalist and post-communist societies. The following sections will explore these claims.

Polls and Democracy in Late-Capitalist Political Systems

In late-capitalist political systems like Britain, there is considerable debate as to the extent to which polls complement and improve democratic practice. Their role is at best double-edged. On one hand, the political landscape is such that political elites need to be responsive to public opinion in order to hold on to political power. This ensures that polls serve as a platform through which the public are able to make some input into political affairs, but this does not include the *control* of political elites. Instead they are a means through which political elites can more effectively compete for political power. Polls provide such elites with the information through which they can be more responsive to the electorate, consider their views in the design, marketing, implementation and modification of policies, and gain feedback as to the public's reactions to these policies, to issues and to events. In this way, polls fulfil a key function in terms of establishing political linkages between the state and society, and in so doing, provide a channel through which the public are able to make some indirect input into the affairs of government. However, polls do not challenge the dominance and power of political elites. Instead, polls generate the data through which these elites might devise strategies to successfully jockey with rival elites and leaders to secure political office and power.

We have seen that in Britain, political parties commission polls in order to win elections to government office (at local, national and European levels). In order to meet these objectives, the competing parties need to sustain the loyalty of traditional core supporters, and win over groups of unattached voters. Thus, polls are used to identify how party policies can be packaged and presented to the electorate in order to maximise their share of the vote in elections. Furthermore, polls are used in an attempt to shape the political agenda in such a way as to undermine the credibility of a party's rivals and elevate its own standing amongst the electorate, by sustaining public focus upon and around issues on which polls suggest it has an advantage over other parties. Because polls perform such a useful and effective role in these areas, parties tend to nurture enduring relationships with the pollsters, and structure polling projects into the heart of their campaigning machinery and strategies. In this way polls may be said to both facilitate and manipulate the democratic process in late-capitalist political systems.

Thus one of the major roles that polls perform in countries like Britain is as a provider of political intelligence in situations where sectional and ideological interests compete for political power. However, we have also seen that the very nature of this rivalry ensures that the public, through its views as measured in polls, have some influence over the outcome of these struggles between elites to capture political office. Through polls, citizens may exercise a degree of control over leaders who are held partially accountable for their actions and for their record in office. Furthermore, polls are able to exert a relative degree of autonomy from their sponsors. They are not usually tied to the state or to any other institution or organisation, but are privately-owned companies. In addition, it is not uncommon for polls to form associations to formalise their independence, and/or set in train codes of conduct to minimise the worst abuses of data by their sponsors. Consequently, polls are often perceived by the public as useful mechanisms through which they may become informed about and help to shape, political affairs.

This demand by the public for information about political affairs, and in particular in terms of the current state of public opinion on major political issues and events, helps to explain the increasing sponsorship of polls by the mass media. Polls are commissioned by these organisations to maximise their share of market audiences and (for private companies) to increase profits. Even state-media enterprises have uses for polls in terms of meeting their objectives as providers of public services, and reporting on all aspects of political news for viewers, listeners and readers. Where these state-owned/controlled media organisations are subject to deregulation and marketisation, polls will be increasingly seen as tools to help compete for audiences with other (private) organisations.

Media-sponsored polls extend the democratic process in late-capitalist societies by disseminating information about political affairs to the public, and contributing generally to the diffusion of political information in society. However, the pursuit of profit by these privately-owned mass media organisations results in a situation where political news is largely 'manufactured' - in this process, poll stories may be amplified, sensationalised, misleading, exaggerated, or just poorly reported. In extreme cases, polls may be commissioned with the intention of actually creating political news to secure audiences. Where data are abused in this way, polls are performing a manipulative function for the mass media which weakens the democratic process. Ultimately, such polls are involved in the artificial construction of political news, rather than the collection and dissemination of political reality.

Polls and Democracy in Post-Communist Political Systems

Polls are likely to have a more profound effect on the democratic process in Central and Eastern European post-communist countries, given the character of the new regimes there, the political inexperience of the emerging elites, and the lack of developed structures and mechanisms for political decision-making and popular participation in political affairs. After decades in which the state has been centralised and bureaucratised, and political power located at an increasing distance from civil society, the collapse of communism has been met with a clamour for democratisation and reorganisation of the state and the political process. In many instances, leaders of the opposition movements have been thrust into positions of political power with little or no prior experience of government, but with a vague commitment towards setting in train the pluralisation of political power, and democratisation of state structures and institutions. Many within the post-communist generation of political leaders have actively sought to devise methods through which they can consult with the public and negotiate new political machinery. In some cases, polls will have proved a useful mechanism in this process. They enable political leaders and the public to enter into a dialogue about the nature of the political process to be pursued, together with the preferred method of involving citizens in political affairs.

Furthermore, the study of polling in Central and Eastern Europe conducted for this research demonstrates that polls help to frame policy by indicating to governments and politicians the concerns and aspirations of the public, their views on different policy-options, their reactions to legislation, and their requirements of the political leadership. In such contexts, polls perform a more formal role than in late-capitalist political systems. In this way, the role of opinion polls in post-communist political systems can be summarised as one in which they perform a core function in developing the movement toward political liberalisation and democratisation. Under these conditions, the public will view polls favourably, precisely because they are understood to be a means through which they can be informed about, participate within, and consequently have some influence over, the political process.

Given three key factors, polls will provide a reliable and valid barometer with which to gauge public opinion:

- political leaders require objective information about the state of public opinion in order to help democratise the state and society;
- polling organisations should be free from any overt state interference, control, or censure, so that they may conduct professional studies with no obvious interests to patronise;

• the public should be willing to participate in polls.

However, polls are often commissioned by various agencies in order to manipulate the public and the political process. The larger political parties commission polls with the same objectives in mind as their counter-parts in late-capitalist countries like Britain: that is, to test their propaganda and package their policies in ways which are electorally appealing to voters. Often the relationship between these parties and the pollsters will be perceived as one of *collusion* by the public, and as a hangover from the communist era in which the pollsters were agents of the state, conducting propaganda to sustain the hegemony of dominant elites.

The poor quality of media-sponsored and media-reported polls intensifies public scepticism of polling, and contributes to a contradiction in the status of polling in these societies. On the one hand, the use of polls by the new regimes for consulting with the public enhances people's positive views of polls, and ultimately improves the reliability of polls. On the other hand, people's experiences of polls used by the political parties and the mass media organisations is often negative, and diminishes the public's confidence and participation in polls. This ultimately undermines the quality of polling. Given that the pollsters have less experience, resources and infrastructure for polls, this has very serious implications for the fledgling polling industry in post-communist countries.

We can conclude this section by noting that opinion polls have potential for improving the democratisation of the state and society in both late-capitalist and post-communist political systems. In late-capitalist societies there is significant scope for polls to strengthen and extend the processes of democratisation, but polls will stop short of challenging the basis of elite power in society. Polls will inform the decision-making processes within different, competing elite groups, and encourage these elites to respond to the demands of the citizenry. In this way, polls may provide a channel through which the public can bring some pressure to bear on those who wield political power. Ultimately however, they do not help to wrest such power from elites. In fact, the information which polls convey actually helps elites to compete for political power more effectively; in reality, polls reinforce the political hegemony of elites. Similarly, media-sponsored polls both contribute to, and undermine the democratic process in countries like contemporary Britain. Media organisations enjoy relative freedom from the state to channel information about political affairs to the public. However, the manipulation of polling data by the mass media is such that the information can often be distorted, and there is significant potential for the public to be misinformed about political issues and events. Consequently, the public's capacity to make informed decisions about political affairs and to hold elites accountable for their actions through polls will be reduced. Opinion polls are therefore to be seen as double-edged weapons in the battle for democracy. They enable the public to channel their views to political elites, but the sponsors of the polls (the mass media organisations and various political and economic elites) have significant capacity to design the polls, to determine which questions are asked of the public, to shape the political agenda, and to influence what political information is available for general consumption by the public, as well as the form that it should take.

In post-communist countries, there will be demand for polling information by political leaders to assist them in establishing new political arrangements and institutions. In this way, polls extend the processes of democratisation by providing a direct link between elites and citizens, and a meaningful channel through which the public can influence the political process. Such conditions are nearest to, but fall significantly short of Gallup's idealised 'direct democracy' in which polls were to provide a means through which political representatives could articulate the views of the public and translate these directly into policy. The inability of successive post-communist governments to solve social and economic problems has led to a withdrawal of the citizenry from political affairs and from participating in opinion polls. The possibilities in the future for the rise of strong, ideological leaderships whose political programmes do not involve any meaningful dialogue with the public further call into question the continued development of polls. The scope that polls will have in the future to influence the democratic process in such countries is therefore bound to the nature of the political landscape in which they operate. We focus upon this issue for contemporary European political systems in the following section.

Polling and Contemporary Political Landscapes

The degree to which polls strengthen democracy in Europe is largely dependent upon their ability to meet the challenge of change which characterises contemporary political landscapes. In this final section, we focus upon the logistics, appropriateness and effectiveness of political opinion polling in both late-capitalist and post-communist countries in the late 1990s. As a reference for comparison, we will group these themes under specific headings which were first encountered in Chapter 3: *Mechanisms for Political Participation; The Policy Process; Political Culture*; and *Party System*. This should enable us to isolate distinctions and similarities between contemporary European societies. Given the unpredictability, changeability, and volatility in the nature of these contemporary political systems, it will help us to analyse the developing prospects for opinion polling in the future, and enable an evaluation of the utility of the notion of

Complex Politics.   That is, conditions for opinion polling which are characteristically *complex* in the sense that there are significant processes of restructuring in societies taking place (especially at the political level) which are combining to produce contexts which make polling a particularly difficult activity. Baumann's concept of *liminality* provides a helpful and cogent summary of such conditions. Here, the very nature of contemporary societies, together with the electorates, value systems, party systems, policy processes, and type and extent of political participation, are largely inestimable in terms of the forms that they may take. These developments are likely to impact on the status, role and efficacy of polls now and in the future in ways which cannot be predicted.

Mechanisms for Political Participation

Late-capitalist and post-communist political systems can be usefully compared in terms of the conditions for opinion polling. The political systems are relatively open, with clearly defined channels of access available for voters to exert some influence over policy-makers. The existence of regular and competitive elections helps to engender a nominal interest in and articulation of political issues and electoral politics amongst voters, and a sense of political efficacy. The *ideal* context for polling existed in countries like Britain in the post-war period up until the early 1970s. Here, polls were likely to be perceived as meaningful mechanisms through which voters could extend the scope of their participation in political affairs, and increase their political influence. As a consequence, there were high response rates in polls for all social groups, ensuring that polls were representative. Furthermore, voters were likely to be active consumers of political information of the type provided by opinion polls. The relatively high levels of demand for such information was met through mass media sponsorship of polls, with polls helping to maximise audience ratings and generate profits. This encouraged increased diffusion of political information generally, and helped to establish lines of communication between voters and policy-makers. As a consequence, the public was likely to possess both a relatively high degree of political maturity, as well as significant levels of expectation about the political process.

In such situations, the scope for polling was particularly favourable, providing a means through which the public could exercise a degree of influence over their political representatives. Occasionally, people could help to set the political agenda through polls, but this was limited; it depended to a large extent on which questions were put to the public in polls, and these were usually determined by the sponsors - the mass media and various political and economic elites.

In the current period where Complex Politics conditions exist for opinion polling, a significant proportion of the electorate feel alienated from the political system in countries like Britain, and perceive it to be centralised, elitist, and out of touch with the aspirations of the public. In other West European late-capitalist countries such as France, Spain, and Italy, the corruption and partisanship of politicians is relatively more obvious, and public cynicism and scepticism of political affairs correspondingly more intense. Government office is often perceived to be monopolised by entrenched elites which promote agendas favouring the needs and interests of particular groups or classes to the exclusion of others. We have seen that in our critical case, Britain, this has resulted in disproportionately high levels of apathy amongst disenfranchised groups, leading to variable response rates in polls, and differential voter registration. Under such circumstances, response rates will be markedly low amongst groups which feel particularly disaffected with both the political set-up and the relative absence of meaningful mechanisms through which they might participate in political affairs. This will have a detrimental effect on the representativeness of polls by introducing bias into the sample. The views and opinions of some groups will be down-graded, resulting in the amplification and exaggeration of those expressed by other groups. Differential voter registration is particularly problematic for voting intention questions - some non-voters may be respondents in polls, and their recorded voting intentions may bias electoral forecasts. This is important where such data, when reported in the media, are demonstrably at odds with the actual share of votes cast at elections for the political parties. The failure of the polls to forecast election outcomes accurately encourages voter scepticism of opinion polling and people's lack of confidence in the results of polls. This further reduces participation rates and heightens response variability.

In these respects, the pollsters in late-capitalist societies are beginning to experience the type of problems prevalent in the newly emergent post-communist societies. In the immediate aftermath of the collapse of communism in Central and Eastern Europe, leaders and citizens entered into an informal coalition to agree new political structures and processes, and this galvanised a feeling of genuine political efficacy amongst the public. Response rates in polls were consequently relatively high, reflecting the publics' interest in both the processes of democratic reconstruction, and in the value of polls for communicating people's aspirations to political leaders. However, the failure of successive governments to solve post-revolutionary economic and social problems has tended to lead to a withdrawal of the public from political life, and to a reduction of participation rates in polls. Furthermore, the processes of information diffusion in both late-capitalist and post-communist political systems are relatively similar. The declining public confidence in the political process is likely to have a knock-on effect in terms of the quality and quantity of information diffusion. Polls are an expensive form of journalism and the media may look to other sources of news to attract audiences where the public demonstrates ambivalence to poll stories. This will result in a decline in the public profile of polls, and may lead ultimately to a reduction in polling.

The net effects of such processes for polling are common in both post-communist and late-capitalist societies. There will of course be differences, but in the current context, these will be of degree only. As a result, pollsters in these countries will be increasingly confronted with problems of non-response and variable response rates which will need to be solved if they are to provide effective polling services in the future.

The Policy Process

The political process in both late-capitalist and post-communist political systems is characterised by regular and relatively open competition for governmental and political office. This ensures that candidates and parties are to an extent, both responsive to voter's needs and interests and held accountable by the electorate for policies implemented and for political actions taken. Polls may be used in these contexts to identify voter preferences, and to monitor their reactions and levels of satisfaction or dissatisfaction with political decision-making. Furthermore, parties will commission opinion polls in their campaigning and marketing strategies to sustain core support and target key groups of unattached, floating voters.

We have seen that in Britain, particularly in the 1950s and 1960s, the major parties tended to be pragmatic in terms of their policy-positions, and polls were often used to identify whether there was a need for any review or revision of programmatic commitments. However, there was often resistance amongst certain factions within parties to the use of polling in this way. The degree and level of support for opinion polling was therefore dependent upon the political balance within a party between *revisionists* and *traditionalists*. The Labour Party provides a useful example to highlight the effect that the ideological complexion of, and balance of forces within, a party will have on the status and activities of polls within that party. Throughout the post-war period, there has been vocal scepticism of, and resistance to polling within the party. However, in the 1980s and 1990s, the consolidation of power within the Party by the revisionists and the marginalisation of the left-wing (traditionally the group most critical of polling) has led to a renaissance of polling within the Party's general campaigning strategies and marketing.

In the post-communist societies of Central and Eastern Europe, the scope for polling within the policy process is uncertain. Many of the initial post-communist governments were led by movements which had their origins in the mass popular opposition to the former Stalinist regimes. Consequently, polls were both perceived and used as a tool for channelling public opinion directly into the policy-process. President Vaclav Havel in the Czech Republic is a typical advocate of opinion polling for this purpose, but the more ideologically-oriented Prime Minister Klaus prefers a minimalist approach to government intervention within the economy and society:

> He (Klaus) believes in 'Economics' - the behaviour of people is best seen in the market, not in opinion polls (Herzmann, 1991).

Furthermore, the growth in public support for authoritarian movements and personalities such as Zhirinovsky in Russia, may lead to the emergence of governments in the future more inclined to rule by decree than by opinion polls.

To summarise, we can see that in respect of the *Policy Process*, there is a relative degree of overlap in terms of polling for late-capitalist and post-communist political systems. Both appear to be exhibiting change and volatility in terms of the role and status of polls in the policy process in similar ways. The future for these types of polls is therefore likely to be as variable in countries like Britain as it is in the post-communist countries of Central and Eastern Europe.

It is in relation to the categories *Political Culture* and *Party System* that the notion of Complex Politics conditions for opinion polling appear most cogent, as Britain and other late-capitalist societies undergo changes which broadly parallel those of the post-communist systems in Central and Eastern Europe.

Political Culture

In the early post-war decades, Britain was an *ideal* context for polling in respect of *Political Culture*. There existed a traditionally strong national political culture, based upon a Butskellite Welfare-State Collectivist consensus. The unity of a core set of values in society provided a stable framework of attitudes and opinions, and these were relatively easy to monitor and measure in opinion polls. There were differences in terms of degree of support for these values, but these differences occurred within certain limits. Where changes in values, attitudes and opinions did take place, these were usually relatively gradual and homogenous; they were national, limited swings, and pollsters usually experienced few difficulties in anticipating and tracing these. Tasks involved in developing national samples of the electorate were relatively straightforward, and low population variability ensured high levels of accuracy in poll results. Society was broadly located into easily identifiable socio-economic groups, based on the predominant social relations of production (labour, and the capital-owning classes). These divisions were only partially blurred by the growth of affluent manual workers and of white-collar non-manual worker groups. Class location predisposed voters towards particular ideologies and to support for social, economic and political solutions. This helped to generate and sustain traditionally strong and stable alliances between voting classes and their parties. This situation was defined by the concept of Party Identification, in which voting was usually emotive, and party support was long-term (for instance, see Butler and Stokes, 1974).

In this context, conventional polling methodology had a proven track record for producing high quality data relating to public opinion on political matters, and polls performed particularly well in forecasting the outcome of elections in terms of party shares of support. As a consequence, polls gained a reputation for reliability and for producing good quality data. There were innovations in methodology which were embraced and implemented by the pollsters, but these changes were introduced only occasionally.

However, since the mid-1970s there has been a steady decline in the post-war consensus, together with the emergence of new and post-class value systems, based upon a variety of cleavages including nationalism, regionalism, ethnicity, feminism, post-material issues and others. In the 1990s, the culmination of these developments in Britain and in other West European late-capitalist political systems will present a complex scenario for pollsters to survey, as public opinion becomes increasingly volatile. The electorate is likely to respond in an increasingly heterogeneous way to unfolding social, economic and political developments, with national reactions replaced by extensive regional and localised swings in the public mood. This may create problems for the pollsters in terms of devising their samples, including selecting sample points, clustering, working with limited sample sizes and so on.

There is a tendency toward the restructuring or dissolution of the traditional class system. A gradual, but accelerating process of fragmentation and heterogeneity is taking place, leading to an increasing atomisation of the electorate into a myriad of different groups. There may be overlapping (and apparently contradictory) complex membership networks. A new era of electoral non-alignment is emerging, characterised by class dealignment, and/or postmodernist political behaviour. Voting behaviour is increasingly affected by a whole range of factors, not just social class, and there is significant voter volatility. Voting will be expressive, and subject to a variety of long-and short-term factors. Such voter volatility is likely to have an important impact upon the ability of polls to measure public opinion effectively. Furthermore, if polling performance deteriorates, this may lead to diminishing media, academic and public confidence in the polls. If this occurs, it will necessitate the reappraisal of methodology and techniques by the pollsters, and the adoption of new approaches.

Britain can be seen to be moving toward a Complex Politics scenario for opinion polling which largely resembles the situation which currently exists in Central and Eastern Europe. Of course, the disintegration and fragmentation of society and of traditional value systems in the latter is at a comparatively more advanced stage. The collapse of communism has been a decisive factor in the emergence of a range of social, economic and cultural groups and classes, membership of which is often temporary and cross-cutting. Consequently, society is in a state of relative flux, and this is reflected in the general processes of opinion formation, where the public has demonstrated a tendency toward volatile and erratic opinion and behaviour patterns. The similarities in the nature of the political landscapes in late-capitalist and post-communist political systems are considerable in terms of their implications for opinion polling. This enables us to speculate that the issues currently confronting pollsters in post-communist societies are likely to emerge in countries like Britain if current trends continue.

The Party System

As has been demonstrated, the tasks facing the opinion pollsters will be least problematic in circumstances where the party system is relatively undifferentiated. The optimum context for polling will reflect the party system which developed in Britain between 1945 and 1974. For such cases, a competitive party system is the norm, usually based on two well-established dominant rivals, providing limited choice for voters at elections. This helps to maintain and perpetuate enduring links between groups of the electorate and the political parties. In such situations, there will be limited sets of political priorities on offer, and these will broadly reflect the interests of the principal competing classes. However, there will be a general consensus on the nature and composition of the party programmes, and this will broadly aim at support for, rather than alternatives to, the social and economic status quo. In this context it will be relatively straightforward for pollsters to gauge public opinion and forecast electoral outcomes, because of the enduring voter-party alliances and the limited number of parties available as political homes for the electorate.

However, the reality of contemporary British politics is that there has recently been a virtual dominant single-party system in operation at governmental level, with a multi-party system in opposition to the governing party. In many of the consociational party systems of Western Europe such as Italy, France, Germany, and Ireland, the complexity is even more evident. The emergence of new, and/or reinvigorated parties provides a variety of political homes for the electorate, and fosters increased tactical and protest voting and general voter volatility.

Opposition parties may enter pre-election pacts or agreements in order to undermine the dominant governing party, and usher in the prospect of hung parliaments, or coalition governments. The policy-programmes of the dominant/established parties will be subject to constant revision as electoral competition intensifies. Programmatic positions will shift between convergence and ideological polarity. New opposition parties are likely to present unorthodox economic, social, cultural and political agendas. As a result, the electoral landscape is increasingly complex for pollsters to survey. There will be greater scope for voters to behave more selectively at elections, and to switch between the parties. Consequently, pollsters are likely to find it increasingly difficult to track voting intentions and forecast electoral outcomes.

Again, as with the three dimensions of Complex Politics discussed above (mechanisms for political participation, the policy process, and political culture), these developments are similar to those currently unfolding in the countries of Central and Eastern Europe. The proliferation of parties which characterised the end of communist political hegemony has not significantly receded with time. The party systems are extremely complex, and are typically composed of large numbers of contestants, often forming temporary alliances and coalitions which later fragment and reshape. The visibility and profile of many of these parties will often be blurred, and the electorates will find it difficult to recognise parties which represent their interests, and will be unlikely to form enduring attachments with them. The process of complexity in these countries is clearly more obvious than in Western Europe. However, the problems which this complexity poses for pollsters will be similar, as late-capitalist countries like Britain continue to undergo processes of restructuring which are re-shaping their party systems along the lines currently in evidence in Central and Eastern European societies.

Complex Politics and Polling Practice

So, what are the practical implications of these Complex Politics conditions for the opinion pollsters in both late-capitalist and post-communist societies? If pollsters are to meet the challenge of change which such developments imply, and produce sound, reliable and valid measures of public opinion in the future, they need to respond in appropriate ways. It is clear from the analysis conducted throughout this book that this involves pollsters reappraising their methods, and embracing technical innovations where research shows these to be relevant, if they are to cope with the restructuring of contemporary landscapes.

The political complexity confronting pollsters in post-communist and late-capitalist societies also implies that pollsters carefully consider the nature of the electorates in their respective countries. This suggests that the methodologies and techniques of polling need to be driven by the social and political environment which they intend to survey, and should evolve to take account of these new conditions and of the new electorates. In our critical case, Britain, the experiences of the polls at the 1992 General Election has given rise to a number of detailed enquiries into polls and voting behaviour in order to establish the chief factors and influences of public opinion formation. As a result, a series of revisions and innovations in polling practices have been suggested, many of which have been tested by pollsters in experiments. In some cases, these experimental practices have been adopted as normal procedure when conducting opinion polls. In countries like the USA, Italy, and France, where social heterogeneity and political restructuring is endemic, pollsters should take similar steps to develop their methodologies.

In post-communist societies where the pace, nature and extent of political restructuring is more marked, pollsters would do well to monitor the effectiveness of such developments in polling methodology in the immediate future. This will provide guidance on good polling practice for the industry in their respective countries. Furthermore, pollsters in late-capitalist countries should carefully observe the processes of restructuring in Central and Eastern Europe which relate to and affect polling, as well as monitor those processes which are embryonic, or fast reaching maturity in their own countries. Through this, they should gain a clearer understanding of how electorates may change in the future, anticipate how they will respond to issues and events, and from such vantage points, assess the likely modifications and technical innovations that may be necessary for opinion polling.

New Directions for Research on Opinion Polling

In the course of this study, a number of issues have been raised or intimated which are beyond the scope of this book, but which warrant further research in order to advance our knowledge of the role of polls in relation to the processes of political liberalisation and democratisation in contemporary societies. The extent and impact of polling in the post-communist countries of Central and Eastern Europe could be explored in a number of ways. It might be interesting to monitor and assess the use of polls by governments which are dominated by former communists who had previously questioned the philosophical and political basis of opinion polling as a study of human consciousness. Another field which has been relatively under-researched is the effect on polls of de-regulation of the mass media, and the concentration of ownership of media organisations. And thirdly, what is the response of authoritarian governments and leaderships to polling in these post-communist countries where democratic consolidation has not been achieved? As they confront the various social, economic and political crises which have beset many of the post-communist countries, will they listen to public opinion as it is communicated through the polls, or, like their Stalinist predecessors before them, will they ignore the polls in favour of their own ideologically-formulated solutions? A final issue for consideration, is the ownership of polls in the post-communist societies. Under Communism, polls were carefully controlled by the ruling Marxist-Leninist parties. However, under the new regimes, who owns the polling companies, and how much independence do they have from the state, the mass media, political parties, and other organisations? We have seen a burgeoning international influence in the development of the industry - if the polling companies are owned by multi-national companies, does this imply that they are able to exercise relative autonomy from national elites?

Other areas for investigation include: the use and role of polls in helping to create a bandwagon for new political parties (such as Forza Italia in Italy); the impact of polls on forms of direct-democracy styles of politics (such as the use of referenda on the European Union throughout the region in 1993 and 1994); the advances in, and effectiveness of new polling technologies of the type currently being considered in Britain, and of their export to other countries; and what alternatives could be developed in place of polls if they are unable to meet the challenges of change which currently confront them?

Recent developments in European politics have highlighted the need to establish sophisticated mechanisms to enable citizens to exert greater influence over both the political process and the political elites who currently dominate it. Opinion polls provide one such channel through which the voice of the people can be heard above the din of competing, and increasingly unrepresentative, elites. However, if we do not conduct such research, then opinion polls will continue to fall far short of the ideal envisaged by Gallup. If we do not take steps to gain a better understanding of the role of opinion polls, then we do a disservice to democracy by leaving them in the hands of entrenched elites, and possibly therefore to be abused. If this is allowed to occur, then the danger will be that polls may be used ultimately to subvert and not to extend democracy.

Appendix: Methodology for the Study of Opinion Polling in Central and Eastern Europe

The methodology used for researching polling developments in Central and Eastern Europe involved conducting a questionnaire study of opinion polling companies there, followed by semi-structured in-depth interviews with other pollsters and with users of the polls. The intention was to gain a sense of the changing conditions for polling and of the development of the industry in these countries.

In the absence of a complete sampling frame of opinion pollsters, a *snowball sampling* approach was adopted, in which initial respondents provided details of colleagues who were then contacted for inclusion in the study. A preliminary list of organisations, institutes and academics conducting polling activities in the region was assembled with the help of leading British pollsters, the World Association of Public Opinion Researchers (WAPOR), and the relevant national Embassies and Chambers of Commerce. These sources provided the contact details of 20 opinion polling agencies from 9 countries. A questionnaire was then sent to these pollsters which included a question inviting respondents to append the contact details of other pollsters working within their country. Because of the nature of the sampling method adopted, the questionnaire study was on-going. Questionnaires were sent out over a period of two and a half years, from the end of 1990 to the beginning of 1993. Two waves of recall questionnaires were sent out to boost the response rate, each reminder two months after the preceding mail-out. Table i.i below sets out a response matrix for the survey. Of the 71 pollsters contacted, 45 returned completed questionnaires, resulting in a response rate of 63%.

The method of analysis adopted for this survey was *descriptive*, rather than *explanatory*. There was no intention on my part to identify correlational links between any of the variables, nor to investigate causality between them. My purpose was to provide an overview of the state of polling in the newly-emerging post-communist societies, to monitor the size of the opinion polling organisations, the scope and nature of their activities, and the range of issues which they confronted when attempting to measure public opinion on political issues, events, institutions, and players. The survey was designed therefore to gather *factual* rather than *attitudinal-* or *value*-based data. The statistics from this study have been reported in chapters 9 and 10. The data are aggregated, and the findings are generalized to the whole region. There is therefore no attempt to differentiate the experiences of pollsters in different countries, because the sample size of 45 respondents is too small for such detailed analysis. Nonetheless, the data provide a useful insight into the status and development of opinion polling in these countries.

Table i.i   Response Matrix for the Survey of Opinion Polling in Central and Eastern Europe 1990-1993

	Number of Pollsters Contacted	Number of Pollsters Responded	Percentage Response
Czechoslovakia	19	13	68
USSR	13	10	77
Poland	11	5	45
Bulgaria	9	8	89
Estonia	3	2	67
Hungary	7	2	29
Lithuania	2	2	100
Latvia	3	2	66
Yugoslavia	4	1	25
Total	71	45	63

This survey-based approach is no different from any other research study, in that it is subject to various *limitations*. Firstly, there was no control over *who* actually completed the questionnaires. This is a common problem in postal questionnaires. However, this investigation was only a *fact-finding* study, and as such only required that respondents be sufficiently informed about polling activities and circumstances to provide the required information. Contacting specific individuals is not therefore a priority with this type of study; what is of importance is that respondents have access to, and the clearance within the organisation to pass on these data. Of those who responded to the survey, all met this criteria, in that they were leading players within their respective organisations. Consequently, the findings reported in the questionnaire study are sufficient to provide an informed summary of the status of opinion polling in the countries contacted.

A second possible problem in the design of the survey is that the questionnaire was written in English, and as a consequence, some polling agencies contacted may not have been able to translate and understand its contents. If this was an attitudinal- or opinion-based survey, then this would be an issue of particular concern: it might be a possible source of response bias, especially if the non-respondents held different views to the respondents. However, given that it is a fact-finding study, sample coverage and response rates are not of such methodological importance, because the intention is not to *explain* patterns in value-formation, nor to look for any causal relationships between phenomena, but merely to provide some insight into the development of the opinion polling industry. Hence, the aim of the survey was first and foremost to build up stocks of factual information, where each additional questionnaire obtained adds to the clarity of the study, rather than to generalise findings to a given population where response rates are at a premium. An English language questionnaire is not a limitation under these circumstances. Where questionnaires were completed, the absence of any *item non-response*,[1] and the quality and depth of the answers given to open questions, suggests that respondents had little or no difficulty in question comprehension.

Thirdly, based as it was on the snowball sampling approach, the study was not representative of the polling community, nor indeed was it meant to be. The strategy was designed to obtain information from as many organisations and academics engaged in polling as possible, and to help develop an appreciation of the development of polling in post-communist societies. The data therefore provide only an *indicative* survey of polling. The snowball sampling method employed is generally considered to be a legitimate one for these purposes (Arber, 1993; Sapsford and Abbot, 1992).

A fourth consideration is that, by itself, the data from the questionnaire survey do not reveal any great detail of the *processes* of political change which have shaped the conditions for polling in post-communist countries, nor the ways in which polling has attempted to adapt to these conditions. This limitation is largely a feature of all survey-based questionnaire studies. This structured research approach is typically constrained by its reliance on a particular set of questions, and the fact that these (and no other) questions were asked. Such a technique precludes exploring an area more deeply with respondents, and operates only at the level of broad factual aggregates, rather than of detailed explanation. To rectify this limitation within the data, the study required a more intensive, unstructured approach to the research, to provide an additional dimension to the findings.

In-depth qualitative interviews were held with pollsters and users of polls in some of the countries within the region. A series of field-trips were conducted in Poland, Hungary, and Czechoslovakia in 1991, and later in Bulgaria and Romania

(1995). Funding was secured from the Faculty of Economics and Social Sciences at the Nottingham Trent University, and from the British Councils in Warsaw and Budapest. The intention was to interview leading pollsters from as many organisations as possible, as well as some users of the polls (government personnel, and national political party figures). In researching the pollsters, the objective was to add depth and clarity to issues which had emerged from the questionnaire study; the interviews with the *users* of the polls were designed to try and identify the rationale for poll sponsorship, how data was built into policy and programmes, and the degree of importance attached to polls in general activities. Details of the fieldwork dates, and number of interviews conducted are given in Table i.ii below for each country.

Table i.ii   Fieldwork Schedule

Country	Fieldwork Dates	Number of Pollsters Interviewed	Number of Users Interviewed
Poland	21 to 27 May 1991	7	2
Czechoslovakia	25 to 30 September 1991, & 4 October 1991	9	-
Hungary	1 to 3 October 1991	3	-
Romania	1 to 7 May 1995	6	-
Bulgaria	8 to 14 May 1995	5	3
Total		30	5

Again, the snowball sampling method was used. Pollsters who had responded to the questionnaire survey were contacted, and many of these interviewed.[2] In some cases, these pollsters were able to provide details of colleagues from other polling agencies, and of poll users who were then interviewed. Interviews usually lasted between one and three hours, and in all but four cases, were conducted with English speaking informants.[3] An interview schedule provided a guiding framework for the discussion, and respondents were encouraged to elaborate on issues, and to offer examples to clarify and illustrate points.

Qualitative interviews of this type are often criticised because they do not employ standardised approaches, and as such, their procedures cannot be made fully explicit for replication and verification purposes by other researchers. In this way, they may be considered *unreliable*, and the findings insufficiently robust for generalisation to the wider population, and quantitative comparisons. This limitation is compounded by the tendency to focus upon *depth* rather than *breadth*, and the generation, therefore, of only a small number of cases for analysis.

However, posing the same questions to respondents in the interviews enabled me to achieve verification and validation of data through cross-checking. Furthermore, the similarity in answers given by respondents suggests that the data provide an indicative summary of the status of polling in those countries visited and of polling issues there. In addition, comparable data would be achieved by other researchers using the same interview schedule. And finally, the data complement the results from the questionnaire survey, in that they tap into similar issues but in a more intensive and probing way.

Overall, it is considered that the methodological aspects of this research were carried out as efficiently and appropriately as possible in the light of resource limitations. As a consequence, the data collected provide a valid and indicative overview of the practice of opinion polling in Central and Eastern Europe, and of the experiences of those conducting such research there. The interpretation of the data is my own, and does not represent the views of those organisations which funded the research.

Notes

1.   Item non-response refers to a situation where individual questions are left unanswered by respondents, either because they lack the confidence to reveal their view(s) about the issue, or else they have not understood the question.
2.   Because of the volatile nature of the industry, not all pollsters from the questionnaire survey survived to be interviewed. Consequently, data in Tables i.i and i.ii are not directly comparable.
3.   Translated interviews were held with: Strzeszewski (1991); Kwiatkowski, S. (1991); Georgiev, Z. (1991); Popov (1995).

Bibliography

Abramson, J.B., Arterton, F.C. and Orren, G.R. (1988) *The Electronic Commonwealth: The Impact of New Technologies Upon Democratic Politics* (New York: Basic Books Inc)

Abramson, P. and Ingelhart, R. (1992) 'Generational Replacement and Value Change in Eight West European Societies', in *British Journal of Political Science*, 22, pp.183-228

Adaméc, C. (1991) *Fear and Hope in 1968*, Unpublished Paper (Prague)

Adaméc, C., Pospisil, B. and Tesar, M. (1947) *What's your Opinion: A Year's Survey of Public Opinion in Czechoslovakia* (Prague: Orbis)

Adaméc, C. and Viden, I. (1947/48) 'Polls come to Czechoslovakia' *Public Opinion Quarterly*, Winter

Adams-Schmidt, D. (1952) *Anatomy of a Satellite* (Boston: Little, Brown and Company)

Allen, J. (1988) *Towards a Post-Industrial Economy?*, in Allen, J. and Massey, D.

Allen, J. and Massey, D. (1988) *The Economy in Question* (London: Sage Publications Ltd)

Almond, G. and Verba, S. (1963) *The Civic Culture* (Princeton, N.J.: Princeton University Press)

Arber, S. (1993) 'Designing Samples', in N. Gilbert, *Researching Social Life* (London: Sage)

Ashdown, P. (1996) 'Electronic Democracy Forum', *Http://www.guardian.co.uk/livewire/ashdown.html*, Sunday 10 March

Asher, H. (1988) *Polling and the Public* (Washington: Congressional Quarterly Inc.)

Attila, A.G.H. (1990) 'The Emergence of the Science of Democracy in Hungary and Its Impact on the Democratic Transition', paper delivered at the conference of the *International Committee for The Study of The Development of Political Science*, Barcelona, May 14-20th

Ball, A.R. (1988) *Modern Politics and Government* (Basingstoke: MacMillan Education Ltd)

Bankowicz, M. (1994) *Czechoslovakia: From Masaryk to Havel*, in Berglund, S. and Dellenbrandt, J.A.

Bankowicz, M. (1994b) *Bulgaria: The Continuing Revolution*, in Berglund, S. and Dellenbrandt, J.A.

Barbalet, J.M. (1986) 'Limitations of Class Theory and the Disappearance of Status: The Problem of the New Middle Class', *Sociology*, Vol.20, No.4, pp.557-75

Barnett, (1989) 'Polls: The Loaded Question' in *The Guardian* January 2nd

Batt, J. (1991) *East Central Europe From Reform to Transformation* (London: Pinter Publishers Ltd)

Batt, J. (1994) 'The International Dimension of Democratisation in Czechoslovakia and Hungary', in G. Pridham, E. Herring, and G. Sanford (eds)

Baumann, Z. (1994) 'After the Patronage State: A Model in Search of Class Interests', in C.A.G. Bryant and E. Mikrzycki (eds.)

Beacham, R. (1984) 'Economic Activity: Britain's Workforce?', *Population Trends*, No.37, pp.6-14

Bean, C. and Marks, G. (1993) 'The Australian Federal Election of 1993', in *Electoral Studies*, Vol. 12(3), pp.253-256 and p.286

Becvar, J. (1991b) Miscellaneous Data From Political Opinion Polls Conducted in Czechoslovakia 1968 and 1969

Bede, B. (1972) 'Forward', in J.A. Piekalkiewicz *Public Opinion in Czechoslovakia, 1968-69* (New York: Praeger)

Bell, D. (1973) *The Coming of Post-Industrial Society* (London: Heinemann)

Bell, D. (1980) 'The Information Society', in Forester, T. (ed.) *The Microelectronics Revolution* (Oxford: Basil Blackwell)

Benn, T. (1982) *Arguments for Democracy* (Harmondsworth, Middlesex: Penguin Books Ltd)

Berglund, S. and Dellenbrandt, J.A. (1994) *The New Democracies in Eastern Europe: Party Systems and Political Cleavages* (eds.) (Aldershot: Edward Elgar Publishing Ltd)

Berglund, S. (1994) *The Breakdown of the German Democratic Republic*, in Berglund, S. and Dellendbrandt, J.A.

Blondel, J. (1995) *Comparative Government: An Introduction* (Hemel Hempstead: Prentice Hall/Harvester Wheatsheaf) 2nd ed.

Blondel, J. (ed) (1969) *An Introduction to Comparative Government* (London: Weidenfeld and Nicholson)

Bojcun, M. (1995) 'The Ukranian Parliamentary Elections in March-April 1994', in *Europe-Asia Studies*, Vol.47(2), pp.229-249

Boorstin, D.J. (1961) *The Image: A guide to Pseudo Events In America* (New York: Athenum)

Bova, R. (1991) 'Political Dynamics of the Post-Communist Transition', in *World Politics* Vol. 44, October, pp.113-138

Boycott, O. (1995) 'Cornish Stake Electoral Claim', *The Guardian*, 30th December

Bradburn, N.M. and Sudman, S. (1988) *Polls and Surveys* (San Francisco: Jossey-Bass Inc)

Bradley, I. (1981) *Breaking The Mould* (Oxford: Robertson)

Bruner, J.S. (1944) *Mandate from the People* (New York: Duell, Sloan Pearce)

Bryant, C.G.A. (1994) 'Economic Utopianism and Sociological Realism: Strategies for Transformation in East-Central Europe', in C.G.A.Bryant and E.Mokrzycki (eds.)

Bryant, C.G.A. and Mokrzycki, E. (1994) *The New Great Transformation?* (eds.) (London: Routledge)

Buchanan, J.M. and Tullock, G. (1962) *The Calculus of Consent* (Michigan: Ann Arbor)

Burke, E. (1976) 'Speech to the Electors of Bristol' in Hill, B.W., *Edmund Burke on Government, Politics and Society* (New York: International Publications Service)

Butler, D. (1989) *British General Elections since 1945* (Oxford: Basil Blackwell Ltd)

Butler, D. (1994) 'Introduction', in *The Opinion Polls and the 1992 General Election*, (London: The Market Research Society)

Butler, D. and Kavanagh, D. (1980) *The British General Election of 1979*, (London: Macmillan)

Butler, D. and Kavanagh, D. (1984) *The British General Election of 1983* (London: Macmillan)

Butler, D. and Kavanagh, D. (1988) *The British General Election of 1987* (Basingstoke: Macmillan Press Ltd)

Butler, D. and King, A. (1966) *The British General Election of 1966*, (London: Macmillan)

Butler, D. and Pinto-Duschinsky, M. (1971) *The British General Election of 1970*

Butler, D. and O'Muircheartaigh, C. (1979) *What is 40%? A note of the Eligible Electorate*, Unpublished Paper, February 13th

Butler, D. and Rose, R. (1960) *The British General Election of 1959* (London: Macmillan)

Butler, D. and Stokes, D. (1974) *Political Change in Britain* (London: Macmillan)

Carey, H.F. (1995) 'Irregularities or Rigging: The 1992 Romanian Parliamentary Elections', in *East European Quarterly*, Vol. XXIX (1), March, pp.43-66

Carter, A. (1982) *Democratic Reform in Yugoslavia: The Changing Role of the Party* (London: Pinter)

Circautas, A.M. (1994) 'In Pursuit of The Democratic Interest: The Institutionalisation of Parties and Interests in Eastern Europe', in C.G.A. Bryant and E. Mokrzycki (eds.)

Clemens, J. (1983) 'The Telephone Poll Bogeyman: A Case Study in Election Paranoia', in I. Crewe and M. Harrop. *Political Communications: The British General Election of 1983* (Cambridge: Cambridge University Press)

Clemens, J. (1984) *Polls, Politics and Pogulism* (Aldershot: Gower)

Cockburn, R. (1993) 'Scare Campaign Brings Labour Level', in *The Times*, March 13th

Collins, M. (1987) *Use of Polls in the 1987 General Election* (SCPR Survey Methods Centre and City University Business School)

Connor, W.D. and Gitelman, Z.Y. (1977) *Public Opinion in European Socialist Systems* (New York: Praeger Special Studies)

Cotta, M. (1994) 'Building Party Systems After the Dictatorship: The East European Cases in a Comparative Perspective' in G. Pridham and T. Vanharen

Crespi, I (1980) 'Polls as Journalism', in *Public Opinion Quarterly*, Vol.44, pp.462-476

Crespi, I. (1989) *Public Opinion, Polls and Democracy* (Colorado: Westview Press)

Crewe, I. (1983) *Surveys of British Elections: Problems of Design, Response and Bias,* (Colchester, Essex: Essex Papers in Politics and Government, University of Essex)

Crewe, I. (1985) 'Great Britain', in Crewe, I. (eds) *Electoral Change in Western Democracies: Patterns and Sources of Electoral Volatility* (Beckenham, Kent: Croom Helm)

Crewe, I. (1986) 'Saturation Polling, the Media and the 1983 Election', in I. Crewe and M. Harrop (eds.), *Political Communications: The General Election Campaign of 1983* (Cambridge: Cambridge University Press)

Crewe, I. (1992) 'Sampling Methods Explain Variation' in *The Times*, March 25th

Crewe, I. (1993a) in 'Suggers, Fruggers and Data Muggers', *Horizon*

Crewe, I. (1993b) 'A Nation of Liars? Opinion Polls and the 1992 Election', in *Parliamentary Affairs*, 45(4) pp.475-495

Crewe, I. (1993c) 'The Changing Basis of Party Choice, 1979-1992', in *Politics Review*, February

Crewe, I. Sarlvik, B. and Alt, J. (1977) 'Partisan Dealignment in Britain 1964-74', in *British Journal of Political Science*, 7, pp.129-190

Crook, S. Pakulski, J. and Waters, M. (1992) *Postmodernization: Change in Advanced Society* (London: Sage Publications Ltd)

Curtice, J. and Steed, M. (1984) 'Analysis of the Results', in Butler, D. and Kavanagh, D.

Curtice, J. and Steed, M. (1992) 'The Results Analysed', in Butler, D. and Kavanagh, D.

Curtice, J. (1997a) 'Are The Opinion Polls Ready for 1997?', in *Journal of The Market Research Society*, 39(2), April, pp.317-330

Curtice, J. (1997b) 'Can we Believe The Polls?, *BBC Election 97 Website*, http://www.bbc.co.uk/election97/analysis/jcpoll2.htm

Dahrendorf, R. (1959) *Class and Class Conflict in Industrial Society* (London: Routledge)

Dahrendorf, R. (1969) 'The Service Class' in Burns, T. (ed.) *Industrial Man*, (Harmondsworth: Penguin)

Dalton, R.J., Keuchler, M. and Bürklin, W. (1990) 'The Challenge of New Movements', in R.J. Dalton and M.Keuchler (eds.), *Challenging the Political Order* (Cambridge: Polity)

Datculescu, P. (1992) 'The Methodology of Pre-election Polls: Criteria of Accuracy and Credibility', Paper prepared for the *International Meeting on "Free and Fair Elections in Romania"*, Sinaia, March 15-17

Datculescu, P. (1993) *How Romania Voted: An Analysis of the Parliamentary and Presidential Elections of September 27th, 1992*, Unpublished Paper

Dejevsky, M. (1995) 'Strong Views May Outlaw Opinion Blackout', in *The Independent*, April 24th

Dejevsky, M. (1995b) 'Final Polls Install Chirac in Elysée', in *The Independent*, April 17th

Dejevsky, M. (1995c) 'Swinging Voters Keeps Contenders on Their Toes', in *The Independent*, April 3rd

Dejevsky, M. and Fenby, J. (1995) 'Jospin Top of Poll, But Way Clear For Chirac', in *The Independent*, April 24th

Dellenbrandt, J.A. (1994a) 'Romania: The Slow Revolution', in S.Berglund and J.A. Dellenbrandt (eds.)

Dellenbrandt, J.A. (1994b) 'The Re-Emergence of Multi-Partyism in the Baltic States', in S.Berglund and J.A.Dellenbrandt (eds.)

Denver, D. (1989) *Elections and Voting Behaviour in Britain* (London: Philip Allan)

Dobbs, M. (1992) 'Wisdom From The Soundbite Scientists', in *The Times*, April 7th

Downs, A. (1957) *An Economic Theory of Democracy* (New York: Harper)

Downs, W.M. (1995) 'The Belgian General Election of 1995', in *Electoral Studies*, Vol.14(3), pp.336-341

Duke, V. and Edgell, S. (1987) 'Attitudes to Privatisation', in *Quarterly Journal of Social Affairs*, 3(4), pp.253-284

Duke, V. and Grime, K. (1994) 'Privatisation in East-Central Europe: Similarities and Contrasts in its Application,' in C.G.A. Bryant and E.Mokrzycki (eds.)

Dunleavy, P. (1989) 'The end of Class Politics?', in *Politics in Transition,* Cochrane, A. and Anderson, J. (London: Sage Publications Ltd)

Dunleavy, P. and Husbands, C. (1985) *British Democracy at the Crossroads* (London: George Allen and Unwin)

Dunleavy, P. and O'Leary, B. (1987) *Theories of the State: The Politics of Liberal Democracy* (Basingstoke: Macmillan Education Ltd)

Dunleavy, P. and Weir, S. (1995) 'Its All Over For The Old Constitution', *The Independent*, 30th May

Dutton, W.H., O'Connell, J. and Wyer, J. (1991) 'State and Local Government Innovations in Electronic Services', *Report prepared for the Office of Technology Assessment US Congress* (Los Angeles: Annenberg School for Communication, University of Southern California)

Dutton, W.H. (1992) 'Political Science Research on Teledemocracy', in *Social Science Computer Review*, Vol.10(4),Winter, pp.505-521

Dynes, M. (1995) 'Belgium Voters Dash For Right Dreams of Power', in *The Times*, May 22nd

Easton, D. (1957) 'An Approach to the Analysis of Political Systems,' *World Politics* (10) 383-400

Easton, D. (1965a) *A Framework for Political Analysis* (Eaglewood Cliffs, N.J: Prentice-Hall)

Easton, D. (1965b) *A Systems Analysis of Political Life* (New York: Wiley)

Ekert, G. (1991) 'Democratisation Processes in East Central Europe: A Theoretical Consideration', in *British Journal of Political Science*, Vol. 21(3), pp.285-313

Ello, P. (1968) *Czechoslovakia's Blueprint For Freedom* (ed) (Washington: Acropolis)

Endean, C. (1996) 'How The Left Took Their Hold on Power', in *The European*, April 25-May 1

European Marketing Data and Statistics 1990 (25th Edition), London

Fenby, J. (1995) 'Balladur Battles Back in The Polls', in *The Independent*, April 21st

Fisher, P. (1988) 'Democracy on the Line', *The Guardian*, June 30th

Fishkin, J.S. (1992) 'Talk of the Tube: How to Get Teledemocracy Right', in *American Prospect*, Vol.11, Fall, pp.46-52

Fishkin, J. (1994) *Power and the People*, Channel Four Television, May 8th

Fletcher, M. (1996) 'Buchanan Packs Punches To Pull Level With Dole', in *The Times*, February 17th

Franklin, (1985) *The Decline of Class Voting in Britain* (Oxford: Clarendon Press)

Freedland, J. (1994) 'Republicans' Hopes of Big Poll Wins fade', in *The Guardian*, October 28th

Freedland, J. (1994b) 'No One Likes Him But He's Still There', in *The Guardian*, November 5th

Freedland, J. (1996) 'Battered Dole Set For Victory In Iowa', in *The Guardian*, February 12th

Freedland, J. (1996b) 'Humbling Dole Gives Buchanan The Big Mo', in *The Guardian*, February 14th

Friedman, D.V. (1993) 'Bringing Society Back into Democratic Transition Theory after 1989: Pact Making and Regime Collapse", in *East European Politics and Societies*, Vol. 7(3), Fall, pp.482-512

Friedrich, C. and Brzezinski, Z. (1965) *Totalitarian Dictatorship and Autocracy* (Massachusettes: Harvard University Press)

Gallup (1992) *Political and Economic Index* (London: Dod's Publishing and Research Ltd)

Gallup, G. (1965) 'Polls and the Political Process - Past, Present and Future', *Public Opinion Quarterly*, Vol.29, pp.545-549

Gallup, G. and Rae, S. (1940) *The Pulse of Democracy* (New York: Simon and Schuster)

Galtung, J. (1967) Theories and Methods of Social Research (London: Allen and Unwin)

Garry, A. (1996) 'Scottish Socialist Alliance Launched', in *Militant*, 1263, 16th February

Gartner, M. (1976) 'Endogenous Bandwagon and Underdog Effects', *Public Choice*, XXV, pp.83-139

Ginsberg, B. (1982) *The Consequences of Consent* (Reading, Mass: Addison Wesley)

Gitelman, Z.Y., (1977) 'Public Opinion in Communist Political Systems' in Connor, W.D. and Gitelman, Z.Y., *Public Opinion in European Socialist Systems* (New York: Praeger Special Studies)

Glasgow University Media Group (1980) *More Bad News* (London: Routledge and Kegan Paul)

Goldblatt, P. (1983) 'Changes in Social Class Between 1971 and 1981: Could these affect Mortality Differences Among Men of Working Ages?' *Population Trends*, No.51, pp.9-17

Goldthorpe, J.H. (1984) 'Social Standing, Class and Status', in *SSRC Survey Methods Seminar Series 1980-1983* (SCPR Survey Methods Centre Publications)

Goldthorpe, J.H. et al (1980) *Social Mobility and Class Structure in Modern Britain* (Oxford: Clarendon Press)

Gramsci, A. (1971) *Selections from the Prison Notebooks* (London: Lawrence and Wishart), edited by Q.Hoare and G. Nowell-Smith

Grzybowski, M. (1994) *Poland: Towards Overdeveloped Pluralism*, in Berglund, S. and Dellenbrandt, J.A.

Gumbel, A. (1995) 'Italy's Contrite Pollsters Stuck in a Web of Lies', in *The Independent*, April 29th

Hague, R. and Harrop, M. (1987) *Comparative Government and Politics: An Introduction* (Basingstoke: The Macmillan Press Ltd)

Hames, T. (1995) 'The US Mid-term Election of 1994', in *Electoral Studies*, Vol 14(2), pp.222-226

Harris, R. (1992) 'We Are a Nation of Liars', *Sunday Times*, April 12th

Harrop, M. (1984) 'The Press', in D.Butler and D. Kavanagh (eds) *The British General Election of 1983* (London: Macmillan)

Harrop, M. (1988) 'Opinion Polls In By-elections' in *Market Research Society Newsletter*, March 1988

Heath, A. Jowell, R. and Curtice, J. (1985) *How Britain Votes* (Oxford: Pergamon Press)

Hennessey, B. (1975) *Essentials of Public Opinion* (California: Wandsworth Publishing Company Inc.)

Henshel, R.L. and Johnston, W. (1987) 'The Emergence of Bandwagon Effects: A Theory' in *The Sociological Quarterly*, Volume 28, No.4, pp.493-511

Hewitt, P. (1988) *Policy Review-Note for Discussion*

Himmelweit, H., Humphreys, P., Jaeger, M. and Katz, M. (1981) *How Voters Decide* (London: Academic Press)

Hodder-Williams, R. (1970) *Public Opinion, Polls and British Democracy* (London: Routledge, Kegan and Paul Ltd)

Hoinville, G., Jowell, R., Airey, C., Brook, L., Courtenay, C. et al (1976) *Survey Research Practice*, London: Heinemann)

Hooper, J. (1993) 'Feint Hearts In The Ring', in *The Guardian*, June 8th

Hooper, J. (1996) 'Felipe Viva', in *The Guardian*, March 5th

Hooper, J. (1996b) 'Idol Flusters Italian Poll', in *The Guardian*, April 2nd

Horrocks, I. and Webb, J. (1994) 'Electronic Democracy: Prospects for Development in UK Local Government', Paper to the *PSA Urban Politics Group*, July (unpublished)

Hungarian Institute of Public Opinion Research (1947), in *The International Journal of Opinion and Attitude Research*, Vol 1

Hungarian News Agency, (1947) *Results of Hungarian Public Opinion Research* (Budapest: Hungarian News Agency)

Huntington, S. (1991) *The Third Wave: Democratization in the late Twentieth Century*, (Norman: University of Oklahoma Press)

Husbands, C. (1987) 'The Telephone Study of Voting Intentions in the June 1987 General Election', in *Journal of the Market Research Society* 29(4) pp.405-411

Ingle, S. (1987) *The British Party System* (Oxford: Basil Blackwell Ltd)

Inglehart, R. (1981) 'Post-Materialism in an Environment of Insecurity', *American Political Science Review*, 75, pp.880-90

Inglehart, R. (1987) 'Value Change in Industrial Societies', in *American Political Science Review* 81(4) pp.1289-1319

Inglehart, R. (1990) 'Values, Ideology and Cognitive Mobilisation in New Social Movements', in R.J.Dalton and M.Kuechler (eds.) *Challenging the Political Order* (Cambridge: Polity)

Ivanian, E.A. (1990) 'The Effect of Perestroika on The Development of Political Science in The USSR' paper delivered at the conference of the *International Committee for the Study of The Development of Political Science*, Barcelona, May 14-20th

James, M. (1989) *Telephone Opinion Polls: Getting The Methodology Wrong and Right*, Unpublished Paper (London: Audience Selection)

Jessop, (1974) *Traditionalism, Conservatism and British Political Culture*, (London: Allen and Unwin)

John, D. (1993) 'Keating Makes Last Appeal as Polls Show Close Call', in *The Guardian*, March 13th

Johnston, R. (1985) *The Geography of English Politics: The 1983 General Election* (Beckenham: Croom Helm)

Jones, A. (1989) 'Soviet Sociology, Past and Present', in *Contemporary Sociology*, 18(3), pp.316-324

Jones, M. (1988) 'Initial Confusion Puts Steel Down the Poll', *The Sunday Times*, March 27th

Jowell, R. (1993), in 'Suggers, Fruggers and Data Muggers', *Horizon*

Jowell, R., Hedges, B., Lynn, P., Farrant, G., and Heath, A. (1993) 'The 1992 British Election: The Failure of the Polls', *in Public Opinion Quarterly*, 57, pp.238-263

Ka-Lok Chan, K. (1995) 'Poland At The Crossroads: The 1993 General Election', in *Europe-Asia Studies*, Vol.47(1), pp.123-145

Karl, T. and Schmitter, P.C. (1991) 'Modes of Transitions in Latin America, Southern and Eastern Europe', in *International Social Science Journal*, Vol. 128, May, pp.269-284

Kautsky, J.H. (1973) 'Comparative Communism versus Comparative Politics', *Comparative Communism*, Vol.6, nos.1-2 (Spring-Summer) pp.135-70

Kavanagh, D. (1983) 'Public Opinion Polls', in D. Butler, H. Penniman, and A. Ranney (eds) *Democracy at the Polls* (Washington D.C.:American Enterprise Institute)

Kavanagh, D. (1992) 'Spirals of Silence', *The Guardian*, April 21st

Kavanagh, D. (1993) 'Private Opinion Polls and Campaign Strategy', in *Parliamentary Affairs*, 45(4), pp.518-527

Kellner, P. (1992) 'Objective Polls Curb Partisan Claims', in *The Independent*, March 23rd

Kellner, P. (1992) 'Opinion Pollsters Divided Over Extent of Labour Bias', in *The Independent*, June 13th

King, A. (1997) "Questions Behind Labour's Poll Position", *The Telegraph*, Issue 698, April 23rd

Klein, G. and Krejci, J. (1981) 'Czechoslovakia', in Welsh, W.A. (eds.) *Survey Research and Public Attitudes in Eastern Europe and the Soviet Union* (Oxford: Pergamon Press)

Kolankiewicz, G. (1994) 'The Breakdown of Welfare Regimes and the Problems for a "Social" Europe', in H.Miall (ed.)

Korobeinokov, V. (1988) 'Opinion Polls in the Soviet Union: Perestroika and the Public', *European Research*

Koschnick, W.J. (1980) 'Opinion Polls, the Mass Media and the Political Environment', in *European Research*, March

Kuusela, K. (1994) 'The Founding Electoral Systems in Eastern Europe, 1989-91', in G.Pridham and E.Mokrzycki (eds.)

Kwiatkowski, P. (1989) 'Paradoxes of Poland's Transition', seminar paper at *Social and Political Change in Contemporary East-Central Europe*

Kwiatkowski, P. (1992) 'Opinion Research and The Fall of Communism: Poland 1981-1990', in *International Journal of Public Opinion Research*, Vol. 4(4) pp.358-374

Kwiatkowski, S. (1989) *The Study of Public Opinion in Poland*, Unpublished paper

Lakeman, E. (1974) *How Democracies Vote: A Study of Electoral Systems*, 4th ed. (London: Faber)

Laudon, K.C. (1977) *Communications Technology and Democratic Participation* (London: Praeger Publishers)

Levine, S. and Roberts, N.S. (1994) 'The New Zealand Electoral Referendum and General Election of 1993', in *Electoral Studies*, 13(3), pp.240-253

Lewis, P. (1993) 'Polands SLD: The Communists Who Came in From The Cold', in *Labour Focus on Eastern Europe*, September-December, pp.29-34

Lewis, P., Lomax, B. and Wightman, G. (1994) 'The Emergence of Multi-Party Systems in East-Central Europe: A Comparative Analysis', in G. Pridham and T.Vanhanen (eds.)

Lijpart, A. (1984) *Democracies: Patterns of Majoritarian and Consensual Government in Twenty One Countries* (New Haven, Conn: Yale University Press)

Lincoln, A. (1905) 'Letter to the Editor(Sanguamo Journal)' in Nicolay, J. and Hay, J. (eds.) *Lincoln's Complete Works*, Vol.1 (Francis D. Tundy)

Linton, M. (1993) 'Labour Cautious About Poll Assumption That Puts Party 16 Points Ahead of Tories', in *The Guardian*, 11th November

Linton, M. (1994) 'Pollsters Inject "Realism" To Reduce Labour Lead Over Tories To 10 Points', in *The Guardian*, 11th May

Linton, M. (1994b) 'Pundits stumped by Unpredictable', in *The Guardian*, June 14th

Linton, M. (1995) 'Strong support for Ban on MPs Taking Outside Jobs', *The Guardian*, 31st May

Linton, M. (1995b) 'Poll Gap "Too Big To Close"', in *The Guardian*, 9th October

Linton, M. and Curtice, J. (1989) 'Rising from Nowhere to be Prime Outside Contenders' *The Guardian*, June 20th

Lippmann, W. (1922) *Public Opinion* (San Diego, California: Harcourt, Brace and Company, Inc.)

Lippmann, W. (1955) *The Public Philosophy* (Boston: Little Brown)

Little, D.R. (1976) 'Mass Political Participation in the US and the USSR: A Conceptual analysis', *Comparative Political Studies*, Vol.8

Locke, J. (1992) *Two Treaties of Government* (Cambridge and New York: Cambridge University Press)

Lockwood, C. (1995) 'Dehaene Likely to Form Next Government', in *The Electronic Telegraph*, May 23rd

Lovenduski, J. and Woodall, J. (1987) *Politics and Society in Eastern Europe* (Basingstoke: Macmillan Education Ltd)

Lukes, S. (1974) *Power: A Radical View* (London: Macmillan)

Lutynska, K. (Year unknown) 'Replies of The Type "It Is Hard To Say" In the 80s And Their Determinants' in Z. Gostkowski (ed.) *Analyses and Tests of Research Techniques in Sociology*, vol.VIII, presented to the author on a research visit, Warsaw, May 1991

Lutynska, J. (Year unknown) *Methodological Studies in Lodz Sociological Centre*, Unpublished paper presented to the author on a research visit, Lodz, May 1991

Lutynska, K. (1969) "Third Persons in Sociological Interviews and Their Influence on The Respondents' Replies", in *The Polish Sociological Bulletin* (2)

Lutynska, K. (1987) 'Questionnaire Studies in Poland in The 1980s: Analysis of Refusals to Give an Interview', in *The Polish Sociological Bulletin* (3)

MacPherson, C.B. (1966) *The Real World of Democracy* (Oxford: Clarendon Press)

Mainwaring, S., O'Donnell, G., and Valenzuela, J.S. (1992) *Issues in Democratic Consolidation: The New South American Democracies in Comparative Perspective*, eds. (South Bend: University of Notre Dame Press)

Mandel, E. (1975) Late Capitalism (London: New Left Books)

Mareš, P., Musil, L. and Rabušic, L. (1994) 'Values and the Welfare State in Czechoslovakia', in C.G.A. Bryant and E. Mokrzycki (eds.)

Market Research Society (1976) 'Report of the Market Research Society' (1976) in *Journal of Market Research* 18(3)

Market Research Society (1992) *Report of the Market Research Society Inquiry into the 1992 General Election Opinion Polls* (London: MRS)

Market Research Society (1994) *The Opinion Polls and The 1992 General Election* (London: MRS)

Marks, K. (1996) 'Asnar Hunts For Allies To Prop Up Regime', in *The Electronic Telegraph*, March 5th

Marsh, C. (1984) 'Back on the Bandwagon: The Effect of Opinion Polls on Public Opinion', *British Journal of Political Science*, 15, no.1, 51-74

Marshall, T.H. (1953) *Class, Citizenship and Social Development* (New York: Doubleday)

Marshall, G., Newby, H. and Rose, D. (1988) *Social Class in Modern Britain* (London: Hutchinson)

Masuda, Y. (1985) 'Parameters of the Post-Industrial Society', in T.Forester (ed.) *The Information Technology Revolution* (Oxford: Basil Blackwell)

McCallum, R.G. and Readman, A. (1964) *The British General Election of 1945*, (London: Frank Cass and Co.)

McIlroy, J. (1989) 'Television today...And tomorrow' in B. Jones (ed.) *Political Issues in Britain Today* (Manchester: Manchester University Press)

McIntosh, M.E. and Abele McIver, M. (1992) 'Coping With Freedom and Uncertainty: Public Opinion in Hungary, Poland and Czechoslovakia 1989-1992' in *International Journal of Public Opinion Research*, Vol.4(4) pp.375-391

McKee, P. (1982) "ITN's Use of Opinion Polls", in R.M. Worcester and M.Harrop, *Political Communications: The General Election Campaign of 1979* (London: Macmillan)

McKenzie, R. and Silver, A. (1968) *Angels in Marble* (London: Heinemann)

McKie, D. (1992) 'Big Survey Gives Labour 2.5pc Lead', In *The Guardian*, April 7th.

McLean, I. (1989) *Democracy and New Technology* (Cambridge: Polity Press)

Miall, H. (1994) *Redefining Europe: New Patterns of conflict and cooperation* (eds.), (London: Pinter Publishers)

Miliband, R. (1969) *The State in Capitalist Society* (London: Weidenfeld and Nicholson)

Miliband, R., (1982) *Capitalist Democracy in Britain* (Oxford: Oxford University Press)

Miller, W.L. (1977) *Electoral Dynamics in Britain since 1918* (London: Macmillan)

Miller, W.L. (1978) 'Social Class and Party Choice in England', in *British Journal of Political Science*, Vol.8, pp.257-84

Miller, W.L. (1987) 'The British Voter and the Telephone at the 1983 Election', in *Journal of the Market Research Society*, 29(1) pp.67-82

Milne, S. and Donegan, L. (1995) 'Scargill Hopes for New Left Party By Next May' in *The Guardian*, November 3rd

Mink, G. (1981) 'Polls, Pollsters, Public Opinion and Political Power in The Late 1970s' in *Telos*, 47, Spring, pp.125-132

MORI (1994) 'The European Union: Attitudes of Citizens in its member states' in *British Public Opinion*, Vol.XXVII, No.5, June/July

MORI (1994) 'Poll Digest', in *British Public Opinion*, Vol.XVII(5), June-July

MORI (1997), British Public Opinion, XX/3-4, April-June

Mortimore, R. (1994) 'Great Britain', in *Electoral Studies*, Vol. 13(4), December, pp.341-343

Moser, C.A., and Kalton, G. (1971) *Survey Methods in Social Investigation* (London: Heinemann Educational Books)

Muir, K. (1994) 'Bland Lawyer Ends Cuomo's Reign', in *The Times*, November 10th

Munck, G.L. (1994) 'Democratic Transitions in Comparative Perspective', in *Comparative Politics*, April

Munro, M. (1993) 'Bolger Re-election Boosted by Economic Revival', in *The Times*, November 5th

Murdoch, G. and Golding, P. (1977) 'Beyond Monopoly - Mass Communications in an Age Of Conglomerates' in P. Beharrell and G.Philo (eds.) *Trade Unions and The Media* (London: Macmillan)

Murray, I. (1992) 'Pole-axing the Pollsters', *Marketing Week*, April 17th

Nicholas, H.G. (1951) *The British General Election of 1950*, (London: Macmillan)

Noelle-Neumann, E. (1974) 'The Spiral of Silence: A Theory of Public Opinion' *Journal of Communication*, Vol.24, 43-51

Norris, P. (1987a) *Marginal Polls - Their Role and Record*, paper at the Conference on Political Communications: The Media, the parties and the polls in the 1987 Election Campaign

Norris, P. (1987b) *Volatility in By-elections* (Glasgow: University of Strathclyde)

O'Brien, J. (1980) *Telephone Interviewing*, Unpublished paper (London: NOP)

O'Muircheartaigh, C. (1997), "Election 97: A Triumph for the Pollsters?", in *Research, The Magazine of the Market Research Society*, 373, June, pp.14-18

Offe, C. (1991) 'Capitalism By Democratic Design? Democratic Facing The Triple Transition in East Central Europe', in *Social Research*, Vol.58(4) Winter, pp.865-893

Pakulski, J. (1986) 'Bureaucracy and the Soviet System', in *Studies in Comparative Communism* 19(1), pp.3-24

Pakulski, J. (1988) 'Poland After Solidarity: Social Movements Versus the State', in *Australian And New Zealand Journal of Sociology*, Vol.24(1) pp.152-153

Pakulski, J. (1993a) 'The Dying of Class or of Marxist Class Theory?' *International Sociology*, Vol.8(3), pp.279-292

Pakulski, J. (1993b) 'Mass Social Movements and Social Class', in *International Sociology*, Vol.8(2), pp.131-158

Park, A. (1994) 'Turning Points of Post-communist Transition: Lessons from the Case of Estonia' in *Government and Opposition*, Vol 29(3) Summer, pp.403-413

Parkin, (1967) 'Working Class Conservatives: A Theory of Political Deviance', *British Journal of Sociology* 18(3) pp.278-90

Parkin, F. (1979) *Marxism and Class Theory* (London: Tavistock)

Pelikan, J. (1972) 'The Struggle for Socialism in Czechoslovakia', in *New Left Review* 71

Pelling, H. (1965) *The Origins of the Labour Party* (London: Oxford University Press)

Phillips, J. (1995a) 'Victorious Berlusconi Presses For June Poll', in *The Times*, April 24th

Phillips, J. (1995b) 'Berlusconi Heads for Surprise Defeat in Local Polls', in *The Times*, April 25th

Piekalkiewicz, J.A. (1972) *Public Opinion in Czechoslovakia, 1968-69* (New York: Praeger)

Pridham, G. (1994) 'Democratic Transition in Theory and Practice: Southern European Lessons for Eastern Europe', in G. Pridham and T. Vahanen, (eds.)

Pridham, G., Herring, E., and Sanford, G. (1994) *Building Democracy? The International Dimension of Democratisation in Eastern Europe*, eds. (London: Leicester University Press)

Pridham, G. and Vanhanen, T. (1994) *Democratisation in Eastern Europe: Domestic and International Perspectives* (eds.) (London: Routledge)

Przeworski, A. (1991) *Democracy and the Market: Political and Economic Reforms in Eastern Europe and Latin America* (Cambridge: Cambridge University Press)

Przybylowska, I. and Kistelski, K. (1986) 'The Social Context of Questionnaire Interview' in *The Polish Sociological Bulletin* (3-4)

Pulzer, P. (1967) *Political Representation and Elections in Britain* (London: Allen and Unwin)

Racz, B. and Kukorelli, I. (1995) 'The "Second Generation" Post-communist Elections in Hungary in 1994', in *Europe-Asia Studies*, Vol.47(2), pp.251-279

Rasmussen, J. in Miller, J. "TV Pollster in the Firing Line" *Sunday Times,* 25th October

Rattansi, A. (1985) 'End of An Othodoxy? The Critique of Sociology's View of Marx on Class' *Sociological Review*, Vol.33, No.4, pp.641-669

Rees-Moggs, W. (1995) 'Seeking A New de Gaulle', in *The Times*, April 27th

Rentoul, J. (1995) 'Nolan Much Too Soft on MPs, Say Voters', *The Guardian*, 30th May

Rentoul, J., Robinson, N., and Braunholtz, S. (1992) 'People Metering: Scientific Research or Clapometer?' Paper to the PSA Conference *Voters, Parties and the Media* (University of Essex) September 1992

Reuter (1990) 'Pollsters Predict Hassle - Free Day When The World Awaits Outcome', in *The Guardian*, London, March 16th

Riddell, P. (1992) 'Pollsters Deny Figures Have Been Wrong For 30 Years', in *The Times*, June 13th

Roberts, K., Cook, F.G., Clark, S.C. and Semenoff, E. (1977) *The Fragmentary Class Structure* (London: Heinemann)

Rogers, L. (1940) *The Pollsters* (New York: Knopf)

Roll, C.W. and Cantril, A.H. (1972) *Polls, Their Use and Misuse in Politics* (New York, Basic Books Inc)

Rose, R. (1976) *The Problem of Party Government* (Harmondsworth: Penguin Books)

Rose, R. and McAllister, I. (1986) *Voters Begin To Choose* (London:Sage)

Rose, R. and Haerpfer, C. (1994) 'Mass Response to Transformation in Post-Communist Societies', in *Europe-Asia Studies*, Vol.46(1), pp.3-28

Rousseau, J.-J. (1968) *The Social Contract* (Harmondsworth: Penguin Books Ltd)

Roxborough, A. (1991) 'Republics Look To The Future After The Fall', in *The Guardian*, London, August 29th

Runciman, W.G. (1966) *Relative Deprivation and Social Justice* (London: Routledge and Kegan Paul)

Rustow, D.A. (1970) 'Transitions to Democracy', in *Comparative Politics*, 2, April, pp.337-363

Sage, A. (1995) 'Balladur Facing First Round Election Defeat', in *The Times*, April 17th

Sakwa, R. (1995) 'The Russian Elections of December 1993' in *Europe-Asia Studies*, Vol.47(2), pp.195-227

Sapsford, R. and Abbott, P. (1992) *Research Methods for Nurses and The Caring Professions* (Buckingham: Open University Press)

Sarlvik, B. and Crewe, I. (1983) *Decade of Dealignment* (Cambridge: Cambridge University Press)

Sartori, G. (1976) *Parties and Party Systems* (Cambridge: Cambridge University Press)

Scarborough, E. (1986) *The British Electorate Twenty Years On* (Colchester: Essex Papers in Politics and Government, University of Essex)

Scargill, A. (1995) *Future Strategy for the Left* (Discussion Paper)

Schattschneider, E. (1960) *The Semi-Sovereign People* (New York: Holt, Rinehart and Winston)

Schmitter, P. (1988) 'The Consolidation of Political Democracy in Southern Europe', Mimeo, third revised edition (Stanford University and European University Institute)

Schmitter, P.C. and Karl, T. (1992) 'The Types of Democracy Emerging in Southern and Eastern Europe and South and Central America', in P.M.E. Volten, ed., *Bound to Change: Consolidating Democracy in East Central Europe* (New York: Institute for East West Studies)

Schöpflin, G. (1994) 'The Rise of Anti-Democratic Movements in Post-Communist Societies' in H. Miall (ed.)

Schulz, D. (1981) 'On the Nature and Functions of Participation in Communist States' in *Political Participation in Communist Systems*, ed. D.Schulz and J.Adams, pp.26-78

Schulz, M. in Worcester, R.M. (1989) 'Opinion Surveys: East and West', *British Public Opinion*, Vol.XI, No.10

Schumpeter, J.A. (1976) *Capitalism, Socialism and Democracy* (London: George Allen and Unwin Ltd)

Seabrook, J. (1978) *What Went Wrong?: Working People and the Ideals of the Labour Movement*, (London: Victor Gollancz)

Seabrook, J. (1982) *Unemployment* (London:Quartet)

Sell, H. (1995) 'Advance Party?' in *Socialism Today*, No.1

Seton-Watson, H. (1967) *The Russian Empire 1801-1917* (Oxford: Clarendon Press)

Shaw, E. (1992) "Labour's Campaigning and Communications Strategy 1987-92", Paper presented at the PSA Conference on *The 1992 General Election: Voters, Parties and the Media*, Essex University, September 18-20

Shrimsley, R. (1992) 'Why the Pollsters Got It All So Wrong', in *The Daily Telegraph*, June 13th

Simon, H.A. (1957) 'Bandwagon and Underdog Effects in Election Prediction', in *Models of Man: Social and Rational* (New York: Wiley)

Slider, D. (1985) 'Party-sponsored Public Opinion Research in The Soviet Union', in *Journal of Politics*, 47(1), pp.209-227

Slomczynski, K.M. and Wesolowski, W. (1990) 'Changing Schema for Class and Stratification Research in Poland', Paper for *The Thirteenth World Congress of Sociology*, Madrid, July 9th-13th

Smith, A. (1978) *The Politics of Information* (London: Macmillan)

Smith, D. (1992) 'Pollsters Now Need To Answer A Few Questions', in *The Sunday Times*, April 12th

Smith, D. (1997) "Tense Pollsters Make Final Checks", *The Sunday Times*, April 27

Smith, G. (1994) 'Can Liberal Democracy Span the European Divide?', in H. Miall (ed.)

Smith, G.B. (1992) *Soviet Politics: Struggling with Change* (Basingstoke: The Macmillan Press Ltd)

Snider, J.H. (1994) 'Democracy On-Line: Tomorrow's Electronic Electorate', in *The Futurist* Vol.28(5), September-October, pp.15-18

Sparrow, N. (1993a) in 'Suggers, Fruggers and Data Muggers', *Horizon*

Sparrow, N. (1993b) 'Improving Polling Techniques following the 1992 General Election', in *Journal of Market Research Society* 35(1), pp.79-89

Sparrow, N. (1997a) *ICM Polls and The 1997 Election*, ICM Research

Sparrow, N. (1997b) "Success, But Little Room For Complacency", in *Research, The Magazine of the Market Research Society*, 373, June, p.20

Straffin, P.D. (1977) 'The Bandwagon Curve', *American Journal of Political Science*, XXI, 695-709.

Studlar, D. and McAllister, I. (1992) 'A Changing Political Agenda? The Structure of Political Attitudes in Britain 1974-1987', *International Journal of Public Opinion Research* 4(2), Summer, pp.148-176

Sudman, S. and Bradburn, N.M. (1987) "The Organisational Growth of Public Opinion Research in the United States", *Public Opinion Quarterly*, 51 (pp.567-578)

Swafford, M. (1992) 'Sociological Aspects of Research in The Commonwealth of Independent States', in *The International Journal of Public Opinion Research*, Vol.4 (4) pp.346-357

Teer, F. and Spence, J.D. (1973) *Political Opinion Polls* (London: Hutchinson and Co Ltd)

Terry, S.M. (1993) 'Thinking About Post-Communist Transitions: How Different Are They?', in *Slavic Review*, Vol. 52(2), pp.333-337

The Guardian, (1989) *Everyone Gets a Fat Lip*, February 25th

The International Guardian (1995) *Shrinking into a Black Hole*, May 6th

The Times (1993) *Polls Apart*, June 8th

Thrift, N. (1989) 'Images of Social Change' in Hamnett, C., McDowell, L. and Sarre, P. *The Changing Social Structure* (London: Sage Publications Ltd)

Todd and Butcher (1982) *Electoral Registration in 1981*, OPCS.

Tonge, J. (1994) 'The Anti-Poll Tax Movement: A Pressure Movement?', in *Politics*, Vol.14, No.3

Valles, J. (1994) 'The Spanish General Election of 1993', in *Electoral Studies*, Vol.13(1), March

Van de Donk, W.B.H.J. and Tops, P.W. (1992) 'Informatization and Democracy: Orwell or Athens?', in *Information and The Public Sector*, Vol.2, pp.169-195

van Steenbergen, B. (1992) 'Transitions from Authoritarian/Totalitarian Systems: Recent Developments in Central and Eastern Europe in a Comparative Perspective', in *Futures*, Vol.24, March, pp.158-172

Varley, P. (1991) 'Electronic Democracy' in *Technology Review*, Vol.94(8), pp.42-52

Veen, H.J. (1989) 'The Greens as a Milieu Party', in E.Kolinsky (ed.) *Greens in West Germany* (Oxford: Berg)

Verdon, T. (1993) 'Poll Stalemate in New Zealand Sets Stage for PR', in *The Sunday Times*, November 7th

Von Beyme, K. (1996) *Transition to Democracy in Eastern Europe* (Macmillan: Basingstoke)

Walker, M. (1994) 'Anti-Clinton Landslide', in *The Guardian*, November 9th

Walker, M. (1994b) 'Humiliated Clinton In Struggle For Survival', in *The Guardian*, November 10th

Walker, M. (1996) 'Buchanan Activists Busy Raising Arizona', in *The Guardian*, February 27th

Waller, M. (1994) 'Groups, Parties and Political Change in Eastern Europe from 1977', in G.Pridham and T.Vanhanen (eds.)

Waller, R. (1987) *Constituency Polling: 1987 General Election*, Paper at the Conference on Political Communications: The Media, the Parties and the Polls in the 1987 Election Campaign

Waller, R. (1992a) 'The Polls and the 1992 General Election', Paper presented at the *Political Science Association Conference on Voters, Parties and the Media*, Colchester, September 18-20

Waller, R. (1992b) 'What Makes Polls So Contradictory' in *The Observer* March 22nd

Walters, D. (1987) 'Telephone Polls and The General Election' in *Journal of Market Research Society* 29(4) pp.413-418

Walters, D. (1988) *Telephone Opinion Polls: Getting the Methodology Wrong and Right. Audience Selection's 1983 and 1987 Election Experiences* (London: ASL)

Ward, B.A. (1981), 'An Overview of Social Research in Poland', in W.A.Welsh, *Survey Research and Public Attitudes in Eastern Europe and the Soviet Union*

Waters, M. (1994) 'Succession In The Stratification System: A Contribution To The "Death of Class" Debate', in *International Sociology*, Vol.9 (3) September pp.295-312

Webb, N., (1986) "The Current Situation of Opinion Polling Round the World", in *ESOMAR, Seminar on Opinion Polls* (Strasbourg) pp.7-17 (Amsterdam: ESOMAR)

Webb, N.L. and Wybrow, R.J. (1974) 'Polls in a Changing World', in R.M. Worcester and M.Harrop, *Political Communications: The General Election Campaign of 1979* (London: Macmillan)

Weiner, S.L. (1977) 'The Competition For Certainty: The Polls and The Press in Britain', in *Political Science Quarterly*, Vol.91(4) Winter, pp.673-696

Welsh, H.A. (1994) 'Political Transition Processes in Central and Eastern Europe?', in *Comparative Politics*, Vol. 26(4), July, pp.379-394

Welsh, W.A. (1981) 'An Overview of the Status of Survey Research in Eastern Europe and the Soviet Union', in Welsh, W.A. *Survey Research and Public Attitudes in Eastern Europe and the Soviet Union* (New York: Pergamon Press)

Welsh, W.A. (1981) *Survey Research and Public Attitudes in Eastern Europe and the Soviet Union* (eds.) (New York: Pergamon Press)

Whale, J. (1977) *The Politics of the Media* (London: Fontana)

White, S. (1979) *Political Culture and Soviet Politics* (London, Macmillan)

White, S. (1995) 'Public Opinion and Political Science in Postcommunist Russia', in *European Journal of Political Research*, Vol.27, pp.507-526

White, S., Gardener, J., Schöpflin, G. and Saich, T. (1990) *Communist and Post Communist Political Systems* (Basingstoke: Macmillan Education Ltd)

White, S., Pravda, A., and Gitelman, Z. (1992) *Developments in Soviet and Post-Soviet Politics*, (Macmillan: Basingstoke)

White, S., Gill, R. and Slider, D. (1993) *The Politics of Transition: Shaping a Post-communist Future* (Cambridge: Cambridge University Press)

Wiatr, J.J. (1970) 'The Hegemonic Party System in Poland', in E.Allardt and S. Rokkan (eds.), *Mass Politics: Studies in Political Sociology* (New York-London: The Free Press and Collier-Macmillan Ltd)

Wiatr, J.J. (1971) *The State of Sociology in Eastern Europe Today* (eds.) (London: Feffer and Simons, Inc)

Wilde, L. (1994) *Modern European Socialism* (Aldershot: Dartmouth)

Wolchik, S.L. (1991) *Czechoslovakia in Transition: Politics, Economics and Society* (London: Pinter Publishers Ltd)

Woodward, S.L. 'An Overview of Survey Research in the Socialist Federated Republic of Yugoslavia', in Welsh, W.A. *Survey Research and Public Attitudes in Eastern Europe and the Soviet Union*

Worcester, R.M. (1980) *A Review of Political Opinion Polling in Britain,* (MORI)

Worcester, R.M. (1983) in 'The Polls, Opinion Pollsters or Opinion Formers', *Marxism Today,* August 1983, pp.29-35

Worcester, R.M. (1987a) 'The Internationalisation of Public Opinion Research' *Public Opinion Quarterly,* Vol.51

Worcester, R.M. (1987b) Letter to Our Readers, *British Public Opinion,* June, Vol.IX, No.5

Worcester, R.M. (1989) 'Political Opinion Polling: Problems and Prospects', in *Contemporary Record,* November pp.15-18

Worcester, R.M. (1991) *British Public Opinion* (Oxford: Basil Blackwell Ltd)

Worcester, R.M. (1992) 'The US Election', in *British Public Opinion,* Vol.XV(9), November

Worcester, R.M. (1992a) 'The Polls Have a Lot to Answer For' in *British Public Opinion* Vol.IV, April/May

Worcester, R.M. (1992b) *British Public Opinion: The British General Election of 1992,* Vol.I, MORI

Worcester, R.M. (1992c) 'Opinion Polls in General Elections', Paper delivered for the *Market Research Society Conference,* March 19th

Worcester, R.M. (1993a) 'A Deliberate Plan for Confusing The Issue', in *Research,* November

Worcester, R.M. (1993b) 'Public and Elite Attitudes to Environmental Issues', in *International Journal of Public Opinion Research* 5(4)

Worcester, R.M. (1993c) *MORI Secret Ballot Experiments 1992-3*

Worcester, R.M. (1993d) *MORI's Question Order Experiments,* Unpublished paper

Worcester, R.M. (1993e) in 'Suggers, Fruggers and Data Muggers', *Horizon*

Worcester, R. (1994) 'Voting Intention', in *British Public Opinion,* August

Worcester, R.M. (1997) *British Public Opinion: The British General election of 1997*, MORI, Vol.I

Wybrow, R. (1993) Letter to J.Camp, 8th November

Zaslavskaya, T.I. (1990) 'Perestroika and Public Opinion' *Unpublished Lecture*

Zinn, C. (1993) 'Poll Leaves New Zealand Facing Crisis', in *The Guardian*, November 8th

Zinn, C. (1993b) 'Double Election Puts New Zealand At The Crossroads', in *The Guardian*, October 28th

PERSONAL INTERVIEWS & CORRESPONDENCE

Abraham, D. (1995) *CURS*, Bucharest, May 3rd

Adaméc, C. (1991a) Former director at *UVVM*, Prague, September 27th

Becvar, J. (1991a) Former director at *UVVM*, Prague, October 4th

Campeanu, P. (1995) *CIS*, Bucharest, May 6th

Clemens, J. (1988), *AGB Cable and Viewdata*, November 26th

Datculescu, P. (1995) *IRSOP*, Bucharest, May 1st

Dohnalik, J. (1991) *OBOP,* Warsaw, May 21st

Duben (1991) *Military Institute of Social Science*, Prague, September 26th

Georgiev, B. (1995) *Centre For The Study of Democracy*, Sofia, May 10th

Georgiev, Z. (1995) *British-Balkan Social Surveys*, Sofia, May 11th

Gjuzelev, B. (1995) *Bulgarian Democratic Party*, Sofia, May 9

Hartl, (1991) *STEM*, Prague, October 4th

Harvey, M. (1994), *TV Interaction,* May 25th

Herzmann, J. (1991) *UVVM*, Prague, September 27th

Hoščalet, M. (1991) *AISA*, Prague, September 25th

Ivanov, A. (1995) *Centre for the Study of Democracy*, Sofia, May 10th

Jasiewicz, K. (1991), *Institute of Political Studies: Polish Academy of Sciences*, Warsaw, May 27th

Kiss-Schaeffer, E. (1991) *GFK-Hungaria*, Budapest, October 1st

Kivu, M. (1995) *IMAS*, Bucharest, May 2nd

Klikova and Komarkova (1991), *AGMA*, Prague, September 25th

Kôppl, L. (1991) *ECOMA*, Prague, September 25th

Kwiatkowski, P. (1991a) *CBOS*, Warsaw, May 22nd

Kwiatkowski, P. (1991b) *CBOS*, Warsaw, May 25th

Kwiatkowski, S. (1991) *GFK-Polonia*, Warsaw, May 27th

Lutynska, K. (1991), *IFiS*, Lodz, May 23rd

Moon, N. (1994) *NOP*, March 25th

Moon, N. (1997) *NOP,* Private correspondence

Moser, A. (1995) *President of The Bulgarian Agrarian Party*, Sofia, May 10th

Muscetescu, A. (1995) *CSOP*, Bucharest, May 1st

Nowotny, N. (1991) *Demoskop*, Warsaw, May 22nd

Partchev, I. (1992) *BAFECR*, Sofia, Personal Letter, May 25th

Popov. M. (1995) *National Committee Member of the Bulgarian Socialist Party*, Sofia, May 13th

Rostocki, A. and Kowalski, P. (1991), *Universytet Todski*, Krakow, May 24th

Sandu, D. (1995) *SOCIOBIT and Vice-President of the Romanian Sociological Association*, Bucharest, May 5th

Somogyi, A. (1991) *MARECO*, Budapest, October 1st

Stoyanov, A. (1995) *Centre for the Study of Democracy*, Sofia, 9th May

Strzeszewski, (1991), *Polish Presidential Office,* Warsaw, May 22nd

Szecsko, T. (1991) *Hungarian Institute for Public Opinion Research*, Budapest, October 3rd

Szymondarski, J. (1991), *Solidarity Presidential Advisor,* Warsaw, May 21st

Tesar and Zahradnícek (1991), *GFK-CSFR*, Prague, September 26th

Waller, R. (1994) *Harris*, March 17th.

Walters, D. (1988) *Audience Selection Ltd*, June 20th

Worcester, R.M. (1994) *MORI*, March 10th

Wybrow, R. (1994) *Gallup (UK)*, March 25th

Index

References from Notes indicated by 'n' after page reference

For Product Safety Concerns and Information please contact our EU representative GPSR@taylorandfrancis.com Taylor & Francis Verlag GmbH, Kaufingerstraße 24, 80331 München, Germany

Printed and bound by CPI Group (UK) Ltd, Croydon, CR0 4YY

08/06/2025

01896977-0014